Bride
in the
Solomons

Books by Osa Johnson

I MARRIED ADVENTURE
FOUR YEARS IN PARADISE
BRIDE IN THE SOLOMONS

For Children

OSA JOHNSON'S JUNGLE FRIENDS
JUNGLE BABIES
JUNGLE PETS
PANTALOONS
SNOWBALL
TARNISH

Bride
in the
Solomons

BY OSA JOHNSON

Illustrated

Houghton Mifflin Company, Boston

The Riverside Press Cambridge

The Riverside Press
CAMBRIDGE · MASSACHUSETTS
PRINTED IN THE U.S.A.

To the boys in the Armed Services,

in the Solomons and elsewhere

throughout the world

Contents

Contents

Illustrations

Bride
in the
Solomons

*Bride
in the
Solomons*

...this is Malaita

*H*ERE is your letter to the District Commissioner.'
The Governor of the Solomons handed Martin an official envelope.

We were boarding a little sailboat at Tulagi, bound for the cannibal island of Malaita. The Governor had come down to the wharf to see us off.

'You will be safe with Mr. Bell,' he said, 'or you would not be going.'

From the beginning, the Governor had done everything he could to dishearten us. He had even sent us a formal communication saying that he would not be responsible for our safety if we persisted in photographing savages. While he was being officially patient, I think he would have been glad to see us go to Malaita or anywhere and never come back.

'A few weeks of this and you will be fed up. If not, and if you persist in this foolishness, I require that you take a police force. Meantime, you will be in Mr. Bell's hands. Godspeed!'

Everyone else had been just as discouraging. Our friends at Chanute out in Kansas thought we were insane. My father said we would lose everything we had — with nothing left to show for our fine dreams. My mother was sure we

1

would die of fever. If we ever did come close enough to a cannibal to get his picture, we would be boiled and eaten, or at least eaten, maybe raw.

Only my grandmother had shown any confidence in us. 'It's no worse than coming out to Kansas from Pennsylvania to fight the Indians,' she had said. 'Your granddaddy and I were almost scalped many a time. It's in your blood, I guess. Getting around and seeing things is good for young folks, anyway, and they have to take some chances if they are going to amount to anything. I wouldn't give much for anybody without some adventure in him.'

The worst objections had come from traders and missionaries on board the steamer as we crossed the Coral Sea. They were old Solomons hands and were full of misgivings, although the missionaries were very kind and solicitous and did their best to give us practical advice.

I asked if they had ever seen a cannibal feast. They had not, but had lost white friends and native crew boys in the jungles and knew there were cannibals on Malaita, Guadalcanal, and New Georgia, and even on San Christobal.

In any case, the Solomons were no place for a woman. On this they all ardently agreed. We were just asking for trouble.

'My advice to you, Johnson, is to leave your wife in Tulagi,' the Captain said.

But I put an end to that. I resented this white taboo and told them I was going wherever my husband went, regardless.

We had no illusions about what we were doing, nor how difficult it would be. Everyone knew that there was cannibalism in the Solomons. But no one had any real proof. Those who had seen a cannibal feast had nothing but their own words to prove the story, and most of the witnesses never came back. We were determined to *prove* cannibalism on film, with still and motion pictures. We would make pictures of everything the natives did, and if we were lucky, pictures of a real cannibal feast.

'All I want is one good shot of them,' Martin said over and

over again. 'Just one good scene of cannibals actually eating human flesh. That will be the whole story, right there on the screen, and nobody can doubt that cannibalism exists. That one picture will be worth all the cost and patience.'

Our chief mistake so far had been underestimating our expense. By the time we had reached Sydney, en route to Tulagi, our money was nearly gone, and with what we had left, we could not have stayed more than a few weeks in the Solomons. But luckily we obtained a theatre engagement of several weeks in Sydney. Martin showed his pictures and lectured, as he had on the Orpheum Circuit at home, and I sang Hawaiian songs. The show was a hit, and we left Sydney with our original capital, of nearly five thousand dollars, restored and the assurance that we could last through two years of exploring if we were careful of our money and wasted no time.

Now, on our way to an officially assured cannibal island, we began to feel we were getting somewhere at last. We might find the 'real thing' at any moment, from this point on.

At Malaita, we had a discouraging reception from Mr. Bell. He seemed more pleased to receive his week's mail than to see us. He was extremely cool and formal, and I was sure he resented our coming.

A large, athletic man, bronzed from his dark hair to the sturdy legs that showed bare beneath his white shorts, he seemed physically equal to his tough assignment here. Certainly he had plenty of stamina and nerve. His jaw was strongly set, and his eyes, like blue steel, seemed to look a hole right through me.

He bowed, without a smile. I winced as he shook my hand, and saw that he was going to be no man to cross. He turned and strode up the path. We followed, in silence.

He was evidently not fond of women.

It then occurred to me that I was not too presentable. I had a pet cockatoo on each shoulder and my checked gingham dress and big straw hat and white canvas shoes must have made a queer combination. These clothes were all I had, and I thought I ought to look my best for a man who saw very few women, and would be lonely and glad for a little feminine relief. But the birds and the costume probably made him wonder what on earth he had on his hands.

We crossed a broad lawn to Mr. Bell's house, a rambling one-storied frame building set up off the ground on six-foot poles. The roof was of thatch and around the house ran a wide open verandah. A clearing extended for at least three hundred yards on each side of the house and on one side down to the sea. Gardens of flowering shrubs and roses and native flowers were planted everywhere.

Toward the sea was a clear lawn, the grass freshly cut. Here, several native soldiers were marching up and down as a native sergeant shouted orders. An armed black sentry saluted as we came up and another stood at the top of the steps on the verandah, saluting smartly. We were evidently in a very military household.

'There will be tea, if you like,' said Mr. Bell abruptly.

He turned to his desk on the verandah and sat down to read his mail. He seemed completely if politely oblivious of us.

The houseboy beckoned, and we followed him around the verandah to a small, neat, whitewashed room. It was furnished with a wooden bed, chest of drawers, and three chairs, all carved out of native wood. The houseboy wore the smartest costume I had seen in the islands — white shorts and coat, severely starched, and a white shirt with stiff collar and plain black tie. His legs and feet were bare, but in the top button-hole of his coat was a great white-and-yellow orchid. He smiled agreeably as he brought tea for us, and for the first time I began to feel at home.

'That boy was probably a cannibal a few months ago,' said Martin. 'He has a fine smile, but look at those wild eyes!'

Exactly as Martin guessed, Mr. Bell had trained his boys and bodyguard from the raw. That evening at dinner, he told us how he took recruits as near to the cradle as possible, believing that he could make civilized human beings out of them.

'They are right out of the bush,' he said. 'Blood brothers of the savages they protect us from.'

His houseboy, cook, kitchen boy, and table boy he had brought down from the hills as mere children, by arrangement with a friendly chief.

'They learn to be clean and obedient and are loyal to death. They have plenty of talent and capacity. I have always believed that our civilization is only skin-deep. Give me a hundred boys from England and put them into this jungle, on their own or with the natives, and they will survive, but will have the same standards as the natives. Take a hundred of these boys and put them through good schools at home and you will have fine English clerks, shopkeepers, and scholars. At least that is my opinion and I am making it work, so far.'

As he talked, he became more and more agreeable, although he never completely dropped his severe manner. He was now freshly dressed and combed and looked extremely handsome.

Mr. Bell addressed everything he said to Martin. I could only conclude that he was another woman-hater, like so many others out here. I hoped he would not be prejudiced against me, for Martin's sake. At best, this was going to be no easy place for us to do our work, and I must find a way into his friendship if we were to have his interest and aid.

'This is the best meal I've had in the Solomons,' said Martin helpfully.

The meal began with pigeon soup, rolls, and tinned butter. There was a delicious stew made from tinned beef. Out of the garden there were yams and bananas, both baked. Our dessert was papaya pudding with a sauce made of passion fruit, lemon juice, and coconut cream. The coffee was surprisingly good, despite the chicory.

'If you had to live here year after year, everything, even

food, would get jolly boresome,' said Mr. Bell. 'This is a
sorrowful land, and when I say sorrowful, I am not just using
a figure of speech. But if you have an ideal, to do a job well
and to make the world a little better for those who come after
us, you can bear it. Otherwise you would surely go mad.
It's a joke that we ever come out here in the first place, but
once here we never get away — victims of routine and habit.
We go home on leave and are miserable until we get back to
these miserable islands.'

I could see that he was not running away from life, but
facing it, and was a man of pride, discipline, and vision.
Everything about the house was spotless. Our dining table
was laid with a colorful, flower-patterned lava-lava and
decorated with a vase of white and red hibiscus and fern
leaves. The silver was old and battered, but good, and the
china was of equally good quality, although it rarely matched
and showed none too careful handling in the kitchen. The
servants were perfectly trained, quick, and efficient. Here
was a man who, in contrast with the escapists, was giving his
life to a kind of Spartan ideal and was getting the most comfort and happiness he could out of the circumstances.

'Do you like music?' said Mr. Bell as we finished dinner
and walked out to the verandah. I assured him that I was very
fond of all music. I wondered if he had a native orchestra
and what instruments they would play. But he turned on a
small portable gramophone, and in a moment John Mc-
Cormack was pouring forth a somewhat cracked and tinny,
but lively, 'Remember' and other familiar airs.

While Mr. Bell played Gilbert and Sullivan and others of
his favorites, principally from musical comedies, I told him
how I had sung in the Chanute church choir at home in
Kansas and then for Martin at his theatre, and how Martin
and I were married before I was of age and hid from our
parents until we finally got their approval by telephone.

'We haven't been married long and this is actually our
honeymoon,' I said.

Mr. Bell laughed heartily. 'What a place for a honey-moon!' he exclaimed.

By degrees he warmed and soon was chatting pleasantly.

When I brought out my ukelele and sang him 'Honolulu Tomboy,' 'Aloha,' and 'Sweet Little Maori Girl,' he began to act as though he had known us always. He asked me to sing 'Aloha' over and over again.

For an hour after Martin and I had gone to bed, we heard the gramophone playing softly. Then we heard only the throbbing tree-frog and cricket symphony, which slowly rose to fill the whole out-of-doors, and the soft steps of the sentry patrolling the verandah.

Next morning I woke early with the sun beating upon my face. Thousands of birds were singing, and through the window I could see great flocks of parrots and cockatoos, warblers and pigeons, fluttering among the trees and bushes. I dressed quickly and slipped out into the garden.

A barefooted sentry wearing only a short skirt of khaki, but armed with a large rifle and cartridge belt, smartly walked 'round and 'round the house.

I followed a path into the rose garden and on through flowering bushes and a low hedge into the open woods. The air was literally filled with the color of birds. Butterflies swarmed over the flower beds taking their fill of honey. I strolled on to a meandering brook and stood there listening to its music.

Suddenly I heard a sharp, shrill police whistle and turned to see Mr. Bell striding toward me. He motioned to me with that stern, superior manner of his as though he were summoning a servant. He was excited and flushed.

'Do you know what you are doing, young lady?' he almost shouted as he came up to me and shook a finger in my face. 'This isn't America; this is Malaita. Don't you ever stir away from that house without a sentry. And without telling me where you wish to go. Do I make myself clear?'

I gave him the best smile I could muster and stammered, 'Why, yes; I'm sorry and I certainly won't do it again.'

We walked toward the house and for some time he seemed unable to speak, or perhaps he restrained himself for fear of exploding. Then he stopped me and pointed to a low hedge.

'Do you see that hedge? I have to keep it cut to knee height and may have to take it up altogether. Last year some hillsmen hid behind it and ambushed one of my sentries. Just shot him full of poison arrows and ran. *Why* do you think I have this clearing and all these men on patrol?'

As if to impress me further with the thought, he took me to the parade ground beyond the house. There his bodyguard of some twenty soldiers, all dressed like the sentry in abbreviated khaki skirts and cartridge belts and armed with old Snider rifles, were marching about. He put them through a routine drill, and they executed all his orders with the smartness and dispatch of seasoned troops.

'They will give a good account of themselves,' he said. 'When we began to train them, I didn't have guns and had to drill them with sticks. But now they can shoot, and they are all skilled in jumping, running, gymnastics, and self-defense. They are fine oarsmen and woodsmen, and are better at ambushing than the wild men up in the hills. They will hold their own. I am not afraid to go with them anywhere.'

Martin came out with his cameras and made several hundred feet of motion-picture film of our host and his 'army,' as he called them. Then Mr. Bell took us back to the house to watch him hold court over a native accused of murder. Martin took still pictures of the proceeding and posed Mr. Bell for several portraits.

'What will you do with the native now that you have found him guilty,' I asked, when the trial was finished.

'Take him back to his village and execute him,' he said. 'We must string him up in the presence of the chief and the villagers. There is nothing else I can do. Just putting him out of the way would accomplish nothing except to wipe out another pest. We have to break this murder madness on the island; we must make a show of force that they will remember every time they want to go on a rampage and give them a picture of retribution they can't doubt and will not forget.'

I asked him if he thought they really understood retribution.

'Certainly,' he said. 'That is all they do understand. We show them genuine kindness as long as they act peacefully and in all our normal dealings with them, but absolute discipline when they commit a crime. When I came here, there was nothing but warfare throughout the island. Whole villages would be wiped out overnight for no reason except that some gang took pleasure in killing or wanted a new crop of heads for a ceremony or to decorate a headhouse.'

He looked out across the garden at the forest. 'One night a village was raided and every male in it was killed, numbering over a hundred. The women were forced to carry the heads down to the conquerors' village. There the women were in turn beheaded and the men had a great feast. Some tribes prefer to eat women. They say the flesh is more delicate and tasty.'

His voice became reflective and almost defensive. 'I have no hope of bringing perfect peace to the island, at least not in my lifetime. But it has given me satisfaction to put this section under control and by example and energy and persistence we will succeed, some day.'

Martin had developed and printed some of our arrival pictures, and he brought them to show us.

Mr. Bell's face beamed. 'By Jove,' he said, 'you are splendid. Could you get me some extra prints of these to send home?'

For some reason his whole manner was changing, and he now spoke in a friendly way as though he were really interested in us.

'I am going to risk taking you up into the hills,' he said at last. 'You will see fine specimens of the lowest type of humanity. I can't promise you anything but protection. And I must depend upon you to be very discreet and to do as I ask.'

He was worried about our photography. The natives had

never seen cameras and taking their pictures was going to be
a delicate business.

'One thing that most native peoples resent,' he said, 'is
interference with their routine ways. If they get the idea that
you are doing "magic" of some kind, as they are almost sure
to do when you point those cameras at them, you had better
be ready for the worst.

'Of course, I think you both are daft,' he went on. 'Although I suppose these pictures will be of great interest, as
you say, to the rest of the world and valuable to posterity, it
seems a great trouble and risk to take just for that. And to
get cannibals in "action," as you put it, will be impossible.
Unless you want them to eat you and your negatives as well.
But you are so earnest and so persistent that I want to do anything I can to help you. We will start tomorrow at daybreak,
and see what happens.'

Next morning we started before the sun was up, hoping to
reach a village in the mountains before dusk and prepared
to stay several days, if necessary. Mr. Bell led off with a
guide and sentries, while behind us trailed a dozen armed
soldiers and a score of boys carrying our cameras, food, and
bedding.

'Those bayonets will be pretty sticky food for any cannibal
that gets hungry today,' I thought, as we swung into the
forest and began to climb up the narrow trail.

Almost immediately the dense jungle closed in and the
towering trees and umbrella of foliage overhead shut out the
light and gave the place a spooky effect. I hurried to keep up
with the long strides of Mr. Bell and Martin.

As we went on, the heat became intense and vapors rose
from the ground, heavy and suffocating with the odor of decaying vegetation, the like of which I had never before
smelled. The whole forest seemed to be rotting.

My hair stuck to my temples and to the back of my neck,
and I perspired all over. I took off my jacket, and in the
dampness the silk shirt felt clammy and chill against my back.

Hornets, wasps, bees, and thousands of mosquitoes and other insects began buzzing around, and I swatted or shooed them with my handkerchief constantly.

As I raised my arms to take off my hat, my foot caught in something and down I went into the undergrowth beside the path. Martin helped me to my feet while a soldier cut away a vine that had caught my ankle. My face and arms were scratched and bleeding.

I was almost ready to explode with one of Martin's good strong words when something bit me in the neck, and I screamed instead.

Martin brushed it off my collar. 'Why, I'm surprised, honey,' he said; 'just a spider; you'd think a cannibal had you, by that yell.'

'I might as well be eaten by cannibals as by these hideous insects,' I grumbled. 'I never did like them and this seems to be their native home.'

To rest a moment, I started to sit down on a log.

'Don't do that!' shouted Mr. Bell. 'That will be full of lizards and stinging ants and probably scorpions as big as your hand. Don't touch anything you don't have to out here in the forest and don't pick things up off the ground. In addition to the insects, much of the vegetation is poisonous and it affects some people violently, so don't go looking for trouble. See there!'

A few feet away a green snake was inching up the trunk of a tree toward a bird's nest. And on the leaves of a bush, lizards were catching mosquitoes and moths on their long tongues. Large caterpillars and centipedes crawled about the ground. A horned frog leaped over a tree root, and a mouse scuttled away. In a giant web a hornet struggled helplessly as a black spider darted out to tie him down. I became aware of an enormous forest population of small creatures, busily at work devouring each other or trying to keep from being devoured.

Moving along the trail, we came into a clearing, so sunny and bright that it hurt my eyes for a moment. Hanging down

from a near-by tree were festoons of creepers bearing white
star-shaped flowers as beautiful as orchids and sweet with a
heavy fragrance. The air seemed filled with butterflies of
every size and color. Cockatoos scolded from overhead and
fluttered about in large clusters, seeming to make the trees
bloom when they lighted. Bird-calls drowned out the insects,
and I called to Martin to stop and enjoy this sudden blaze of
beauty.

'That seems to be the way of the jungle,' he said. 'Wherever there is great beauty there is danger, and wherever there
is extreme danger there is some beauty to compensate. Who
could ask anything lovelier than this, but what a place in
which to find it!'

'See the pigeons!' I exclaimed, reaching for my gun. 'Shall
I get them?'

'Not pigeons,' cautioned Mr. Bell, with one of the first
chuckles he had made since our arrival. 'Those are butterflies. Nine to ten inches across their wings and certainly as
large as pigeons, probably the largest in the world.'

I was sure he was fooling me until I took the binoculars
and saw for myself.

'This is a land of freaks,' he continued. 'Rats as big as cats,
cockroaches one and a half feet long, lizards as large as small
crocodiles, snakes that fly, toads that eat flesh, and fish that
climb trees. There is even a bird that hatches out of its egg
fully feathered and flies away.'

He was evidently in dead-earnest.

'Here on Malaita there is supposedly an ape-man that
walks on all fours, lives in trees, and comes in and steals
bananas and yams. *That* would be something for you two
young naturalists to find. The natives are terribly afraid of
these ape-men, and are so positive about them that I am beginning to believe the story myself. Nothing is improbable
to me, after living on these islands and seeing what I have
seen here.'

In the afternoon we passed through our first village. It

was a cluster of bamboo and thatch huts, all apparently
empty, although fires were smouldering and smoke issuing
from some of them. Wishing to invite no trouble and to save
time, we moved on.

Soon we came upon a woman in the trail. She was bending
over a baby, apparently about to tie it on her back. Seeing
us, she was terrified. Trembling like a wild animal, she eyed
us for a moment, then fled, leaving the baby in the trail. We
hurried past and left the squalling child where its mother had
deposited it.

'That's the way they are,' said Mr. Bell. 'The scariest
creatures in the world. They live in constant fear of one
thing or another. Even their warriors aren't brave. They
fight by ambush, stealth, trickery, and treachery. That
woman probably thought we were coming to chop her head
off, or that we had bad blood and if she came near us she
would be cursed. Or perhaps it was seeing a white woman,
the first one ever to come into the Malaita interior. They will
think you are some kind of a ghost, Mrs. Johnson. You are
going to be quite a curiosity, but that will be a protection for
us.'

We passed clearings where there were yam and taro
gardens under cultivation, and then we entered another and
more pretentious village.

The place was absolutely deserted. There were nearly a
score of houses. One was built of great bamboo logs four feet
high, laid horizontally as with our log cabins at home. It had
a steep, inverted V-shaped roof about fifteen feet high, heavily
thatched. In front of the door was a tall idol resembling a
totem pole. This was about twenty feet high and was carved
with grotesque heads and human figures.

'The chief's house,' explained Mr. Bell. 'You have a look,
Johnson, but your wife will be taboo. There seems to be no
one about, but someone will be watching from the forest or
one of these huts. I'd rather not take any chances; they
might ambush us all.'

Inside, Martin said there were dozens of heads hung about the walls and rafters, with pig tusks and spears and what Mr. Bell called 'other mementoes of the chief's head-hunting days.' I began to feel that we were very close to the 'real thing' that we were after.

In the late afternoon, we came to the village which was our destination. Spread over a considerable expanse of mountainside, it made an impressive settlement. Smoke from the thatch roofs showed that dinners were being cooked. Men were bustling about, carrying spears, and women were bringing in loads of firewood.

Mr. Bell stopped us in a clearing among the huts. Natives peeped at us from the doorways and there were surprised exclamations from all sides at our appearance.

Here was another large house, with a high roof and carved door posts. From this strutted forth a stalwart but potbellied black man wearing a very brief and dirty loincloth and an old felt hat.

'The chief,' said Mr. Bell. 'I gave him the hat, last time I came here.'

Mr. Bell saluted the chief smartly. I expected him to shake hands, but he did not. Martin and I followed his example. The chief returned the salute and drew himself up haughtily. He looked down at me, and his large, wild eyes seemed to pop with incredulity. He turned to his men, who had now come up behind him, pointed to me and jabbered away to them excitedly. Then, collecting his composure, he sat down on a large bamboo chair that had been brought for him, evidently his 'throne,' and motioned for us to sit on a log near-by.

I noted that his feet were very large, and he had great, strong big-toes, somewhat separated from the others, like those of an ape. He was as black as a gorilla. Scars of yaws and other sores showed on his legs, and his skin was filthy. His face was shiny black, seamed and weatherbeaten, but there was a touch of vanity in a scraggly mustache which drooped from his upper lip and in that felt hat on his head. Those wild eyes followed our every movement, but he just stared, and never once smiled or made any sign except of astonishment.

His wife now came up to join him, the first woman we had thus far seen at close range. She was probably the chief's age, but looked much older, for she was very thin and somewhat stooped. Her only clothing was a dirty loincloth which looked as though it had been cut from the chief's. About her neck hung several necklaces of porpoise teeth and shells. She was chewing betel nut, the juice of which drooled down at the corners of her mouth and colored her lips a livid red. She seemed too tired or bored to be interested in anything.

While Mr. Bell ordered the tobacco unpacked so that he could make a present to the chief, he confided to me that this was probably the oldest of the wives, but not the favorite. 'Otherwise,' he said, 'she would have many more necklaces and bracelets, for the porpoise teeth especially are valuable and the women like to show off all they possess.

'Here on Malaita,' he added, 'the men marry only virgins and they make a great fuss if any girl loses her virtue. I have known brothers to kill their sisters for the offense and parents sometimes inflict horrible punishments. In some other islands the opposite is true and virgins are unknown. This gives me hope for Malaita, for I feel they have a sense of discipline here. All they need is proper leadership and a little enlightenment.'

The boys brought a case of tobacco. In the meantime, about a score of the chief's men had drawn up behind him and stood there leaning on their spears, eyeing us with curiosity. I felt no uneasiness, probably because I was so interested and well guarded, but there seemed no particular cause for fear.

Mr. Bell opened the tobacco and took out a few sticks which he handed to the chief with a great salaam. I expected him to pass the treat around, but he closed up the case and ordered it away.

Women now came with steaming yams. They served the chief, then Mr. Bell, and the rest of us. The skins were burned to a crisp, but the yams tasted good and we made a great show of appreciation.

After this reception, we followed Mr. Bell to a building where he said we would spend the night. Our boys had already deposited our luggage there, had set up our camp cots, and were preparing dinner.

The structure was merely a broad thatched roof, supported by stout poles. It had no walls and only a dirt floor. Mr. Bell said that he built it for his official visits here and had purposely omitted the walls. The openness seemed a great comfort in these surroundings, but with sentries patrolling the place all night and fires going we would be safe enough.

I was too tired to eat anything. I took off my shoes and rolled into my blankets with my clothes on and fell so soundly asleep that even a cannibal raid wouldn't have disturbed me.

Next morning I wakened to find the sun already up and the birds chorusing loudly as they seemed to do everywhere in this jungle. We were two thousand feet above sea level and I felt the sharp cold despite my ample clothes. The fog banked in deep clouds in the valleys below, and above us the mountain peaks were completely enveloped in mist.

I climbed out of bed and shook out my shoes to make sure there were no scorpions, centipedes, or lizards in them. Then I rubbed my eyes with amazement.

Near-by were several dozen natives, squatting on their heels, and eyeing us with silent curiosity. Every one of them was naked except for a few who wore loincloths. I wondered how on earth they stood the morning cold and then the change at noon to tropic heat. I wondered, too, what my mother and dad would think if they could see me waking up here among these hungry-looking savages, separated from them by only a few feet and protected only by a patrolling sentry.

'Get dressed, Osa; here comes the chief,' said Martin as he came over to me. 'Those are his wives. We met only the head wife. Mr. Bell says he has fifty or more!'

The chief came across the clearing toward us, followed by a dozen women of varying ages. He still wore the slouch hat, at the same angle, the same scant loincloth, and carried himself with the same hauteur.

'He Mary belong me,' said the chief, with a wave of his hand toward the women, as he addressed Martin and Mr. Bell. He still scowled as he had the day before.

The wives came toward me, holding out their hands. I thought they meant to shake hands, but Mr. Bell restrained me.

'Go easy,' he said. 'Don't alarm them. What they want is tobacco. Shake hands later.'

Martin gave a stick of tobacco to each wife. Of course, the chief had put them up to this, for he would get the tobacco. None of them smiled. Their mouths drooled betel-nut juice. They had lost most of their teeth. Some were probably as young as fifteen or twenty, but they all looked middle-aged or older, from drudgery and exposure. Their breasts sagged and were quite emaciated, their bodies were filthy, and their legs were caked with dirt from wading about the gardens. Certainly, they never took a bath.

'The more children they produce, the more the chief likes them,' said Mr. Bell, 'and the more he is respected by the village.'

Now I must shake hands with them. To my horror, I saw they were covered with ringworm and yaws and other sores, especially about the legs and arms. But if Martin were to make pictures, we must have the chief's good will, and this attention to his women would please him.

I stepped out and offered my hand and shook the leathery hand of each wife in turn. They giggled bashfully, and one of them turned and ran for all she was worth. But the chief thawed perceptibly, and grinned at me in approval. Then, while Mr. Bell talked with the chief, I quickly went to the rear, got out my medicated soap and gave my hands a good scrubbing.

While our boys served us tea and biscuits, Martin set up his cameras to take advantage of the good light and the opportunity to photograph the chief.   Mr. Bell explained to the chief as best he could what pictures we wanted, that our cameras were harmless and the lenses were not guns, all in his best colloquial.

'This fellah no belong musket,' said Mr. Bell as he turned the motion-picture camera upside down and held it for the chief to examine.   'Him no sing out.   Him fellah black bokkus.   You look along this fellah black bokkus; him good fellah too much.'

For added assurance, Martin turned the camera away and began grinding the crank.

'Ah,' sighed the chief.   'Me savvy.   Black bokkus, good fellah too much.'

Completely at ease, the chief ordered his throne of bamboo, and seated himself on the edge of it.   Martin quickly made motion pictures of him and then several still portraits.   The natives who stood about seemed quite relieved that the black box did not explode, and everyone relaxed.

I motioned to the head wife and had Mr. Bell ask her to be photographed with me.   Except that she kept wiggling her toes throughout the performance, she seemed as bored as ever and acted as though she had always posed for cameras.   I think she was too stupefied by the narcotic nut she was sucking to know what it was all about.   Suddenly she spat a perfect stream of betel-nut juice, at least six feet, just like an old hillbilly in the Ozarks, and went on chewing.

Martin then posed me with a dozen native men, all carrying spears.   I looked at the weapons apprehensively.   Mr. Bell had said that if natives were unarmed, I could be ninety per cent sure of their peaceful intentions, but if they carried spears, to be on guard.   These men seemed friendly enough, so I stepped in among them and faced the camera.   The smell of them was sickening — from rancid coconut oil rubbed into their hair and the dirt and sweat of their bodies.

There was an awkward pause while Martin changed a film magazine, and I tried to jolly the men in my scant *bêche-de-mer*, the trade language of the Solomons. They looked at me with their shifty eyes, but not one smiled. Probably they were too bewildered, or were disgusted with this 'black bokkus' nonsense and the idea of posing with a woman.

Encouraged by his success, Martin took pictures of the scrawny children and one after another of the villagers who came into view. After each picture, even of the children, he gave everyone who posed a stick of tobacco, and I wondered if the supply would last. Then he turned to the chief's house and was still photographing it when Mr. Bell came quietly over to me.

'Notice the people coming in?' he said. 'The news has got around to other villages.'

Small groups were moving into the clearing from all sides and others were standing at some distance, trying to get up courage to come nearer. There were very few women and the men all carried spears.

'Too many of the blighters, and too cocky to suit me,' said Mr. Bell. He paused for a moment. 'The boys are packing and we are going down the mountain right now. No especial danger, but I don't want the responsibility . . .'

Mr. Bell said a few words to the chief in the native language, and I saw that he had resumed his severe manner and was leaving no doubt about who was superior. Then he saluted. His sergeant saluted. All the sentries saluted. Martin and I clicked our heels and imitated Mr. Bell.

We left as hastily as we could without revealing any concern. The sergeant led our little procession. Mr. Bell, Martin, and I followed, and our sentries brought up the rear, with what seemed to me quite a show of dignity and authority.

Riding ahead on the shoulders of the police boys were our cameras and magazines. The 'black bokkus' and our films were intact, and they carried the first motion pictures of Malaita and her people.

... as popular as poison ivy

I AM TRYING TO SHOW these people that we mean peace,' said Mr. Bell, as we walked briskly down the trail. He spoke reflectively, as though he were thinking out loud. 'Here, in this section of the island, they now have a little sense of order and begin to understand what justice means, but I never know when they will break out.'

There was a sharp sound in the bush and Mr. Bell froze in his tracks. We all stopped. His mouth was set and his eyes were fixed on the jungle. He stood thus for a few moments, and I wondered if the arrows would begin to fly. Then he relaxed, watching the jungle still, and resumed where he had been interrupted.

'It would take a full army just to keep them from fighting each other,' he said. 'There are probably a hundred thousand natives on Malaita, and they are always looking for trouble, it seems. I demand respect for Government by force of arms and example, and in time we will get them under control.'

We resumed our march. Presently, as we crossed a small side-trail, there was a shout from the forest. Standing at some distance down the cross-trail were several women, carrying on their backs and strapped to their foreheads great loads of bananas and firewood. Some of the loads had babies perched on top.

The women eyed us as though scared out of their very wits. Then they dropped their loads, snatched up their babies, and all scrambled into the bush, yelling, 'Ooo-ay! Ooo-ay! Ooo-ay!' as they disappeared.

'Poor things,' I said. I was feeling sorry enough for myself, with the heat and the insect bites, but the sight of these poor creatures made me realize what a long way women had come from these primitive conditions to my own state of freedom and comfort.

'Don't feel too sorry for them,' cautioned Mr. Bell. 'They like their way of life just as much as you do yours. They are brought up on hard work and have never known anything else. Come along, I'll show you their gardens.'

He posted sentries behind us in the main trail and took the others with us. We followed him down the slope and into a cultivated clearing. This was surrounded by a loose fence, about four feet high, made of upright bamboo poles bound together with jungle vine. Within the clearing perhaps two hundred small holes had been dug into the soil about fifteen inches apart. Yams had been planted in some of the holes and the earth filled in and from each 'hill' protruded a short pole for the yam creepers to climb upon.

In the center of the garden was a large pole with a bunch of areca leaves attached to its top. The areca would keep away the evil spirits, bring fertility to the garden, and work an evil charm on enemies who might venture in, explained Mr. Bell. The bamboo fence would keep out the wild pigs and other animals and discourage marauders. More areca leaves were tied to the entrance poles and at intervals around the fence.

'They make a big show of their planting,' said Mr. Bell. 'Of course, the women dig and do all the drudgery. The men simply lay out the garden and watch the women. The first yam planted is blessed by the medicine men and the warriors then dance around it to give the crop an auspicious start.'

'The Malaita men have the right idea,' said Martin. 'Let the women do the work.'

Mr. Bell showed me great clusters of ripening plantains in the forest outside the garden wall. 'Malaita never starves,' he said.

'But we had best get you out of here, Mrs. Johnson. None of us is supposed to be in here, and a woman is absolutely taboo.'

We left the enclosure and started back up the trail.

'If the natives saw you and the crop turned out to be no good, they would swear the strange woman's "bad blood" had cursed the garden,' Mr. Bell continued, 'and they would go after the head of the next white man they saw. There may be someone watching us through the fence right now.'

'I feel as popular as poison ivy,' I said.

'Well,' said Martin, 'you can see what would become of you if anything happened to me. You would be carrying yams and babies up and down the mountain and gathering tons of firewood and cooking for that pot-bellied, betel-nut-chewing old chief we stayed with last night.'

'I'd rather be dead,' I said. 'I don't think that's funny, and I should think these women would murder their husbands.'

'The funny part of that is,' said Mr. Bell, 'they love their husbands as much as you love yours.'

'But I wouldn't carry a ninety-pound load around in the hot sun for any man; not even Martin Johnson,' I snapped.

Mr. Bell smiled one of his rare smiles. 'But you do follow him all over the jungle!' he said.

Back at the main trail, we found the sentries jabbering away to an old man who stood there holding by the hand a little girl, about eight years old. I saw that the child was covered with buckwa, a ringworm disease which leaves great patches of dry, scaly skin.

'You wanta buyum this one fellah?' said one of the sentries to me with a grin.

I knew he was not being fresh, but I resented the idea. 'What name belong you? Me no wanta buyum,' I said.

'Man belong him; he speakum, him good kai-kai; good fellah too much,' said the sentry encouragingly. 'Suppose you givum plenty stick tobac, him sellum this one fellah Mary belong you.'

I saw that he was in real earnest. 'Does the old man actually think I want to eat the child?' I asked Mr. Bell.

'Sure he does,' exclaimed Martin. 'He hasn't any use for the poor little devil. And with no medicine, he can't cure that awful disease.'

'Yes,' said Mr. Bell sadly. 'The disease is contagious and they probably want to get rid of her. He can't sell her to a man for a wife and she won't be much good at work. So he would rather have the tobacco for her than nothing. And she may be one of his own daughters. He will most likely sell her to another tribe to eat. It's often done.'

'Let's buy her, Martin,' I said. 'I'm not going to see her eaten. We can take her down with us and send her to a missionary station.'

I could see that Martin agreed. But Mr. Bell must think he had his hands full, with us buying native children, in addition to causing him so much other concern. I remembered suddenly how my father used to object every time I came home with a stray cat or dog to add to my menagerie. But Mr. Bell did not protest.

'How many sticks of tobacco did he say?' asked Martin, who was digging into one of the duffel bags.

'Give him the whole lot,' I said impatiently.

The idea of buying a human being, and especially with chewing tobacco, made my stomach turn over.

The sentry counted out forty sticks of tobacco and handed them to the old man, who smiled broadly at this handsome bargain, saluted the sentry and then Martin, and went off holding his precious winnings.

Turning to me, the sentry pointed to the child and grinned, as much as to say, 'She is your property now.'

'Forty cents!' I said to Martin.

The little girl looked at me meekly with her big brown eyes, as though she gave me her confidence. As we started down the trail, she fell into line behind the leading sentry and, with an occasional glance back at me, toddled along like an ugly little black doll.

The heat was becoming more and more oppressive. As we hurried on, it struck me in the face like a hot blast and I struggled to breathe.

I stopped to rest and wiped the sweat from my face and neck and arms with my bandana, wishing I had a turkish towel. I saw that the sky was overcast and that black clouds were rolling down swiftly from the mountain peaks above us. The jungle was growing dark as night.

'This is rain,' said Martin. 'Let's push along.'

Almost before he finished, there was a whistling in the treetops, the upper branches began to weave and swish, and there was a blinding flash of lightning and a clap of thunder. Flocks of birds swept overhead to shelter.

Then, down pelted great drops of rain in such a deluge that the trail became slushy and soon was a brook up to my ankles. Trees creaked and groaned and crashed about us in the heavy wind. Lightning struck again and again, and I stood terrified, for I had always been frightened by lightning. I sank into the muddy path, too afraid to leave it for the worse jungle muck on either side.

Mr. Bell was motioning to me, and Martin came to lend a hand. We picked our way along the slippery incline to a banyan tree, where the soldiers were already clustered. The tree spread out over its many trunks to at least forty feet, and although the ground beneath it was spongy enough, it afforded some refuge. We were all so drenched that it mattered very little where we stood.

Martin lit a long cigar and Mr. Bell took out his pipe. I leaned against the tree and shut my eyes to avoid the lightning. The jungle roared and crackled and seemed to be exploding with the storm. Between thunder bursts there was the sound of water tumbling and cascading all about us. The air was more suffocating than ever, and now there rose from the rotting jungle a stench like pungent gas.

I heard Mr. Bell saying to Martin: 'Down on the coastline we had a hundred and fifty inches of rainfall last year. The peaks of the mountains are almost continuously covered with cloud and mist, so that I suppose there are well over two hundred inches up there.'

The little girl whose liberty we had purchased sat on the soaked earth near-by, unmoved by all the bombardment, and eyed me with a fixed stare, as though she thought I were the queerest thing she had ever seen. If she wondered at all, I suppose it was about the new kind of drudgery we would give her at the end of our journey.

Mr. Bell was telling Martin of his first brush with a cannibal chief. He had just taken over the station and was making a trip up the river when he was ambushed.

'Arrows flew from every side,' he said, 'but we fired into the bush and stopped the attack. We never did see the at-tackers.'

Next day the chief had sent a messenger with a warning that Mr. Bell had violated a sacred taboo and to stay away from that area unless he wanted to leave his head. Mr. Bell sent back word by the same messenger that if he heard any more such nonsense, he would wipe out the chief and the en-tire tribe, but that he was not offended and if the chief wanted peace to let him know.

'In a few days,' he continued, 'the messenger returned. He carried in a basket the bloody head of a native. That was the last word in a peace offering. The peace has always been kept and we are on very friendly terms.'

Fully an hour passed and the storm stopped abruptly. There was a gradual lifting of the humid weight on our lungs, and a cool breeze came to us for a few minutes. Birds began to come alive and sing above the sound of the rushing water. They hopped about the ground greedily picking up cater-

pillars, worms, and insects washed off the leaves. Nature
was giving them an easy banquet.

I saw a snake swallow a toad at one gulp. Then I screamed.
A rat, as large as a cat, ran almost across my feet. I had always hated rats, even worse than snakes and crocodiles, but I
had never seen anything to compare to that ugly monster.
Other rats, just as large, were scurrying after prey. The
jungle was rousing again to its business of eating and being
eaten.

Even the banyan tree under which we stood was a picture
of ruthlessness and survival through 'fitness.' Throwing out
its great umbrella-like branches and putting down buttress
after buttress, it had shut off light from above and nutriment
from below until other trees had been stifled or starved, and
it had cleared the wide area where we now were.

The sun came out, and I stepped from under the tree to
dry. The jungle had begun to steam. Clouds of vapor rose
from the vegetation and the odors were revolting. The heat
had also returned and my shirt felt as though it were boiling
on my back.

'I've got a chill,' said Mr. Bell. 'My bones are full of
malaria. How about some quinine?' He called for his
medicine kit.

I was worried about Martin, for he had malaria and I
knew he would soon be feeling the fever after this wetting.
I got out a sweater and made him put it on in spite of his
protests.

The sentries already had a fire going and were heating
water. They were getting out yams and taro to roast for
themselves. Martin and Mr. Bell took their quinine and soon
we all had tea.

'Why won't you take quinine?' Mr. Bell asked me. 'You're
stubborn.'

'No, I'm not stubborn,' I corrected him. 'But I don't like
it; it makes my ears ring.'

'Well,' said he sternly, 'you get a dose of fever and see what it does to you. You will be glad to have your ears ring, to get rid of it for a few hours. If you are going to survive in the jungles, tea and quinine are your best friends.'

Hot as I was, I sipped my tea. Nothing had ever tasted more delicious. But what I would give, I thought, for a nice sweet-smelling clover field back in Kansas and ground clean enough to lie down upon!

Suddenly the air was full of color and I saw bending over us, in a broad band, a brilliant rainbow. It seemed almost near enough to touch. And it must have done something to the birds, for they redoubled their chorus and the forest throbbed with pleasant and exciting sound.

We waited for the water to run off and the trail to dry a little, while the boys cooked yams and taro in the fire. They brought me some of each.

The taro, a starchy, tuberous root, had been pushed into the hot coals for several minutes. I scraped off the charred outside crust and the rest tasted like a flavory and somewhat sweet baked potato. With salt and a little tinned butter, it was delicious. I swore then and there that we would have taro wherever we went in the jungles. Mr. Bell assured me that it was enough to keep one going, if other food gave out.

A large lizard, marked with browns and yellows like a malacca stick, scurried across the ground near-by. Right behind him was another that looked full of fight. Both stopped and looked at me and flashed their long tongues impudently. They reminded me of rattlesnakes, and I felt chills go up my back, but I said nothing, for I didn't want the men to think I was a sissy. There seemed to be thousands of lizards everywhere and I would have to get used to them.

'What does a scorpion look like?' I asked Mr. Bell.

'Like a lobster with a long needle on the end of him,' he said. 'If he sticks that into you, you'll remember what he looks like.'

The sting wouldn't be fatal, he explained, but I would be delirious for a day or two, my veins would stand out and my temples throb, and there would be agonizing pain.

'The wound will be very sore for about ten days,' he said, 'and you will keep your eyes open after that. Shaking out your boots and your bedclothes and watching where you sit down will get to be a regular habit.'

Centipedes were worse, he thought, and the natives dreaded them more.

'Horrible horny legs,' he said. 'They inject a shot of poison and the spot goes numb for several days and you go straight out of your head, with plenty of pain. The natives make an herb poultice to take out the sting and are soon up and around again. After several bites they seem to become immunized. In fact, you get so many insect bites here that the shock soon wears off and you give them very little attention.'

On our way again, we found the forest blooming after the rain. Great tree ferns, banked on either side of the trail and diamonded with drops of moisture, looked cool and fresh against the still-steaming jungle. In the towering hardwood trees, orchid clusters gave little splashes of brown and white color. There were even orchids on the ground and one of the sentries picked a spray of them for me — a cluster of over twenty beautiful white flowers, the size of large pansies.

'Pretty soft,' said Martin. 'Even queens can't afford to have their path strewn with orchids. And there must be thousands overhead.'

White flowers covered several trees. On the ground and climbing over fallen logs were flowering creepers, all now freshened by the rain and brilliantly visible. Some had blossoms of red and crimson and yellow and one had great purple blooms. Against some of the tree trunks I saw climbing sweet peas in yellow and pink. A red flower resembled balsam, and others our garden begonias.

Mr. Bell warmed to the loveliness around us and what he called the 'magic' of the place and I saw that his remaining here was not entirely a matter of ideals and official duty, but that the natural beauty of the islands had captivated him.

We passed through a small village and several young men

stood and glared at us. They were unarmed. In their hair were small white flowers which I had seen in the jungle.

'Those flowers are as good to smell as to look at,' said Mr. Bell. 'They are supposed to be good-luck charms, and are worn by the young bucks while courting. The perfume is hypnotic.'

'Ugly as they are,' said Martin, 'they seem to be great ladies' men. Jungle scents and cannibal allure.'

The plant itself was one of the marvels of the jungle, Mr. Bell said. After blooming, the flowers and leaves fell off and the creeper seemed to die, but a few days later it leafed out and bloomed again. It was almost miraculous, and the natives revered it.

Although we hurried on through the forest, the sun was setting when we came into the open and caught our first glimpse of the sea. For some reason I felt a rushing sense of comfort and escape. The tension which had taken hold of me now let go. With all the talk of head-cutting, and with the closeness of the jungle, the alertness of our guards and the solicitations of Mr. Bell, I had begun to feel a sort of subconscious alarm which now seemed very silly and unwarranted.

When Mr. Bell's house came into view, it seemed to me one of the nicest homes I had ever seen. Simple and rough as it was, the comfort and security it offered were at least as good as any castle.

We were all exhausted, but Mr. Bell, always the Commissioner, promptly inquired of the houseboy whether everything was in order and asked in great detail about what had occurred during the last two days. Then he said he would at once make an inspection of the barracks. As he turned to go, he called the boy again and ordered hot baths for us — one of the best ideas I had ever heard.

'And by the way,' he added, 'I will see that your little girl goes to the missionary station — tomorrow.'

An hour later Mr. Bell sent us word that he had gone to bed with the fever. We went in to see him, but he said, 'Just let me alone. My disposition is bad enough, but when I have this, it's unbearable.'

Darkness had come when we finished dinner, and with it millions of fireflies. The night was pricked with little flashing points of light and the combined glow made even the bushes in the garden discernible. Martin and I stood on the verandah, watching the display and listening to the soft night sounds of the woods. He put his arm around me. I knew that this was one of those moments of great happiness which we found so often together here in the islands.

'Osa,' he said at last, 'this is a very important day for us. We have managed to do something no one else has done. If our pictures are good, the world will have its first movies of Malaita's cannibals. Even if we didn't see them eating each other, we have their portraits and pictures of how they live. We've made a real beginning and I feel more encouraged than ever in my life.'

I told him how proud of him I was. But my words trailed off and I could scarcely keep my eyes open. The long journey and the jungle lullaby made me too sleepy to talk or stand.

As I crawled into my bed a few minutes later, I said, 'Tonight, I won't care if a lizard falls on my face or a spider crawls up my arm. Nor even if a coconut crab bites off a couple of fingers.'

3 〰〰〰〰

. . . artificial islands

*T*HESE ARE THE PACIFISTS of the Solomons,' said
Mr. Bell, 'and a very superior lot. Probably the most intelligent people I have to deal with here.'

He was taking us across the Langa Langa Lagoon to a
small cluster of atolls visible from his residence and not far
offshore. This was just a routine inspection trip for him, but
it was a chance we had been hoping for — to see Government in action 'in the raw,' and to watch the reactions of
natives to authority. He seemed very proud of the islanders
and spoke of them with an almost paternal air.

'Those islands are actually artificial,' he said, 'built by the
natives to escape being murdered on the mainland. Incredible patience! Originally the islands were mere coral
knobs or rocky outcroppings. The natives walled them up,
gathering coral stones on the reefs at low tide or along the
shore of the mainland, and then filled in the enclosures with
earth brought from Malaita, giving themselves little spots of
real land.'

He told us that there were more than sixty of the islands,
some only large enough for a single family. There were no gardens of any consequence, for the space was too restricted and
the islanders could trade with Malaita hillsmen for all the yams

and taro they wanted. But they had planted coconut palms and, for shade and shelter, banyans and other sturdy trees.

'These fellows are none too cordial,' said Mr. Bell. 'And they are just as nervous and shy as the mainlanders. They are always on guard against attack, even out here, and survive only because they are ready to fight for their independence at any moment. A kind of *militant* pacifism. They are no sissies.'

I was sitting in the bow of Mr. Bell's official, native 'war canoe.' The canoe was a magnificent thing, fully twenty feet long, its sides inlaid with mother-of-pearl from end to end. An elongated and curving prow rose to more than twelve feet, and reminded one of the prow of a Viking ship except that it was decorated with white cowrie shells in unmistakable Solomons fashion, and topped with a cluster of areca leaves for protection against the evil spirits of the sea.

Our soldiers helped the boatboys to man the twenty paddles and, as they swung into rhythm, they began a grunting kind of chant. The canoe spun along as smoothly as a sailboat and, except for the muffled click as each blade was drawn back against the canoe at the end of the stroke, not a paddle made a sound. Under the fluttering Union Jack at the stern sat a helmsman, tense with concentration and self-importance.

The jade-green sea was almost completely calm, and as we cut through it, I could see below us schools of bonita and dolphin and bright little sardines. Other fish of all shapes and sizes scattered before us, and porpoise leaped and dove again almost under our prow. In the dazzling sun the low-lying islands seemed almost to be floating about on the surface, propelled by their plumed palms, and I could understand how they must have attracted the imaginative people who had taken them for homes.

As we neared the first of the islands, which looked like only a speck from shore, I was astonished at its size and development. At least forty coconut palms and breadfruit trees covered its two acres. Extending entirely around it was a stout wall about twelve feet high, with a foundation of large stones which must have been extremely difficult to move, and a superstructure made up of thousands upon thousands of smaller stones. A real monument to human independence and persistence.

Natives were peering at us from above the wall. They fled as we drew near, except for three fearless little boys who stood and gaped down at us. We pulled up to a small landing at which several dugout canoes were moored. Mr. Bell climbed ashore and we followed.

'Whew! What a smell!' I said, holding my nose. The stench that struck us was something new, worse than the rotting forest of the mainland.

Mr. Bell smiled. 'Only fish,' he said.

Then I saw that poles jutted out from the top of the wall above and that suspended from these were rattan baskets filled with tiny whitebait or petite sardines, left here to dry. In the bottom of the canoes beside us were thousands of the tiny fish.

I was reminded of Benjamin Franklin's remark that after three days fish and guests smell.

We followed Mr. Bell up a pebbled ramp and through a slit in the wall which was apparently the only entrance.

At the top of the ramp, the earth was nearly level with the wall. A path led inland through a row of houses, making a narrow street. Somehow, I had expected everything here to be in miniature, but the houses were of normal size and of the usual bamboo and thatch construction, although they had a neater appearance than those of the mainland. Not a soul was to be seen anywhere. Only pigs roamed about looking for food, walking in and out of the houses at will.

'The women always scatter,' said Mr. Bell. 'They aren't much to look at, but the men seem very jealous of them.'

Presently, we saw the chief coming down the pathway toward us — a plump, middle-aged, chocolate-brown native with short woolly hair and powerful features. A large shell crescent hung over his chest. In his hair were several small, white, rose-like shells; through his nose was a six-inch shaft of bone tapered at each end, and his long earlobes held double rings of mother-of-pearl. Wampum armbands were bound tight around his muscular arms and in one of these was stuck a clay pipe. A scanty G-string was his only clothing.

He smiled genially and saluted Mr. Bell, who returned the salute. I eyed the bone in his nose and tried to make out whether it was a human shinbone, as I suspected.

'This is Sua, the smartest chief in the Lagoon,' said Mr. Bell. 'He has traveled extensively for one of these people and is a great organizer. Quite a trader, and certainly keeps well fed. His hobby, which we have to watch, is dealing in children, and he also recruits laborers on Malaita for the Guadalcanal and other plantations. He will do practically anything for money.'

Lots of people are like that.

Our headman brought out the customary tobacco and the chief made excited exclamations in *bêche-de-mer*, as the boy gave him a handful.

Then he turned to Martin and me and, with a fine salesman's smile, he said, 'Me wantum one fellah bullamacow.'

Our versatile headman magically produced two tins of bully beef and the chief was now expansively happy.

'He wants to show us through the village,' said Mr. Bell. 'But I am sorry, Mrs. Johnson; you are taboo, so you must stay here on the women's side. Two thirds of the island is for men only and beyond that bridge no woman is ever permitted to go. We might persuade him, but would be risking trouble with the Gods and his people, so I will leave a sentry here with you while we make a quick trip to his clubhouse.'

Martin chuckled. 'Probably the only place in the world where men have been able to get away from their wives and have any real privacy,' he said as he gave me a hug.

Although I resented this constant repression, there was no use to protest, and it was pictures we wanted, after all.

An old hag poked her head out of a doorway. Her short

hair was quite gray and her face seamed with age. She gave me a long stare and a toothless half-smile and backed away.

I heard other women giggling inside the hut and walked over to investigate. There, on the earthen floor, were sitting two old women and three girls, one of whom held a baby to her breast. A fire smouldered in one corner, and filled the top of the hut with smoke. No wonder they all had sore eyes. Strewn about were clay pots, several large wooden bowls, and a half-dozen dilapidated grass sleeping mats. On the walls hung shell ornaments, bamboo water shafts, coconuts scooped out for drinking cups and other coconut-shell containers with wooden plugs, which the sentry told me held precious spring water from the mainland. From above hung several clumps of areca leaves and long strings of shell. The women all seemed to have skin rashes and the smell of the place was almost as bad as the drying fish outside. They all seemed very shy and hid their faces and giggled, so I gave them a salute and left them.

As I walked along the 'street,' the huts were all as silent as a cemetery. I saw that they were crowded close against each other, to take every advantage of the limited space. There was little privacy here.

At the far end of the village was a newly built hut. It was more pretentious than the others, so I made for it. From within came a metallic sound, something like a muffled anvil. I peeked in. On the floor sat a middle-aged woman and several young girls, all busily at work. They were surrounded by small piles of red and white shells. Some were hammering the shells, others filing the edges and drilling holes, and others polishing with what seemed to be pieces of sharkskin. The women paid no attention to me.

'Money belong him,' whispered the sentry. 'Good fellah too much. Buyum plenty taro, plenty wife.'

So here was the 'mint,' and here the precious red shell money about which I had heard.

'Two fellah buyum one fellah wife,' said the sentry, pointing above to hanging strands of the shells, each about three feet long.

Shells buy wives and wives make shells into money, I thought. A mounting spiral of prosperity for the chief and probably one of the reasons for his reputation as an organizer. This was surely a simpler way of making a fortune than we had found at home.

It was obvious, however, that even here finance was a shell game — a game of women and money.

Attracted by youngsters shouting, I walked down to the shore and peered over the wall. Splashing around in the water were a lot of little boys, some not over five or six years old. They dove and swam as though they were part fish and reminded me of a school of brown-bodied porpoise. On the beach were several piles of the same red shells I had just seen in the 'mint,' several fine starfish and two large tortoises, evidently the haul from their morning's work and play. If there were sharks here, the youngsters were either paying no attention whatever, or were depending for protection upon their noise and commotion, or perhaps on the areca leaves which their mothers had hung up at home.

A canoe swung around the projecting wall and the native in it froze at sight of me. A sort of white devil-devil, he no doubt thought. His canoe was filled with squirming sausage-like shapes, resembling salami that had come alive.

'What are those horrible things?' I exclaimed.

'Chinese soup!' answered Mr. Bell, who had come up quietly behind me. 'And very much prized. Actually they are sea-worms, no fins and no tails, just like big fatty garden worms. We call them sea-slugs and the natives call them *Bêche-de-Mer*. You can stretch them just like rubber. They crawl all over the sea-floor and into the crevices and rocky holes from which these boys and the fishermen drag them. They are very sluggish and are scavengers, of course, but the natives say they are fine eating. The Chinese cut them into strips and dry them for soups and medicines and pay a thousand dollars of your money for a ton.'

Osa in Mr. Bell's garden with Pollyanna the Parrot and Cocky the Cockatoo

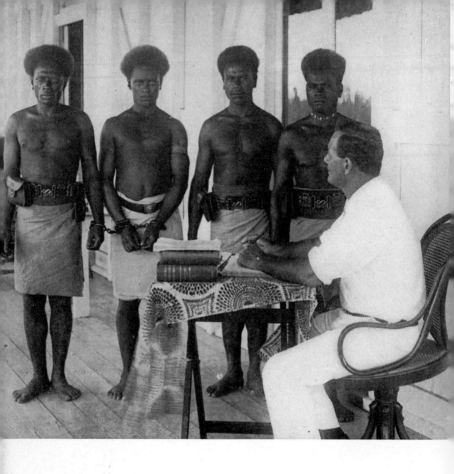

Mr. Bell holding court. The shackled native (second from left) was found guilty of murder, taken to his village and executed.

*Mr. Bell's houseboy.   He wears the smartest costume in the islands —
white shorts and coat, stiff collar and black tie, yellow orchid in the top
buttonhole.*

Malaita chief and wife on his bamboo throne. He wears a felt hat; his wife chews betel nut which stains her lips vivid red.

Malaita mother and children. Even young women look old from drudgery in the savage Solomons.

Across the Langa Langa Lagoon to the artificial islands built up by natives to escape being murdered on the mainland.

*An artificial island with its stone wall, palms, and thatched houses.
The natives live on fish, coconuts, and hope.*

Sua, chief of the artificial islands, poses with his favorite wife and son and one of Mr. Bell's soldiers. The most intelligent and powerful of the Lagoon chiefs, he would do practically anything for money. That made him chief.

Martin arrived with the chief and several warriors. He was elated, and quickly set up his cameras. The warriors were very athletic and healthy-looking, and all were decorated with shell ornaments in their hair and with colorful wampum necklaces or armlets. Some carried knives and flint tomahawks and others spears or clubs, but whether because of their finery or their intelligence or Mr. Bell's assurances, they did not look especially menacing. Not even those who had bones through their noses. They were shy, but smiled agreeably and seemed friendly.

'They are the bankers and jewelers of the Solomons,' said Mr. Bell. 'They live surrounded by a gold mine of shells and they make the most of it. The money they coin and those beautiful mother-of-pearl ornaments they carve are much sought after by the natives of the mainland, who are too lazy or too stupid to do this work themselves. This money circulates all over the Solomons.'

'Have they really given up cannibalism?' I asked, as I eyed the bones in their noses.

Mr. Bell smiled, and said, in an undertone, 'I wouldn't be surprised if they had a bit to eat now and then, just as a special treat or for a ceremony. But I don't think they would do the killing. After all, they are rich and can buy anything they want.'

Martin posed the chief and then his favorite wife and little son. The wife was a buxom creature and her pot belly protruded in a bulge over the top of an abbreviated grass skirt. She was dirty, but she was loaded about the neck and wrists with wampum and shell ornaments. Her eyes were red and sore from the smoke fires and her hands were evidently accustomed to heavy work. She never once smiled, and I was sure she had little in her life of drudgery to smile about. When Martin finished, she promptly turned and fled, her grass skirt wagging behind her.

When we asked the young boys down on the beach to pose, they seemed to know just what we wanted. They held up

their starfish and dove and swam and, like all children, were
unafraid and enjoyed showing off. They weren't concerned
about what we had in the black box, and they behaved as
though they had always acted for the movies.

'No wonder they are so athletic, with nothing to do but
swim and fish and play for a living,' I said, enthusiastic about
the first real show of energy and enterprise we had seen in the
islands.

'They learn to paddle a canoe and swim before most children at home are out of a perambulator,' said Mr. Bell. 'Real
sea-urchins. And I believe they are half brothers to the
sharks, for the place is full of the vermin and I have never
known one of these youngsters to be bitten.'

We stepped into our canoe to leave, and I saw a school of
mullet swimming only a few yards away. I shot blindly at
them with my rifle. One mullet floated to the surface, and a
youngster retrieved it for me.

'By Jove, that's perfect,' said Mr. Bell. 'Right through the
eye. I think you'll do in the jungles.'

On the way home we skirted island after island of the group.
Some were so tiny that there seemed scarcely room for a house,
and only two or three tufted palms rose above the wall of
stones. The tide was rising and the islands seemed about
to be submerged.

'How on earth do they keep from being washed out to sea?'
I thought out loud.

'They take quite a lot of punishment in bad weather,' replied Mr. Bell. 'But the Lagoon is usually calm and about as
idyllic a place as man could find. And what is a little wind
and water, to escape from bloodthirsty Malaita and live in
peace?'

Great flocks of birds were now on the wing, skimming from
island to island, lighting in the trees for a moment and then
taking off again. Gulls and herons fishing for their evening's
meal and making spectacular splashing dives into the sea.
Cranes wading about the beaches for crabs and whitebait and

whatever they could find.   Royal blue starlings on the prowl, scolding at the top of their voices.   Scarlet and red parrots in clusters of fifty or more.   White and yellow cockatoos, scouting for bits of banana and coconut thrown away by the islanders, or attracted by the smell of fruit in the trees.   We sped homeward among these winged rainbows and floating jungles, and I could see in the Commissioner's face the exhilaration he felt, enjoying his lonely liberty and his little empire of untamed beauty.

Coming to the mainland I saw a hundred or more natives seated along the beach.   Offshore were a number of canoes, with an oarsman in each.   The people were quite animated and I asked what was going on.

'That is our market,' said Mr. Bell proudly.   'I have had the bush cleared as you can see, and encourage the natives from the islands and from the mainland to come here and do their trading.'

Better to have them in one place and where he could keep an eye on them, he thought.

'The sentries collect and hold all weapons during the trading.   And we keep the men out of it as much as possible. You see, the mainland men stay back there on the shore and the island men sit in their canoes, while the women mingle and do the trading.   The women are better bargainers anyway and have more sense.   It was difficult to begin, but now the market is quite a success and is making the natives more agreeable.'

We walked up the beach, but the women were so busy they ignored us.   They were chattering like cockatoos, bartering fish for yams and shells for pigs with excited gestures.   I could imagine them saying: 'But we have had bad luck and the yams have not done well this year, even though we have had new ground and our men have prayed and protected the gardens with many areca leaves.   Every day we have cultivated and nursed the gardens.   These yams are the best of the crop and are surely worth more than those few fish.'

While the island woman replied: 'These fish are the best. See how fat they are, and how juicy and sweet. But the fishing is hard. Nets have been lost in the storms and the sharks have torn them and new ones have had to be made, again and again. Our men have worked from morning to night every day this week, for only a few bonita. You dig a hole in the ground and nature does the rest, but we have to slave for every fish we catch, and use much skill. Five more yams and we will call it a bargain.'

Mr. Bell was listening intently. He smiled and I saw the deep pleasure and satisfaction he felt in this reward for his patient discipline.

4 〰〰〰〰〰

. . . my own head some day

ARLY THE NEXT MORNING I was wakened by a woodpecker lustily boring into a near-by tree. The air was heavy and still and humid and I could not get back to sleep. At intervals the hammering continued, and the whole out-of-doors began to buzz with sound. I dressed and went outside.

Every insect and bird seemed at work. Bumblebees droned about and honeybees sipped nectar from the hibiscus, frangipani, lemon, and orange blossoms. Spiders were finishing off great webs in the bushes. Fruit-eating pigeons, cockatoos, and parrots fluttered among banana and papaya trees. Moths and butterflies darted everywhere. And all the mosquitoes in the garden seemed to be alive and on the wing.

Beyond the clearing the sea was glassy-calm, and I could see fish jumping, like trout in a pond. In the heavy heat, the water looked very inviting, and I was struck with an idea. I would go for a dip before anyone was awake and have a nice appetite for breakfast.

Tiptoeing back for my bathing suit, I quickly put it on and stole out across the parade ground. The dew was still heavy on the grass and my canvas shoes were soaked with it by the time I reached the beach. I carried my shoes and walked barefoot along the water's edge. The sand was freshly fur-

41

rowed and marked with thousands of tracks of birds, turtles, lizards, rats, frogs, and crocodiles, as though they had all just been there for a bazaar.

Down the beach I saw several little boys playing on the sand and started toward them. As I approached, they all scampered into their canoes and paddled out to a safe distance to watch, calling at me like imps. I waded into the water and tried to tell them that I wanted one of those canoes.

'Me takum this one fellah canoe belong you,' I said, beckoning to the nearest little fellow. 'Me go ketchum two fellah tobac. Givum father belong you.'

I continued to ask for his canoe and promise him tobacco for his father, and at last he put up his hand and nodded. With two or three quick thrusts of his paddle, he was ashore. He climbed out of the canoe, showing no fear of me.

Then, as I stepped into his canoe and pushed off, he laughed and clapped his hands, as though he had just accomplished the best joke ever. And indeed he had, for I spun around and around in the little dugout, and almost capsized, and got nowhere at all. The boys all howled and splashed water and made quite a circus of the white 'Mary' who could not even paddle, and they were soon all around me, looking me over to see what I would do next. When I finally caught on and made off in clumsy strokes, they applauded noisily.

Being afloat was exhilarating, and I paddled vigorously. The youngsters had now become my escort and were merrily paddling ahead of me and motioning me on. We came to a small river and the boys turned into it. The stream was sluggish and calm. It was overhung with a lacework of trees and looked very cool and inviting, so I followed.

The sides were overgrown with mangroves which at a little distance looked like great banks of dark green rhododendrons. But the tide was out and as I entered the stream, I saw that the mangroves were a gnarled mass of ugly roots and branches and the exposed mud stank with a rotten smell. Huge oysters clung to the trunks and great bats hung upside down from the branches. Cranes started up with a great beating of wings, their feet trailing the water. Turtles plumped into the stream and a great monitor lizard rattled off a branch and fell with a splash. Big frogs eyed me fearfully, and tree-climbing fish, which I had been wanting to see, scuttled down the mud banks. A baby crocodile stuck his nose out of the water and swam quickly away. I wondered what I would do in this tiny canoe if I met a big crocodile.

One of the little boys paddled back to me and handed me a spray of fragrant white flowers from a creeper. 'You wantum this one fellah?' he asked in a piping voice, and I thought him very gallant for his tender age.

Around a bend in the stream was a landing, from which a wide path led to huts just beyond. Here the youngsters had pulled up and were waiting for me. I was exhausted and glad for a little rest, but I didn't want to admit it. I reached up for an overhanging branch to pause and watched the youngsters climb ashore. They seemed to have adopted me by now and to expect me to visit their village. The idea seemed just the thing to do, and after a few minutes I climbed out and followed the boys a short distance through the bush to a cluster of shabby huts.

Outside the first hut was a very old hag busily at work weaving a mat. Beside her was an even more emaciated old man, who sat stolidly and looked at me. The old woman hardly looked up, but grunted at the boys and spat betel-nut juice and went on with her work. The place was unspeakably dirty.

Farther on, a middle-aged, buxom woman was wrestling with a pig in a doorway. She straddled the pig and held it between her knees, and began looking it over as a mother monkey does her baby. Then she picked fleas out of its hide, one after another, and cracked them between her fingernails, as if she were very satisfied with her find.

The village seemed deserted. The women were probably in the gardens and the men off on a holiday. Three youngish women came in with loads of yams and tossed them down with grunts of relief. They gave me a curious stare, but seemed too busy or too stupid to care and went off again in the way they had come.

Mangy dogs and pigs waddled in and out of the houses. The dogs looked mean. They showed their teeth and circled around me, but my strange white skin must have affected them, for they put their tails between their legs and crept away.

I turned to go and something caught my eye through the trees. Men were coming. They were Mr. Bell and Martin and several sentries. Like a person coming out of a dream, I was suddenly aware of my surroundings.

Mr. Bell strode toward me and I could see in the fixed, firm cast of his jaw and mouth that I was in for it. If his look could have killed, I would have been slain on the spot. For a moment his lips trembled as he struggled to control his anger. I smiled my best smile, but I could think of nothing to say.

'What are you up to now, young lady?' he boomed.

'Why, I am only having a little fun with the children,' said I meekly.

'Fun!' he snapped. 'Thank God, you're not potted meat.'

I looked beyond him at Martin, who looked as though he were going to shake apart. His lips were moving, but he seemed unable to speak.

'Martin, can't I do anything in this place but be tabooed? You all treat me like a sissy, and I'm sick of it. All this talk about cannibalism; I think the whole thing is exaggerated.'

Mr. Bell exploded. After all the tension, all he could do was to swear. I was frozen with the suddenness and fury of his attack.

'You're a bloody little fool. That is the mildest thing I can say to you. And I tell you, here and now, that the British Government will have no more of this responsibility. I risk my head enough every day, without having to account for your bloody nonsense in the bargain. The sooner you leave

for Tulagi or for America, the better we all will like it, do you
understand?'

We started toward the river.   Mr. Bell struck savagely at
the trees with his walking stick every few feet, but he ignored
me completely.   We climbed into the war canoe that was
waiting at the landing.   I kept very still.

I was terribly sorry.   Slowly, I began to realize the serious-
ness of what I had done.   This might easily be the end of our
visit and the ruin of Martin's plans, so successfully begun, to
find 'the real thing' on Malaita.

When we reached the house, Mr. Bell was still so angry that
his hand trembled.   'Sit down,' he said, with the cutting
coldness of a piece of ice.

'There is just one more thing I want to remark,' he continued, looking through me with his gaze.   'Your reference to
cannibalism just now.   Exaggerated!   I can put down such a
statement to only one thing — abysmal ignorance.   What do
you think I have been doing here these many years; sleeping?
Do you think I have built this establishment and trained these
guards, and that Government has gone to all this expense and
exercise, for some mild pleasure?   This is all serious business,
too serious for your inexperience to comprehend.   Do you
know that hundreds and probably thousands of people have
been murdered within sight of where you are sitting at this
moment?   And that I spend every hour here at my peril?
On those trails in the mountains, I was fearful that something
would pop out at us around every turn.

'You were blissfully aware only of the birds and butterflies.

'I have been willing to give you this protection and assistance
because I was asked to do so, and because I have liked you
both.   But when you talk such drivel as to call these perils
exaggerated, you infuriate me.   Every minute you have been
here, you have been in danger of being attacked, and the
mere fact that you are white and a stranger has increased the
hazard.   I have expected the house to be rushed any night and
have had special guards posted constantly.   And I have had

your every movement watched by the guards, one of whom trailed you this morning. Exaggerated! Why, this place reeks with murder and head-cutting. And I will not be surprised if they have my own head some day.'

Martin was white with all this unpleasantness. But he composed himself enough to say, 'Mr. Bell, I have talked to the trader who came in yesterday and he has offered to take us to Guadalcanal and Tulagi. If we may have your permission, we will accept.'

'Capital,' exclaimed the Commissioner. He promptly left us for the drill-ground.

How justified Mr. Bell had been in his apprehensions I only found out ten years after we had left the Solomons, when I learned that he himself had been murdered.

To show the savagery of the natives and what happens if the white man relaxes his vigilance even for a moment, I am going to quote from the official report of the commissioner appointed by the British Government to investigate this killing.

Under the heading *Malaita Murders*, the report says:

On 4th October, 1927, between 11 A.M. and 12 noon, Mr. W. R. Bell, District Officer, Malaita, was murdered by being struck on the head by a gun barrel at Kwaiambe in the Sinarango sub-district of Malaita. The attack was prearranged, and, in the mêlée which immediately followed, Mr. K. C. Lillies, a cadet in the Administrative Service, a clerk named Marcus, and twelve members of the Armed Constabulary, Government employees, or domestic servants, who accompanied Mr. Bell, were also killed.

I visited the scene of the outrage and received a vivid description of what happened from an eye-witness. About 11 A.M. some 250 Sinarango natives arrived at the small clearing round the 'Tax House' at Kwaiambe. They were nearly all armed with native weapons, and in addition carried a small number of 'Sniders' — a generic term for any form of old rifle — which they had been told to bring with them to surrender. They apparently expressed their dissatisfaction at having to give up their 'Sniders' and Mr. Bell addressed them, telling them to put down their weapons, come and pay their tax, and that he would afterwards discuss the 'Snider' question with them. This does not appear to have been done in all cases, but at any rate those who came up to pay their tax did lay down their arms. The situation was then as follows. Two tables had been put out in front of the 'Tax House,' Mr. Bell was seated at the right-hand table and Mr. Lillies at the left, the clerk Marcus was standing in between, and at each table there were also two constables, not as a guard but to take the tax money as it was handed in; the remainder of the escort was, by Mr. Bell's orders, inside the house; the queue of natives extended from Mr. Bell's table right round the house to Mr. Lillies' table. After about twenty people at each table had paid their taxes, one Basiana, who was the leader in the affair and who had laid down his gun barrel some twelve feet from Mr. Bell's table and gone up to pay his tax, returned behind the queue, picked up his gun barrel, broke through the queue, and struck Mr. Bell, who was bending over the table, on the top of the head, killing him instantly. Basiana, as he struck, shouted something in his native tongue, and instantly the sides of the house, which were only of leaf, were battered in and the police inside caught in a trap.

It is unnecessary here except briefly to recapitulate the steps taken to arrest the murderers. H.M.A.S. 'Adelaide' of the Australian Navy was sent from Sydney. A local defence force of volunteers from among the planters, recruiters, etc., was raised, and a number of ex-members of the Armed Constabulary re-engaged, and, with assistance from friendly natives, by February, 1928, all opposition was at an end and practically the whole of the adult males of the Sinarango tribe had been rounded up and lodged in gaol in Tulagi.

Subsequently a Judicial Commissioner was sent from Fiji to hear the cases arising out of the murders, with the result that seven natives were condemned to death, of whom six were executed and one reprieved, and seventeen others were sentenced to various terms of imprisonment.

… plenty copra … plenty taboos

HAT ISN'T BRONZE,' said Mr. Creswell, the trader whose boat we had just boarded, when I admired his color. 'That's malaria. And jaundice. Everybody in the islands has that kind of bronze. A few months down here and you'll have it like the rest of us. It's the mark of the Solomons.'

I breathed a silent prayer that whatever happened to me it would not be malaria. I had seen enough of Martin's chills, that made him shake from head to foot. I dreaded his burning fever and delirium as much as he did. 'You feel just as though you were going to die, but you don't,' Martin had said. I was grateful for the health with which I had always been blessed.

'But wait till you get blackwater fever,' said Mr. Creswell. 'That's the prize of them all. I had my go of it and never came closer to kicking the bucket. A little mosquito sneaks up and nips you and you go down for weeks, completely out of your head. Tremendous temperature — you vomit everything you eat — and there's pain you never could imagine. A fine thing to forget.'

We had left Mr. Bell's place at Auki and were skidding down the wave-washed shore of Malaita, in Mr. Creswell's schooner, bound for Guadalcanal and the copra plantations, and then Tulagi. The mass of the island rose from the ocean like a captive piece of the Sierras, wooded and majestically beautiful. Plumes of white cloud clung to the towering four-thousand-foot peaks and contrasted sharply with the blue of the sea about us. It seemed almost incredible that in this place, so blessed with beauty, there should be so much lurking evil.

'I have a few stops to make,' said Mr. Creswell. 'Some copra waiting for me down here, I hope. And I'll show you some of Malaita's "best people." The farther south you go, the worse they seem to be, but I wouldn't give you much for any of them. All I ask is that they let me alone to do my work, but you never know what's next in this place.'

Our skipper, Thomas Creswell, was one of those earnest and ardent speculators of the islands, dreaming of riches, but going about money-making the hard way. He had evidently prospered at his peripatetic trade, for his schooner was an expensive little craft, well designed and fitted with the best of everything. He kept the ship in apple-pie order, from her neat sails to her polished brass, and he himself had the air of one who was accustomed to living well.

His strong face and chin, cool blue eyes, close-cropped, sandy mustache, and blond hair reminded me of a handsome English colonel we had met in Sydney. He piqued my curiosity. I wondered if he had come from some military family at home and had run away to the end of the Empire, as so many others had done, to escape some family unpleasantness or love affair. Certainly he was no ordinary sailor or roustabout, although he was as strong as any of them, and his crew gave him a respect that showed they did not want to mix with his fists nor his reprimands.

'There is an old chief down here who will make you a fine picture,' he said. 'The worst old blighter I ever met. Has hands and toes like an ape and almost makes the ape-man legend of Malaita come true. But he's a coward. Every time I see him, I know he'd like my head, but hasn't the nerve to come and get it. He once went raiding over on the islands, they tell me, but the natives out there put him in his place, killed most of his men, and he was glad to get back home alive and all in one piece. That gave him something to remember, and saved Mr. Bell a punitive expedition. He used to look like my "Satan" over there.'

He pointed to the helmsman. A devil Satan surely was. Out of his bushy black hair, standing straight up from his head, protruded two bone ornaments that looked exactly like yellowed horns. His face was very black, and strong with fierce cunning. He was a powerful fellow, and the muscles in his arms and back bulged and rippled as he swung the wheel. In his ears were shell earrings and from his nose hung a large ring of bone. I was fascinated by that flopping bone ring in his nose and wondered how he ever managed to eat with such a piece hanging over his mouth.

The rest of the crew were almost equally picturesque, but with a less-exaggerated barbarism. One was the fattest man I had seen in the islands. His stomach and jowls bulged and his neck and back were padded with flesh. He wore no clothes but a G-string, and no ornaments except a cluster of three cowrie shells in his long woolly hair. Unlike most of the scowling natives we had seen, he was always smiling and everything seemed to strike him as funny; a fine trait to encourage in this over-solemn part of the world.

One of the boys looked exactly like an Irishman, with his long upper lip and a shortened and upturned nose. His nose was just like mine, Martin said. But he was as black as the ace of spades.

Another looked surprisingly like a chimpanzee. He had the sloping brow, abbreviated head, and enlarged mouth, and he even spat like one. As he went scampering about the deck, he seemed to walk with a chimpanzee's shuffling and swinging gait. And when he finally climbed the mast, gripping the ropes firmly with his toes, I was sure there must be some relation.

'Around that point,' said the skipper, 'we go ashore and pick up my copra. And there is your chief, if he's at home.'

We anchored in a small and attractive bay, the shore of which was banked with coconut palms. Climbing into the whaleboat with a large supply of trade tobacco, beads, and calico, we made for the beach. Some fifty natives, all men and all armed, waited for us there.

'Usually that means trouble — only men, and especially when they are armed,' said Mr. Creswell. 'When they are up to mischief, they hide their women or order them away. These fellows will be expecting me and will be all right. If they make any warlike motions, it will be just to show off.'

But he turned the whaleboat stern to shore, I noticed, and strapped two revolvers to his belt.

Then, followed by his tough-looking boys, all well armed, he waded ashore. Martin followed. Satan carried me on his back.

As I climbed down on the beach, I hoped Satan didn't have ringworm.

Natives were moving out of the bush on every side, but as we walked toward them, I saw that Mr. Creswell was already presenting the chief with an entire case of tobacco, and was slapping him familiarly on the back and smiling as he talked.

After Mr. Creswell's glowing description, I was disappointed in the chief. His face was rugged and fierce enough, but he no longer had Satan's youthful and athletic figure, and all the commanding power seemed to be gone out of him. He was wrinkled and nearly bald and bent forward on a crooked walking stick that reminded me of Harry Lauder's. His legs were even more spindly than the rest of him and were covered with scales of earth or of some disease.

We saluted as Mr. Creswell presented us and the chief gave us a toothless grin, for he apparently had only four front teeth left. His watery eyes and senile mouth gave him a leering look, but he seemed quite tame in other respects. Around his neck he wore several strands of porpoise and dogs' teeth,

and shell ornaments hung from each elongated ear lobe.
About his arms were bands of colored, woven grass, and from
a waistband of attractive small shells hung a loincloth of
hammered treebark.   His hands were large and his arms
overlong, and these, with his distended feet and swinging gait,
did give him an apelike cast, as the skipper had predicted.

'Gottem plenty copra, belong me?' asked Mr. Creswell.

The chief grinned broadly.   'My word, me gottem plenty
copra belong you one fellah,' he said, in a deep guttural.

The beach near the treeline was piled with small pyramids
of coconuts, ready for the taking.   Our skipper gave the supply a satisfied look and, without a moment's delay, he and the
chief began bargaining.   Soon the chief grunted and nodded
his agreement, and motioned to his men.   They promptly
made for the coconuts and began loading them into the
whaleboat and making them into rafts for floating out to the
schooner.

I saw that our skipper's policy was, *No sooner said than done*.
He supervised the whole proceeding with the assurance and
confidence of a major-general and showed his experience and
skill in managing these people, a skill which I envied him and
hoped that we could acquire.

Everything now seemed so agreeable that Martin began
making motion pictures of the natives at work and of the chief
and his armed bodyguard.   Mr. Creswell came up and explained to the men that they were all now inside the black
bokkus, 'all same belong eye belong you,' although they were
actually still outside.   The chief grunted, uncomprehendingly,
but did not seem to be too alarmed.   He was probably more
interested in how he could extract another case of tobacco
than in whether we had any magic powers.   Presently he
beckoned and we all followed him through the towering
trees and along a pathway to his village.

There was a bustle of work in the village clearing as we
entered.   Fires were blazing and I smelled the appetizing
scent of roasting pork and nuts and the sweetish aroma of
baking yams.   I became violently hungry.

'This is going to be a relief from bully beef,' said our skipper. 'And don't be afraid to eat! These people are clean, as Malaitans go.'

Not one of the women wore a stitch of clothing. They might look clean to the skipper, but they looked to me as though none of them had had a bath for months. Their legs were caked with dirt, and there was dirt in the wrinkles of their necks and elbows.

They spread fresh banana leaves for us to sit upon, and others to use as plates. Then they brought us each, on a small piece of banana leaf, a juicy chunk of roast pork with a kind of sauce of grated coconut and milk. It was delicious. There followed a pudding made of steamed yams, mashed and mixed with chopped, roasted almonds. Other yams had been baked in their shells, the skin broken and wild honey poured in. Baked fresh plantains (red bananas) came in their charred skins, and the inside was most succulent and tasty. Roast fish, freshly caught in the sea that morning, was delicate and juicy and tasted much like our channel bass. Fresh papayas, with cool coconut milk to drink, gave us a real feast.

'They may be primitive,' said Martin, as he stuffed. 'But those women are certainly artists at the campfire.'

The skipper must be pulling our leg about this headhunting chief, I thought. The old man seemed too agreeable and this life too settled. But I noticed that the skipper kept his revolvers unstrapped and ready, and that Satan and two of his men stood near-by, leaning on their Snider rifles. He was evidently taking no chances despite all the show of politeness.

'Mary belong me, makum good fellah kai-kai,' said the chief, smacking his lips.

'Mary belong you, good fellah too much,' replied the skipper appreciatively.

'You gottem plenty Mary belong you?' asked the chief, turning to Martin.

Martin chuckled and winked at the chief. 'Me gottem one fellah Mary; him here,' he said, pointing to me.

'My word,' said the chief sympathetically; 'suppose you givvem me one bokkus tobacu, me givvem you two fellah Mary belong me. Makem good fellah kai-kai belong you.'

'Don't laugh, Osa,' said Martin seriously. 'But just think. I paid thirty-five dollars for your wedding hat and here I can get two wives for a dollar's worth of tobacco twist. That ought to keep you in your place for a while.'

'The chief probably paid a pig for his best wife,' said the skipper, 'and maybe a few porpoise teeth and ornaments to the father, to top the bargain. From her looks, I suppose she is from another tribe — that is a practice of theirs — to bring in new blood.'

Martin turned to the chief, and with what he meant for a gesture of gratitude, he said, 'Me no wantum two fellah more Mary, Chief. One fellah Mary belong me, he trouble too much.'

The chief grunted. Then he looked me over critically, wondering, I suppose, what could make me worth fifty women to Martin. To make sure that he was not offended, Martin had our spare case of tobacco brought out and presented to the old fellow, who was as pleased as any child at a Christmas tree.

Presently, the chief began talking to us in rapid and guttural *bêche-de-mer*. He was inviting us to visit his headhouse, Mr. Creswell said. I rose and started to accompany the men, but the chief turned on me sternly.

'Name belong you, Mary,' he said. 'You no go along big house belong Master.' He seemed very indignant.

'You see how it is,' said the skipper apologetically. 'It's a man's world and you will just have to get used to it.'

The whole thing seemed very silly. Grown men being as secretive as little boys over a grass shed, full of skulls and bones and shells and mumbo-jumbo paraphernalia. I had a puckish impulse to go and walk right into the headhouse after them and challenge the whole mystic nonsense. I wanted especially to crack this repression of their women. Somebody would have to be the first to do it.

But Martin and I had agreed that we would always treat every primitive person we met with respect. Just as though his ways were as reasonable and intelligent as our own. We had resolved to be only observers and not reformers.

For a bodyguard, Mr. Creswell had left me one of his men. I looked at the boy's woolly head and ignorant face, and at the old Snider rifle which he probably couldn't shoot if he wanted to, and wondered whether he would be any real protection. I would probably be just as safe with the old savage chief.

The women had now gathered in little groups and stood staring at me, as though I were a museum piece or some evil spirit, and I wished I could talk to them.

One of the women held a tiny baby not over a few weeks old. It was cute and chubby, and I had an impulse to go and hold it. I decided to try and started toward her, smiling and speaking as assuringly as I could in *bêche-de-mer*. She shrank from me and held her baby close, but did not run.

How shall I get her confidence? I thought. If I am going to get along here, I must learn, and this will be the test.

I looked at the mother and almost cooed, in English this time. She was panting with fear, scowled at me, and mumbled something that did not sound too friendly. The baby was a little girl, a pretty little thing, and I began talking to her and then trilled like a canary. She looked up at me and smiled. The mother melted, and smiled. Then she spat a stream of betel-nut juice and to my delight she gave me the baby.

I hugged and rocked the child and went on imitating birdcalls, and she seemed fascinated. She was clean and fresh as a flower, and I recalled Mr. Bell's remark that if these children could only be taken at this age and given proper care, they would grow up as bright and good as any children at home. I dreaded to think of all the toil and abuse she would have to suffer, until, like her mother, she would be old in her twenties.

'Right at home, I see.' Martin had come up behind me. 'Good girl!' he said approvingly.

I handed him the child, but he was never much with babies and handed it gingerly back to its mother, who scowled and spat and disappeared.

The skipper was now anxious to be off, and we started for the beach, accompanied by the chief and what seemed to be the entire village. The coconuts were all aboard. The skipper talked with the chief in *bêche-de-mer*, assuring him that he would call again soon for another cargo, and we climbed into the whaleboat and rowed away.

'That red silk handkerchief you are wearing, Mrs. Johnson. That would be worth the whole copra cargo,' said the skipper. 'I think the old boy would rather have it than the heads of all three of us.'

The schooner was so loaded with coconuts that she rode low in the water. There were masses of the cargo everywhere. The nuts, tied together with strings of vine in bundles of twenty or thirty each, were piled all about us and even choked the passageways. There was scarcely room on deck to walk, and in the hold below every available inch was taken.

'With this load I think we will go straight to Guadalcanal,' said the skipper. 'Smooth water and a slight breeze will give us a fine trip over.'

The moon rose and made a writhing silver pattern on the billowing sea. I put out several fishlines, each baited with a strip of white rag for a 'fly,' to catch bonita or kingfish for our breakfast. The lines made little phosphorescent streaks behind us in the wake. One by one the stars came out. The constellations were strange to me, except that I knew the Southern Cross, but the Milky Way looked just as it did in Chanute, Kansas.

As the three of us sat on the hatch and the skipper and Martin smoked their pipes, I asked my usual multitude of questions. Especially about the women: how did they live together with one man and not fight; how did they bear their children with no apparent comforts; how did they survive all the work, illness, and abuse?'

'That is simpler than you think,' the skipper said. 'It is a matter of what a person is used to or has a liking for that makes him bear his lot. You like this life, but I daresay many a woman wouldn't.'

'But I have some protection against disease and I am not exactly abused,' I said.

'These women don't feel abused either,' he replied. 'They are just naturally strong. Why, one of these women will give birth to a child, right out in the garden or the forest or wherever she may be, without a doctor or even midwife, and the next day she will be back at work again.'

'I wonder if they could stand civilization?' asked Martin.

'They would probably die of pneumonia or boredom or lack of the foods they like,' Mr. Creswell said. 'After thousands of years they have adapted themselves to the Solomons and are masters of this climate and way of life. And they are at their best right up against nature in the raw.'

He became enthusiastic about the beauty and simplicity of life in the islands, and I could see that he, like Mr. Bell, was a little touched by them. He was obviously remaining here because he liked the life and not just for profit.

I asked him again how women could get along so well together, all being wives of one man.

'Polygamy is pretty much a state of mind,' he said. 'With an economic twist. On a farm at home, a man likes to have a large family of children to help with the heavy work. Here, a man has wives enough to take care of his gardens and household — as much for this reason as for vanity or self-indulgence.'

The first wife ran the show and looked after the younger wives, as though they were her children, he explained. And she treated all the children of the household with as much consideration as though they belonged to her.

'These people are kind to their children. To be sure, some of them sell off the surplus when they have too many, but they don't go around abusing the youngsters as the natives do over in New Hebrides and in some parts of New Guinea. The chief wife keeps strict discipline over the girls, especially here on Malaita; she spies on them and sees that there is no monkey business of any kind, and she is mother to the whole lot.'

'I still think the men are brutes,' I said, trying to provoke him to talk.

'They look that way to you, but they aren't much different from the rest of us,' he said. 'Some day the idealists, like Mr. Bell, will calm them down and show them that they can get along better with each other by peace than by war, and by reasoning better than by magic and superstition. Then the only remaining difference between them and us will be color.'

'Their taboos against women are disgusting,' I said, getting back to my pet annoyance. 'They are just selfishly imposed by the men who are better bullies than the women.'

'Go easy with them, nevertheless,' he said earnestly. 'The taboos restrict your fun, but they will save your head some day and maybe your husband's. The way to be a success in the Solomons is to be careful and be lucky. Here are a few primary "don'ts" that I have learned to follow. Remember them if you are going to get along down here:

'Don't make the advances; let the natives make them.

'However peculiar they may look to you, treat them as though they were very wise and entitled to every respect.

'Always be pleasant; nothing is so disarming and reassuring as a smile. But don't let them think you are making fun of them.

'Don't go unarmed anywhere. The natives never attack unless they are sure they can get you. They regard a woman as weak and they may take chances with you that they wouldn't take with me or your husband. Show a rifle or revolver; it is a fine way to keep them from starting anything.

'Don't turn your back and don't let them surround you

'Keep the stern of your boat to shore and within good running distance, unless you are well covered or very sure of your ground.

'Don't get too close to a native. He may have some superstitious reaction, and do you damage before you know it.

'Don't go into any dwelling unless you know it is safe.

'Don't pick flowers until you know which are taboo and
which are not. And the same for creepers and leaves. The
areca, for example, is a charm; let it alone. And so, also, the
little white star-flowers the boys wear in their hair. Anyway,
some of the foliage is poisonous, so that is just as well.

'Don't touch arrows and spears. They may have poisoned
tips, and are sure death. Some of the poisons are so potent
that they last for years or forever.

'And you, Mrs. Johnson, must be very careful. Don't walk
down a trail unless your husband or a guard is with you, and
even then have both eyes open, for many trails are taboo to
women. Give your attentions only to women and girls, but
even then be careful. In many islands you cannot walk on
the beach past their headhouses or clubhouses, and certain
landings and other spots are taboo to women.

'Don't be too cocky; just be agreeable. You are not in your
own country, and these people think that they are actually
better than you are.

'I know this must be pretty discouraging, but I don't want
your head, with those blonde pigtails to hang in some Solomons headhouse. And I want you both to get home with
those pictures.'

6 mmmm

. . . one moment of carelessness . . .
your life is over

'THANK GOD for good weather this morning,' said
the skipper. 'This is the trickiest channel in the Solomons.'
He stood at the wheel, watching the open water ahead.
'Many a time, I've anchored outside, to ride out a squall or
an ebb tide, rather than risk it.'

With sails furled and with only the power of our little fifteen
horsepower 'kicker,' we crept inshore from the sea toward
Guadalcanal. The land ahead seemed more like a continent
than an island, and this spot might easily have been the
Santa Barbara coast. Behind the low shoreline rose an entire
range of mountains, nearly eight thousand feet in height, the
upper slopes half-hidden in billows of cloud and the deep
ravines banked with gray and purple mists. Heavy forests
covered the range. Through the binoculars I could see thin
columns of smoke from native fires, curling upward. Peaks
thrust skyward above the clouds, as white in the morning sun
as though they were glacier-covered. But I knew the glaciers
would be only exposed rock.

Satan was taking soundings with a weighted line. 'Six
fathoms, me hittum bottom belong ocean,' he shouted.

'My word!' yelled the skipper, turning his wheel sharply over to the left. 'You no gottem eye belong you? Me no wantem ship belong me sleep along this one fellah reef.' Then, with a curse, he muttered: 'The bally blighters! If I don't watch every one of them, I'm a goner. A hundred times I've made this channel and he picks today to hang us up.'

But we did not hang up, thanks to his skill.

A great shark fin broke the water beside us. I looked after it and saw a shadow that seemed twenty feet long. Several dolphins leaped and dove and another great shark shot after them.

'No place for swimming,' said the skipper. 'Every sailor who goes into this passage wonders if he will land in a shark's belly. In the old days the natives would come out from shore and take your head if the sharks missed you.'

For more than an hour we picked our way in a zigzag course through the choppy water. A boy in the rigging and another in the bow yelled warnings to the skipper, who somehow managed to find his way, and keep his calm and good disposition through the ordeal.

'Me lookem beacho!' shouted the boy in the rigging.

'Righto,' shouted back the skipper. 'Good fellah boy.' And then, to us, he added, 'That means clear water.' He wiped his brow and seemed to relax for the first time.

The crew boys were now jumping about and working with terrific energy and excitement. Like all sailors, they were evidently anticipating their shore leave — the girls they would see, the feasts they would have, and the dancing around the campfires. The skipper bellowed to them to keep their wits about them.

One of the crew came to relieve the skipper at the wheel. I saw that he had a narrow band tied around his head. It was so tightly drawn across his forehead that it almost cut into the skin.

'What name you gottem this one fellah belong head belong you?' I asked.

He looked at me as though he thought I was very stupid and said, 'My word, Mary, me gottem sore head belong me.'

'That is an old headache cure,' said the skipper. 'Probably gives them a counter-headache, so the first one isn't noticed. If you see fir leaves, with yellow berries, hanging around their necks, that is to cure a cold or sore throat. A plaster of leaves, tied on with a string, will be to draw a boil to a head — they cook the leaves and make a poultice. For rheumatism they rub the limbs with betel-pepper leaves, then crush the leaves and throw them into the sea or the fire. They tell me it succeeds, but I haven't got rheumatism, and their cures don't seem to work for me anyway.'

We were entering a wide-sweeping bay. The shores were heavily grown with coconut palms, thousands upon thousands of them. Along the water's edge ran a beautiful white beach on which we now saw native boys coming out to watch us. Our immediate destination was the famous plantation of the Hardings, associated with Lever Brothers, the soap manufacturers, whose dealings in copra were the principal trade of the Solomons. Our skipper would sell his cargo to the management.

In a few years, the skipper told us, the plantation, which had covered a few acres to begin, had been expanded to more than seven thousand acres. This enormous coconut garden included extensive 'works' for curing and shipping the dried copra. There were so many workers needed that recruiters were kept busy bringing them in from Malaita and other islands.

A rich, sweetish aroma drifted out to us, suggestive of roasting coffee, peanuts, and popcorn combined.

'Copra,' said the skipper, as he sniffed the air appreciatively. 'And say, what food you're going to get! You'll have real luxury for a change. Real steaks, for they have their own cattle here. Broiled crawfish, better than any lobster. And the most delicious roast pork you have ever tasted. American salads, made of coconut palm hearts and fresh lettuce and

real tomatoes right out of the garden. And what cream —
you can't cut it with scissors — made by grating green coconut into fresh coconut milk, and letting it rise overnight —
you will never know it isn't cow's cream. You've got a big
treat coming.'

I was overcome with appetite. My mouth watered as the
skipper talked of delicacies I had not tasted for months. I
thought of my dad, back home in Kansas, for he would now
be in his garden that he loved, tending the sweet corn and
peas and new potatoes and strawberries. A longing for home
swept over me and I tried to keep from crying. But I
knew that this was getting me nowhere, so I struck out into
conversation and asked the skipper how long he meant to
stop here.

'A few days,' he said. 'Give me a chance to settle my accounts and polish up the ship, and you a little time to look
the place over and get back into the bush, if you want to see
this part of Guadalcanal.'

I asked him about the managers of the plantation and
whether they had white or native wives.

'You're going to meet a Baroness,' he replied. 'The manager married a Spanish Baroness Eugenie, a Castilian. They
are madly in love and very romantic and she has wonderful
clothes, right out here in the jungle, and excellent furnishings
and tableware and every possible luxury. Both seem to be
going a little native, but they are very practical about running
the plantation. They call the place "Penduffryn" — I don't
know why, but it's poetic.'

We anchored at some distance offshore, and presently we
saw a cutter coming out to us. In it was Mr. Bernays, the
plantation manager. He climbed aboard our schooner and
greeted the skipper warmly.

Mr. Bernays took my hand and then Martin's, as the skipper
presented us, and spoke in a warm and friendly tone. He
was a handsome Englishman, of middle age and medium
height, blue-eyed, with long black eyelashes and black hair.

He wore a mustache and goatee, and when he smiled, showed dimples and fine teeth.

'Glad to see an American,' he said to Martin enthusiastically. Then he apologized for being dressed in a native lava-lava, a patterned white cloth of knee length, tied around his waist, and for his bare feet. 'I wasn't expecting guests,' he said, and then, pointing to Mr. Creswell, 'This old blighter is one of the family.'

Mr. Bernays had taken off his large felt hat, a 'Baden-Powell,' and I saw that in his ears were small gold earrings. Around his neck was a gold chain and a locket, with a picture of a stately beauty framed in it. On a finger of each hand was a gold ring, one containing a huge white pearl and the other a black pearl of equal size.

I resolved to have pearls just like those if I could ever afford them, and I wondered if they would cost more than fifty thousand dollars each. As if an explorer would ever possess that vast sum! I promptly gave up the idea of having such pearls, though I continued to stare at them as we went ashore and walked down the dock.

Mr. Bernays was pointing out new buildings and other objects of interest in response to Martin's questions. 'We plant the coconut trees thirty feet apart,' he said, 'so they have ample light and air. The result is those fine large nuts, the best that grow. Natives have always cultivated coconuts, but their trees overrun and suffocate each other and the nuts are small. For centuries they have used coconut oil for their hair, cooking-fat, and other uses. We whites have just now caught up with them and gone them one better.'

Despite the wide planting, the fronds of the great trees reached each other overhead and made a green mat against the sky. In the grove beneath, scores of native boys were working at great piles of coconuts. With quick thrusts of a kind of dagger of hardwood, they split off the shaggy husks. Other boys took the nuts, and with long steel blades split them in half, and then, with a flip of the knife, scooped out the white meats. These were tossed into small piles, where collecting crews were picking them up and taking them off to the driers. Other crews were gathering the husks and removing them for burning.

Seeing us approach, the headman yelled orders and put on a great air of authority. Mr. Bernays chuckled, but saluted him and appeared to be very impressed. The boys were especially athletic, clean and well fed, and were among the best physical specimens we had seen. They worked with a will and were anything but lazy.

'Most of them are from Malaita,' said Mr. Bernays, 'but from all the other islands as well. Straight out of the bush. I think they show the effect of being well cared for and looked after, and are proof of the health they all could have with decent hygiene and discipline.'

Native girls were coming down the path, their grass skirts swaying from side to side as they walked. They looked like a troupe of dark-skinned ballet dancers. As they passed, they eyed us shyly, stared at me, giggled, and hurried on. Baskets were strapped to their backs — with food for the cutters. They all scorned foreign food, Mr. Bernays explained, and were content as long as they had enough yams, fish, and occasional pork. Their chief delicacy was 'flying fox,' the big fruit-eating bat.

We now came into a large compound with several substantial buildings in the center. These were surrounded by gardens, filled with blooming flowers and colored foliage, laid out in patterned beds. The beds were edged with croton hedges, conch shells, or coral stones. Neat paths, paved with crushed shell, led up to the main house. Here and there were giant clam shells filled with growing flowers. Several garden boys were at work, and each of them wore a flower behind his ear or in his hair. This was surely gardening in the best English tradition, and the Hardings were making the most of the climate to give themselves the illusion of home and the pleasure of greenery and color.

The main house, built up on stilts to avoid the pests and provide a good lookout, sprawled over a large area. It seemed enormous to us, who had seen only huts for so long. We were shown into a great living room, comfortably and tastefully done in European furniture. Mats covered the walls and gave the effect of paneling, and against these were bookcases filled with books. On the walls were hung natives' shields, spears, and other trophies, many of which were museum pieces. There were flowers and growing plants everywhere about the room and they showed a woman's fondness for them and skill in arrangement. In one corner was a wild boar's skull, and from it hung a growing creeper, much like our hunter's robe. In other receptacles were potted orchids. Through the open windows came a pleasant scent of flowers and earth and sea.

Mr. Harding came in and greeted us warmly. He was a big, handsome, blue-eyed man with a roundish face and an affability that at once made us feel at ease.

Seeing how much I admired the place, he showed us the other rooms. An adjoining 'recreation room' had a large billiard table and other game devices, and comfortable chairs of native hardwood. The dining room had a table large enough for at least twelve people, and great cabinets filled with fine china and glassware. Beyond, were serving pantries and storerooms, stocked with enough tinned provisions for a grocery store. And the kitchen was equally oversized and well equipped.

'My wife is in Sydney with Madame Bernays. She will be sorry not to see you, but let me show you her rooms,' Mr. Harding was saying.

He led us into an apartment occupying one wing of the building. A large bedroom was furnished with a handsome French suite, brought from home. The bed was a four-poster, and there were ample chests, and a dressing-table loaded with cosmetics, perfumes, and eau-de-colognes which I was dying to smell, but didn't. The fine mirrors made me aware of my disreputable jungle make-up, and I wished that I had a decent dress to wear. In an adjoining dressing-room was a tin bath-tub and all the fittings of home, except for the porcelain and nickel. All this was a fine compromise with the jungle for one who enjoyed luxury, but was determined to make the most of Guadalcanal.

In our own room Martin and I found tea ready. But he looked worried.

'Don't you feel well?' I asked anxiously.

'I feel all right,' he said. 'But Mr. Harding said to dress for dinner, and you know I haven't any clothes with me but what I have on.'

'I'll wear the little dress I wore at Mr. Bell's and that will make up for both of us,' I assured him.

I took the dress from my duffel-bag. It was a simple blue-and-white, checked gingham-taffeta, with organdy collar and cuffs. The dress fell apart in my hands. 'What on earth!' I exclaimed. I examined it and saw that it had been cut from top to bottom, as though with sharp scissors.

'Silverfish!' said Martin, and he laughed as though he had just heard the best joke in the world. 'I can't help it, Osa. I know what that dress means to you, but it *is* comical. Your last hold on respectability, and a mere insect eats right through it with his little nippers. Eat your dinner in your best breeches — and you'll probably enjoy it a lot more.'

So I dragged out the only garment I had left, a plaid cotton dress with an organdy blouse and black satin bow. I did my hair into a psyche and put on a pair of high-heeled patent-leather pumps, now terribly shabby. At least, I would be clean.

Embarrassed as we were, we found that our host was the only one who had dressed. In his white mess jacket and black tie and black trousers, he looked extremely fashionable, but I knew that he was not putting on airs. Like all the men who ran things out here, he was only trying to keep his self-respect under the punishment he had to take in his daily work. And he was also maintaining, in this way, his connection with home and the society from which he came.

Two new men had arrived in addition to Mr. Creswell and Mr. Bernays. They were introduced to us as Mr. Tomlinson and Mr. Darbishire. The former was a slight and rather fragile man, with olive complexion and thinning hair, and was dressed in a wrinkled white suit. The latter, similarly dressed, was taller and stronger, but his skin also showed yellow from the ravages of fever, and his blue eyes and light hair were burned out by the sun. Like typical Englishmen, both men were reserved, but they immediately put us at ease with questions about our trip, our work, and our ambitions.

Our host seemed exhilarated to have guests in the house, and he was as excited and jolly as though he were giving a party in Mayfair. We entered the dining room and he drew back my chair for me. After over a year in the jungles and a thousand and one taboos that had begun to give me a sense of nonentity, that little attention made my heart flutter. I looked at Martin and wanted to say to him, 'This is what I want you to do for me every evening hereafter.' But I knew he would call me a sissy if I mentioned it.

Several serving boys, in white lava-lava and each with a flower behind his ear, stood about the dining room. Candles burned brightly in candelabras of French crystal. The fine tableware and silver and linen made me feel even shabbier in the dress I wore. I was almost overcome with excitement and happiness and swallowed hard to keep from crying.

The dinner was as lavish as I might have expected in such a place: green turtle soup with sherry, broiled spiny lobster, new potatoes, green beans, corn on the cob, lettuce and tomatoes, fresh butter and real cream, delicious cheddar cheese in port wine, steamed pudding and fruit, several wines and rich coffee. I ate everything and was ashamed of my appetite.

'Tomorrow you can ride horseback all over the place,' Mr. Harding assured me. 'And you can sleep as long as you like.

Native children on the artificial islands. These sea-urchins learn to paddle a canoe and swim before our children are out of the carriage. They are completely unafraid of sharks and are seldom bitten.

Looking across Langa Langa Lagoon. These native isolationists are superior to the primitive mainlanders who do not even own canoes.

Osa in an outrigger. She is paddling down an estuary on the coast of mountainous Malaita.

A Malaita boy at Penduffryn, Guadalcanal. The scars, nose ring and battered wristwatch earring all are signs of beauty.

Mr. Bernays at Penduffryn, with workers from the copra plantation.

On the Balesuna River near Penduffryn. The heavy jungles are full of flowering vines, orchids and rare, colorful birds.

Osa at seventeen, before the Tulagi jungle expedition.

*The Johnsons' home at Tulagi.   A climb up two hundred steps to a
bungalow that seemed palatial after jungle huts and the little schooner.*

and have your breakfast in your bed or on your verandah any
time from daybreak to noon.'

I couldn't believe that I was awake and in the Solomons.
But I came back in a flash, for Mr. Bernays was talking to
Martin — about cannibals.

'Yes, New Georgia, Guadalcanal, and Malaita are the
worst in the Solomons, although I daresay that if you lived
on any island long enough you would think that one was the
worst. The boys here are picked from hundreds and hundreds
of recruits, and some of them have been born and raised on
the plantation, so they are fairly well disciplined, but you
don't have to go far into the hills to find raw savages, on the
warpath every day of the year.'

'Has the plantation ever been attacked?' I asked.

'Hah!' said Mr. Harding. 'We have had some rather bad
messes here, but we have put the rascals in their place. They
have found out we can handle our guns. By the way, how
would you like to see our arsenal?'

Finding that we were interested in guns, Mr. Harding led
us off to his bedroom, where in an alcove he had exactly what
he had called it, an arsenal. Cabinets built into the wall, with
strong locked doors, contained a rack of rifles of varying size
and make. All were polished and oiled and looked very
businesslike. In other cabinets hung revolvers in holsters,
ready for action.

We sat down in the living room to visit, and I heard Martin
planning with Mr. Bernays to make a trip up the river and
back into the hills to see what he could find for pictures.

The world seemed so quiet here and so snug and secure that
I wished Martin would rest and forget cannibals for a few
days. I knew, however, that every moment counted, and that
he would be impatient with me if I even suggested such a
thing. All that worried me was the danger.

I asked Mr. Harding if he had ever been attacked by the
natives.

'You know,' he replied, 'a soldier never likes to talk about a war he has been in, probably more because he wants to forget the experience than for any other reason. But you can't live here and have a bed of roses. Danger and struggle are just part of the day's work. You have to be geared to battle and enjoy being top dog, or there is just no use. We have all had our experiences, but we manage to keep things in good order, and we don't go out of bounds looking for trouble.'

'Then tell me your *worst* experience,' I urged.

'My worst was another man's,' he said. 'My best friend down here was Oliver Burns. His ship was raided and burned at Morovo Lagoon, New Georgia. He was toma-hawked and his entire crew captured and killed, in one hor-rible way or another. This followed the burning of several other schooners hereabouts and the killing of their masters, but his murder came closer home to me. Burns was a splendid character, very kind, an excellent shot, and thoroughly self-reliant. All of which makes you realize that it takes only a moment of carelessness down here at the wrong time and place, and your life is over.'

I resolved that I would be Martin's insurance against care-lessness if I could.

Next morning I woke to find Martin gone. It was nearly noon. He had left at dawn with Mr. Bernays, the houseboy told me, and had asked them to let me sleep.

That seemed excuse enough to stay at home and luxuriate, so I ordered a hot bath and soaked in it for half an hour. I was soon having breakfast in the best of style on the sun-flooded verandah overlooking the flower garden. Never had a meal tasted better: papaya and lemons, both fresh out of the garden, fresh boiled eggs, piping hot scones with Australian marmalade, and aromatic coffee with thick cream. With every bite I made up for weeks of breakfasting on tea and biscuits.

'Will you please bring me more coffee?' I said to the boy.

I started as someone came up behind me. It was Mr. Harding trying to be pleasant and to frown at the same time.

'Don't be timid with these boys,' he said sternly. 'When you ask for something, show them that you mean business. With Malaitamen like that, there must never be a moment's doubt about who is Master. Raise your voice and be firm. That is the way their chiefs treat them and the only authority they understand.'

I wanted to challenge this. I couldn't feel uncomfortable with these natives, and they seemed to respect me when I smiled at them and treated them as I would anyone else. But Mr. Harding knew the Solomons, and I decided that I would stick to my gentleness, but keep my eyes open as well. I remembered his warning that one moment of carelessness was enough.

Keeping his promise of a horseback ride, Mr. Harding asked if I would like to make the plantation rounds with him. A stableboy brought two beautiful thoroughbreds. The saddles were of the finest leather and workmanship. I felt that I was rapidly being spoiled, but I was enjoying it.

We rode through the vegetable gardens and across acres and acres of shady coconut groves, alive with scarlet and green paraqueets and beautiful white cockatoos with crests of delicate yellow, all scolding and screeching as usual. Beyond were more vast acres of rubber trees, now fully grown. They were being tapped by native workers, mostly Malaita boys, under the supervision of Mr. Darbishire.

The Malaita boys were a wild-looking lot. All had long fuzzy hair and were very black. Several had bones or sticks of wood through their noses, and in their enlarged ear lobes an assortment of things they had picked up on the place, from safety pins and nails to a trade penknife, a battered wrist watch and the wheel of an alarm clock. They were new recruits, and looked as though they would take plenty of watching

We rode on through the orchards, where everything had been laid out on the most generous scale. Experiments were being carried on with dozens of fruits for the export trade.

There were several kinds of bananas and lemons, limes, grape-
fruit, pomelo, and oranges. When ripe, the oranges were
small, and half-green, half-yellow in color. They were
deliciously sweet. Pineapples grew abundantly, along with
mangoes, papaya, passion fruit, granadilla, breadfruit, and
bellfruit. The karambola, a yellow fruit, known as the 'five
corner,' was sour, and was used for making drinks. With a
knife I scraped out the cottony pulp of my first custard apple.
It was very sweet, appetizing, and juicy, and each taste made
me want more.

Then came great gardens of vegetables, all needed for the
use of the plantation. Here was everything familiar to us at
home, even squash. Several boys were at work weeding,
with native knives and spiked sticks. If this soil and climate
would produce so abundantly, here was a job for future agri-
cultural missionaries, and a means to win the cannibals over to
a new and better way of life, I thought. If they could only
manage to keep their heads in the process!

I noticed a cluster of wild kapok trees. Because of the
growing demand for kapok, Mr. Harding thought that he
would some day get around to cultivating them for trade.
He said he had already used them for stuffing pillows and
mattresses. He could not have anticipated that kapok was
to be important among the materials of a great war in the
Solomons years ahead.

The flower gardens made my heart leap. Here were
beautiful hedges of croton, the leaves making a rich variety
of reds, yellows, and many shades of green. Hibiscus in
several colors, frangipani, bougainvillea, and a dainty white
waxlike blossom with a delicate yellow center and exquisite
fragrance, and other tropical plants and shrubs.

In the trees were sprays of beautiful yellow orchids brought
in from the forest. Wired or grafted to a crotch, they quickly
attached themselves for good, and soon bloomed. In other
islands, said Mr. Harding, they had distinctive colors: at
Tulagi white, pink, or purple, and in the Shortlands, a very

pure white. The Shortlands orchids were so sweet that they filled a room with their fragrance. Others made beautiful house plants with leaves of every hue and shade.

Leaving the gardens we came to great galvanized iron sheds. Inside the sheds, coconut meats, on racks suspended over ovens of wood coals, were being dried by hot air. The air reeked with the heavy, sweetish smell of copra. The dried and shrunken copra was being sacked for shipment to Sydney, where it would be shredded for confections and turned into oil for soaps.

'The white man couldn't get along without the Solomons nowadays,' said Mr. Harding. 'Copra is part of our lives. Would you believe there has almost been war in Europe, several times, over these little pinpoint spots in the Pacific?'

I didn't believe then. But I know now.

He told me about the squabbles which big commercial and shipping interests had already had over the trade. And that the Germans, French, and British were still jealously watching each other's every move in the Solomons. Even the Japanese had large copra ambitions.

'But the black man saw it first,' he continued. 'Copra is not just a luxury with him; it's an absolute necessity. And I suppose there isn't another tree in the world that offers so many benefits and services. There are hundreds — almost a couple of thousand.'

Up to now, I had thought of coconuts as just an easy way to a drink or a meal.

'From the trunk of the coconut tree, he makes his canoe,' said Mr. Harding. 'And his house, fence posts, rafts, and other structures. The leaf makes a thatch for the house and skirts for the women. The midrib of the leaf makes walls for the house, fence staves, and arrow shafts. Dry and green leaves tied together make torches. The leaf-fibre makes floor mats and mattresses, baskets and wrappings. Toddy is made from the sap of the flower stalk. Heart of palm makes an excellent salad. Fibre from the husk of the nut is twisted into twine — useful for building houses and canoes and also making fishnets and fishlines and belts and straps. The coconut shell makes household utensils.'

It was literally 'the tree of life,' he assured me.

He gave me a green nut meat to taste. It was just like the white of an egg. I made a wry face, but Mr. Harding went on enthusiastically.

'Everything lives on coconuts down here,' he said. 'The pigs eat those green meats by the ton, and the dogs and chickens get fat on them. The trade which has brought the whites here has kept the black man alive for centuries past. That is the chief reason the black man fights. He is satisfied with his simple way of life and is going to defend it against all intrusion.'

For one of the primary 'intruders' I thought he showed an unusual understanding and consideration.

'You haven't seen our crocodiles,' said Mr. Harding as we rode on through more coconut groves to where the Balesuna River swung past Penduffryn to the sea. It was evening, and the boys were running home in groups, shouting and laughing, and hungry for their sweet potatoes. Overhead, thousands of birds were chirping and calling at once, and the air was full of flashing color and feathery traffic. Clusters of butterflies fluttered languidly about, and occasional bats whisked close to us.

The small brackish river looked like a harmless creek at home. But as we reached it, a monitor lizard slithered away into the mangroves, and crabs scuttled down the bank. Mullet were jumping, and amongst them I suddenly saw a splash, as a crocodile plunged into the stream for his evening's meal.

We turned downstream and found several boys tugging at a line, on the other end of which was a struggling crocodile, threshing about and trying to regain the water. Mr. Harding drew his rifle and, with one shot into the brain, dispatched the reptile. The boys shouted and danced. Having made sure the beast was dead, they went forward, and with their knives cut out of its gullet a great shark's hook attached to a chain.

'We bait them with chicken and often catch three to six a day,' said Mr. Harding. 'The crocs are bad enough medicine for our pigs, but especially so for the boys, who have to come here for bathing and for water for the gardens. We have caught hundreds, and have at least made the place habitable. But between the cannibals and the crocodiles, there's never a dull moment on Guadalcanal, even for a man with a gun and a good shooting arm.'

I felt something crawling over my cheek and smacked it. There in my hand was a large black fly, as big as a blowfly, with a yellow head that gave it a vicious look. Another was crawling up my arm, and as I brushed it off, several others attacked my head as though retaliating. Mr. Harding chuckled to see me fight them.

'Some of our little pests,' he said, 'and there isn't anything you can do about them. You get so used to things crawling over you and taking a bite out of you that you ignore them all after a while.'

'I'll never get used to them,' I retorted. 'I hate them, and flies worst of all.'

'The only way to take flies,' he said, 'is with the interest of the naturalist. They aren't entirely enemies of man. Up in the hills some of the natives actually use these big fellows for food; they eat them roasted and fried in coconut oil.'

I shuddered and looked to see whether he were joking, but he was in earnest.

'And they are food for the birds you like so much,' he continued. 'Those beautiful paraqueets and cockatoos have to have something to eat. Even our chickens like them, and the fish get a full meal out of a few flies. Flies prowl around the flowers and blossoms and help pollinate the garden. You live here in the Solomons long enough and either you get to be philosophical about the insects or you go out of your mind.'

'What about the diseases they carry?' I asked.

'Guilty there,' he said, 'but only one fly in thousands carries a disease germ. And only one mosquito in a million carries a malaria bug. Here's an interesting thing. Flies live for only a few hours or days and actually need very little food. They do their feeding and most of their growing in the larval stage. Very often the adult male fly takes no food, and often the female fly takes food only to mature her eggs.'

Some were predatory and fed on other insects and worms, he went on. They liked the soft-bodied things, and had legs specially modified for catching and holding their prey. Some injected a poison into their victims and paralyzed them, and some sucked blood.

'But usually their food is just a sip of honey or pollen or fruit juice or decaying vegetable matter,' he said, 'or the sweat of animals or human beings. That fellow who annoyed you a little while ago wasn't going to bite you; he just liked your aroma.'

As he talked, I thought I would rather take my chances with cannibals. Against them one was at least a fair match, but against these unseen little murderers, there was no protection. Much as I hated the feel and smell of coal oil, I would go and douse myself with it as soon as I got back to the house to keep from being eaten alive.

Mr. Harding was still rhapsodizing. 'Imagine their doing thirty miles an hour on those tiny wings — much better than our launch — and for long distances. Some of them can hover motionless in the air and land straight down, as easy as you please. Others can skate around on the water without breaking the surface. And I wish I could walk up a smooth wall or across the ceiling like one of them. God has certainly given them enough advantages. They must be intended to survive for some good purpose.'

We were returning through the coconut groves, now deserted by the workers, but still noisily alive with hungry birds, all looking for their dinner. They were pecking at the tree trunks or catching insects in the air or grubbing in the earth and grass. Nature was providing them with a lavish feast.

And that seemed 'purpose' enough for most of the microscopic pests. Perhaps, when we had finished recording the cannibals and headhunters and apes, we could explore some of this vast world of infinitesimal things with our cameras.

Late that evening, Martin returned, worn out but jubilant. 'The best pictures yet!' he exclaimed. 'These natives are real men. Big, husky fellows with a lot more intelligence than those Malaitans. Just wait till you see what I got today!'

Before we finished dinner, it was agreed that while he developed his films in the morning, I would go up into the hills with Mr. Harding and Mr. Darbishire to make still pictures and see the people and the country for myself.

'If you don't mind butterflies,' said Mr. Harding, with a wink, 'we will take nets and binoculars and see that other world of mine.'

7 　wwwww

. . . rhythms . . . haunted me

Y OU WILL SEE fine natives today,' said Mr. Harding.
'Not as tough as on Malaita, and I know you want them
tough. But better specimens. These Guadalcanal fellows
are really handsome.'

We were paddling up the Balesuna River, flanked on either
side by a heavy growth of mangroves and slithery mudbanks.
Cranes and other birds startled as we passed and flew on
ahead, to light again and look us over. We had brought Mr.
Darbishire and a dozen boys in two canoes, for whatever
might develop during our visit to the hills. And we had left
Martin in his bathroom laboratory, to take advantage of the
cool of the early morning for his developing.

Our boys were so expert at paddling that they made almost
no sound, or else it was lost in the throbbing sound of the
jungle about us.

Crocodiles dozed along the river's edge, but they did not
budge, and if they heard and saw us they gave no sign. Suddenly, one did plunge into the water only a few feet away. At
that close range he seemed gigantic, and I grabbed my gun,
for I was sure he would strike us. But he dove and disappeared
in the muddy water. To be chewed up by a crocodile was one
kind of death I did not want.

But Mr. Harding was unconcerned, and without mentioning crocodiles he told me about the other wild life: the lizards, cranes, parrots, butterflies, and the insects which swarmed everywhere. He seemed to know them all and to enjoy showing them off with an almost proprietary interest.

'What little I know about the forest,' he said, 'I have learned from these boys. With all their superstitions about good and bad charms, they know every vine and flower and bird. And the more they tell me about the out-of-doors and its meaning to them, the more I respect their superstitions. They have one of the oldest and most refined of all the religions of the world — they are really a part of Nature.'

Every boy in our canoe wore some flower in his hair. One had a red hibiscus, which went very well with his bushy mane and dark skin. Another wore a spray of small, white, waxlike flowers. And another had a bandeau of snug little blue flowers, very much like bachelor's buttons.

'They love color and they make the most of it,' said Mr. Harding. 'My houseboy fills the vases with flowers every morning, and I see him arrange them and then stand off and scowl, and arrange them again and again until he has the artistic effect he wants. Then he stands and admires them. Bloodthirsty as they are on the warpath, they are aesthetes through and through, and not a bit of beauty escapes them.'

Mangroves along the river banks were now so heavy and closely matted that one could not possibly get through unless he cut his way. The slime out of which they grew smelled revoltingly of rot and decay. Crabs, crawfish, lizards, frogs, and turtles prowled around in the muck hunting for worms and insects. Balanced on a branch, a monitor lizard reached out his long, flashing tongue for mosquitoes and gnats, and completely ignored us.

'Monsters of the mangroves,' said Mr. Harding, pointing to the lizard. 'We killed one the other day, and he was so fat, we cut him open. There, inside him, was a rat — one of our big ones — a foot long. They are very fond of crabs and

birds' eggs. They dive with great ease and swim long distances. I've seen them grow as long as five and a half feet —
looked like some prehistoric beast. Like a python, they have
a very fat belly, and can live on their fat for a long time without food in the worst heat. The natives like them to eat.'

Soon the mangroves gave way to the bright and lacy foliage
of nipa palms, their drooping fans making shadowy patterns
on the water. Small trees and ferns were massed in banks of
greenery, above which tree ferns pushed up to fifteen and
twenty feet. Then fan palms appeared, their top fronds wav-
ing plumelike in the trade wind. Here in the sunlight were
orchids and hibiscus and flowering vines. In the fertile soil
and balmy sun, Nature was being pushed to her limit of
growth. But decay was just as rapid, and the odors of decomposing undergrowth seemed to be magnified.

Banyans began to appear, throwing out their great but-
tresses, to give the forest a cathedral-like touch. At the center
of some could be seen the rotting trunk of a sturdy tree upon
which the parasite had climbed for support, and which had
paid with its life for this assistance. Mr. Harding told of the
native legends about this endless battle — of the other trees
banding together to fight the banyan.

'But the banyan always wins,' he added. 'A perfect case
of might and persistence triumphing and a theory which
Nature never contradicts in the Solomons.'

Tall forest trees, festooned with orchids and flowering
creepers, began to arch above us. Wild plantain, and a great
variety of palms, ferns, arecas, and small shrubs grew everywhere. A tree, which Mr. Harding called the 'lowasi,' was
heavily laden with white flowers, as beautiful as spray orchids,
and gave us a breath of its fragrance. The larger trees became more numerous and towered to a hundred and fifty feet.
Beneath them long, clean corridors led back into the deep
forest. The light now lessened and came down to us only
through rents in the heavy roof above, where some giant tree
had fallen or had been torn by the wind. Bird-calls echoed

sharply through the silent aisles and the falling of a branch took on an exaggerated sound.

Suddenly I heard a groan overhead and a sharp report. We all ducked and the boys stopped paddling. There was a breath-taking silence. Then came a thud like thunder, and an explosion that echoed and re-echoed through the air. But nothing was to be seen of the huge tree that had crashed, and we were on our way again.

'When one of those giants comes down,' said Mr. Harding, 'there is enormous destruction. Hundreds of small trees are crushed. Small animals and young birds perish. Tons of rot are added to the decay on the forest floor for ants and cockroaches and vermin to feed upon and to nourish the other plants for decades.'

Coming to higher ground, we moored the canoes and started inland over a well-worn trail. We curved about the trunks of gigantic trees, the tops of which could not be seen among the mass of foliage overhead, and walked under great, spreading palms and banyans. The forest was gloomy with a strange half-light. We stumbled over roots and obstructions that we could scarcely see. There were no flowers except for occasional creepers that took advantage of a pool of light to unfold their blooms. The glades I had seen from the river were an illusion, for the abundant undergrowth was heavy, and except for the trail we would have had to cut our way. There was a sense of dead air and dank cold, and the smells were worse than those of an abattoir.

As we climbed upward to perhaps five hundred feet above the sea, the air cleared somewhat of its stickiness. Now we felt for the first time the fanning breeze of the trade wind. At least it helped to blow away the clouds of mosquitoes, gnats, and flies. Below us, the sunlight rioted over the boundless greenery, picking out shades of color in such variety that the effect was stimulating.

Great banana palms thrust out over the darker ferns, mosses and fungi, wild yams, taro and castor-oil plants, and masses of cane grass. The bananas caught the light on their spearlike fronds so that some seemed almost white. Tree ferns fought for the open spaces, and I saw that one had leaves marked with olive-colored leopard spots. Beyond rose the higher fan palms, almond trees, and arecas, making a crazy-quilt of greens.

All around us there were now brilliant clusters of flowers. Birds were feeding everywhere among the flowers and foliage, and the air was bursting with their song and chatter. A covey of grouse, about the size of our bob-white, flew up and quickly took cover. And I saw a family of bush fowl, resembling our prairie chicken, dash across the trail ahead of us.

Seeing my interest, Mr. Harding gave me the binoculars and singled out birds I had never seen. 'That little brown sparrow with the white-tipped tail is the fantail,' he said. 'And the yellow breast, like a hummingbird, is the sunbird, drinking nectar from the flowers while poised in the air. The little green one is the flower-pecker. He has a fringed tongue with which he also sucks nectar from the blossoms.'

A flock of vivid green birds settled into the branches of a palm. 'The dwarf parrot,' said Mr. Harding. 'The smallest parrot known — only nine inches long. He's a lively little insect-hunter and likes fruits and seeds.'

There was a flash of yellow above us.

'The yellow-breasted lory,' Mr. Harding supplied. 'He is a charmer, with his red body, green wings, and yellow band across his breast, and makes a fine house pet. He differs from all other parrots — has a fringed and hairy tongue for drinking nectar.'

But he didn't take it on the wing, I noticed. Instead he picked himself a nice solid perch where he could do his sipping safely.

'He crushes flowers and buds with his beak, so he gets his wine and salad all in one,' Mr. Harding added, 'the true lotus-eater.'

The coconut lory and others of the family varied in color through reds, blues, and yellows.

My favorites were the fruit dove, green, with a bright red head and a little red cape around his neck — resplendent in the sun. And almost as attractive were the little black-and-white flycatchers, as fresh as though they were just out of a bandbox.

I saw my first mynah bird, glossy black, with orange patches about the eyes, and white on its wings, a relative of the oriole and starling. I meant to have one of these for a pet some day and see if it were true that they could be trained to speak like a parrot.

We moved on and saw more fantastically colored parrots in hundreds. A great scarlet fellow, at least a foot long, looked like an exotic orchid as he perched on a vine and eyed us suspiciously. The females hung upside down and looked very foolish. Less obvious were the big green parrots, which Mr. Harding said were extremely destructive to the fruits and heartily disliked by the natives.

Hornbills, with yellow beak and white neck and white tail, were making their booming call and behaving like fan-dancers. There were white cockatoos with yellow topknots; crested long-tailed pigeons, a rare variety, found only here; swifts, catching and cracking insects as they flew, but on the lookout lest they be struck and killed by bats; finches; king-fishers, and warblers; and flying foxes (large bats), asleep and hanging by their feet in the trees.

Great birds, resembling hawks, soared overhead. They were coasting up the wind in follow-your-leader formation, and their swift, smooth, effortless flight was a joy to watch.

'Brahminy kites,' said Mr. Darbishire, who had been silent up to now, but who evidently also knew his birds. One of the handsomest of the lot. A red-and-brown body, white head and breast, and roundish tail. Probably the nimblest of all birds of prey. They can strike faster than anything you have ever seen and will take a bird or frog, lizard or snake, quicker than sleight-of-hand. They even catch bees and insects in midair with their feet and eat their prey as they fly. Very loyal to their flock — if one is wounded, the others hover around the spot for hours.'

Soon came a flight of eagles, and Mr. Darbishire explained that their chief delicacy was the cuscus, but they often became scavengers, like vultures, when really hungry. Osprey and hawks abounded and several kinds of owl, one of the rarest of which was found on this island. Guadalcanal is a happy hunting ground for future ornithologists.

'Another Solomons freak,' said Mr. Harding, 'is the Nicobar pigeon, with a gizzard that cracks nuts! He even cracks the hard seeds the natives use for necklaces. The gizzard is halved and under the thick muscular wall are two cartilaginous lumps — hemispheres, with the flat sides opposed to each other, and covered with a horny membrane. Between these flat sides, the nut is caught, and the muscles contract and crush it. And a pebble of quartz inside the gizzard also helps.'

I asked why a quartz pebble.

'Just his whim,' Mr. Harding said. 'Odd, because there is very little quartz on the islands and plenty of coral and volcanic rock, but quartz it always is. Of course, the fruit-eating pigeons have no such equipment. They feed on soft, fleshy fruits and spit out the seeds. Between them these two pigeons have undoubtedly brought us the wild fruits we have here — from New Guinea, Australia, the East Indies, and the Asiatic continent. They are really the sowers of the Solomons.'

Reaching a thousand feet of elevation, we came to our first bamboos. Great masses of them banked against the mountainside, swaying gracefully in the wind like giant ostrich plumes.

Deep among them, natives with large knives were chopping down the stalks, which they cut into sections and tossed into piles. The larger stems would be used for carrying water from the springs and for storing it, for giving themselves baths, and even for piping water short distances. The smaller would be taken down to the coast to trade with fishermen for poles and net supports, or else used for building their own houses and a thousand useful articles.

The men were clean, sturdy, and much better-looking than the Malaitans, but their eyes were wild enough. They began talking to our boys and laughed in a friendly way. I felt at once that I was going to like these people.

Their village, a dozen houses in a symmetrical row, was set on a small tableland. It was probably an illusion, but everything seemed very clean. Even the clearing looked as though it had been swept.

Several women, in pandanus skirts, sat on the ground with a number of little girls of varying ages, and all were busily working at a pile of pandanus leaves. Some were making thatch for the roofs; others, mats which would be both a bed and a covering. The children were making bracelets of the fibre. In a few years these little girls would be mothers and must learn now to manage all the household arts.

Although we distributed tobacco to the women, they only grinned and grunted and paid little attention to us. They all went on with their work, probably because they could think of nothing else to do. I had already noticed that these primitive people had a way of keeping their dignity intact by pretending indifference when they met something they did not understand or know how to manage. I dug out of my jumper a few beads for one of the children. It caused a flurry of excited appreciation among them, and all the youngsters held out their hands to me, but I had no more.

'The women run the show here,' Mr. Harding confided. 'They do all the heavy work, but they also own most of the property. Inheritance is matrilineal. When a woman dies, her property goes to her heir. A man's property goes to his sister's heir. Women have more freedom and more respect than on Malaita, where they hardly dare make themselves heard. In fact, the men often help the women do their work, and the men make a great fuss over the children. I have seen a father spend half an hour carefully bathing a child and treating it with the same tenderness and affection you would expect from a mother.'

A warrior had come up and stood leaning on his long wooden-shafted spear. The point was a slender piece of bone which at once caught my eye. It was a human shinbone, a favorite spear-point here, according to Mr. Harding, but the bones of swordfish and sawfish were also prized and obtained in trade from the salt-water people at the shore. The fish-bones were whiter than human bones, but human bones were harder to get. A fishbone spear-point would cost a canoeload of bamboos or perhaps ten strings of shell money — a very heavy price and as much as some wives would cost.

'They aren't as bloodthirsty as the Malaitans,' said Mr. Harding. 'They are bad enough when provoked, but aren't always looking for a fight. If they get the idea that some other village has insulted them or practiced sorcery on them, they may go and wipe the place out. But they often hire some other community to do the dirty work, for they are well off. The chief's headhouse over there is full of skulls and I know they aren't all his ancestors'. Two he showed me had cracks in them that only a steel tomahawk could make.'

They had all the usual spirits that haunted the other islands, he said. The shark and snake and eagle spirits especially. The shark spirits protected their water voyages. The snakes guarded their crops and punished garden thieves by chasing the culprits. The eagles were the souls of their ancestors. They carried a general blessing over the whole village and were never molested.

'The dead have two souls,' he continued. 'One goes to the spirit-land, from which the eagles come; the other goes into the headhouse with the skull. The natives destroy the property of the dead, unless it is something of special value for the headhouse. When the head of a family dies, they put on a big feast, eating up all the person's pigs and yams, and with this compliment the soul gets a good start toward the other world. Mourners come and wail for several days and all the visitors are given porpoise teeth or some other fine token.'

Seeing the chief and his men coming, Mr. Harding got out

the tobacco and made the chief a generous gift. Then he introduced me. The chief was a tall, stalwart, bushy-headed fellow with a fine smile and the best teeth I had yet seen here. He wore a necklace and a bracelet of porpoise and dogs' teeth and ear pieces of shell, and in his hair was a band of cowrie shells. His muscular and bronzed men all had great mops of bushy black hair, and most of them had the same fine teeth, but few decorations and no clothes. They seemed so friendly that I could not believe we were in cannibal-land.

'They are going to dance for us,' said Mr. Harding. 'Quite a compliment. They like to show off, but it usually takes a feast to work them up to it.'

I hurriedly got the still camera ready and wished that Martin were here with his motion-picture machines and his superior skill, for we might not again have a dance on Guadalcanal by daylight. It was past noon and the light was perfect.

The men filed out of their houses carrying spears and small wicker shields. They now wore beautiful armlets of black-and-white wampum, woven grass, and porpoise teeth. All wore anklets of shell of varying sizes and colors, which made a musical clinking sound as they walked. Some had cockatoo feathers, cowrie shells or flowers in their hair, and others, necklaces of teeth or seeds or shell. One wore a necklace of at least five hundred dogs' teeth, a great fortune in itself. He must have been one of the wealthiest men in the mountains.

They lined up in a column, four abreast. Singers in the center of the group began a high-pitched chant. Slowly they all began to move, swinging in a wide circle which became narrower and narrower. They stamped their feet and quickened their pace. I began taking pictures. Faster and faster they whirled, and the chant died out and became a series of sharp yells, shouts, and deep-toned guttural grunts that had the feeling of muffled drums. They worked up to great excitement, now doing all sorts of acrobatics and thrusting with their spears, probably at some imaginary enemy or evil spirit.

I saw that they danced with their whole bodies and not with their feet alone. They began to imitate birds, especially the soaring and dipping flight of the eagle. Every movement was done with exquisite grace and rhythm and practiced skill. I finished a score of camera shots and stood watching the dance with such absorption that I felt as though I were a part of it. It was barbaric, elemental, and gripping. I knew that nothing I could put on film would capture the swaying beauty of those bronzed bodies nor the power and grace of the dance nor its haunting sound.

Wanting to reach home by nightfall, we showed our appreciation for all this reception, and said good-bye to the chief.

A little girl, who had been standing near-by, staring at me, toddled after me as I moved away. I stopped and patted her little black bottom. She pointed to my gold wedding ring, which had apparently fascinated her. I shook my head, and tried to find something in my pockets for her. I had nothing suitable but a cheap bead bracelet, and this I gave her. She held it and stared at it a moment and then walked over to the chief and dutifully put it in his hand. Without a smile, he hung it over his ear.

'Just as well you haven't earrings,' commented Mr. Harding. 'One of these fellows might take your head for them.'

We hurried off down the trail. The moment we entered the forest, we were surrounded once more by thousands of birds on the wing. They seemed to have multiplied.

King parrots, each a foot long, the males green-bodied with red sides and the females a brilliant red, lighted in a single tree and were so astonishingly beautiful that I stopped and gaped at them.

Another flock of large birds were doing queer acrobatics. They were a brilliant green and blue and had vivid red bills. As they flew, they opened and closed their tails and puffed out their throats, and every now and then one would turn over as though doing a somersault in midair.

I asked what on earth was the matter with them.

'Rollers,' said Mr. Darbishire. 'Just showing off. They actually do somersaults, and when the mating season is on, they are a complete circus. They breed in holes in the earth, making a bed there for the eggs, instead of building a nest. And they have a ravenous appetite for frogs and small reptiles as well as beetles, grasshoppers, worms, and flies. One species has even been seen in Britain, but very little is known about them.'

In the branches above us were hundreds of little wagtail flycatchers, glossy black with white bellies, busily getting their dinner. Like a swallow, one would dart swiftly into the air and seize a bug, or miss it, and then return to his perch. They seemed to be working harder than any birds in the forest.

Just as lively were the cuckoo shrikes, small reddish birds with gray heads and hooked beaks, so alert and nimble that no insect would have half a chance of getting away from them.

A black hornbill with great yellow beak beat across our path with the rumbling sound of a motor and perched on a high branch to watch us.

'Just like a goat,' said Mr. Darbishire. 'They will eat anything in sight, especially if it's bright and shiny. We had one for a pet, and he downed thimbles, buttons, safety pins, coins, and even silverware from the table. He was a nuisance. A flight of them sounds like an express train and they can out-talk any parrot alive. They're the clowns of Guadalcanal.'

Millions of butterflies fluttered about the clearings in the mellow sun. Some flew in barrel formations and others in ragged flocks, filling the air with vivid yellows, greens, blacks, browns, blues, and whites. With his net Mr. Harding caught a giant bird-winged male, fully nine inches across his fore-wings. He said he had seen them as broad as fifteen inches. The wings were black, green, and translucent gold, with black dots along the outer margin. The head and antennae were black. Others we caught had blue on the wings. The females were brown or beige and quite colorless in comparison, but were even larger than the males.

Moths, great and small, flew up from the trail as we walked,
but they seemed very shabby after the butterflies. Those we
caught were about three inches in wing-spread and were a
variety of browns, some with bright orange patches on the
hind-wings. I saw that Mr. Harding was keeping several for
his collection, another evidence of his affection for his island
and everything it contained.

There were easily twenty-five thousand different moths
and butterflies here, he thought. And just as many beetles.
And thousands of varieties of flies, wasps, mosquitoes, ants
and termites. With the heavy jungle above and deep mat of
decaying vegetation underfoot, insect life multiplied to a
maximum.

'It is a wonder the insects haven't driven man out of the
Solomons,' he said. 'They may actually do so some day
unless man can find some way to protect or immunize himself and strike a balance with Nature.'

He told me how to spot the fever-bearing anopheles mosquito.

'When he stings, he stands up on his forelegs and bores into
you,' he said. 'Looks as though he were standing on his head.
You are probably immune to malaria or you would have
caught it by now, but smack one of those fellows every time
you see him. No use to take any chances.'

'What about snakes?' I asked him. 'There must be thousands in this lush growth.'

'Plenty!' he said. 'But they seem to mind their own business unless attacked. One of my boys stepped on a snake with
his bare foot not long ago, and I think the snake was more
scared than he was.'

He explained that their brown-and-yellow bodies and backs
of olive or grass-green camouflaged them well among the
foliage. Some were vicious-looking and nearly thirty inches
in length, and the natives had the same fear of them that we
had.

'If you do see one,' he said, 'let him alone. He may look

horrible, but he will run away if you keep your head and give him a chance. Or you can pin his head down with a forked stick. You will see very few, and most of them aren't poisonous. Snakes will be the least of your worries in the Solomons.'

Mr. Darbishire had gone on ahead and had the canoes waiting when we reached the stream. Now the boys' skillful paddling was welcome. I was thoroughly bitten by mosquitoes and scratched by vines and thorns, and I was hungry enough for two dinners.

Silently and swiftly, in the gathering dusk, we sped downstream. It was dark when we reached Penduffryn and found Martin and the others waiting for us at the landing.

As we dined, I heard Mr. Bernays saying, 'The deeper into the hills you go, the less hospitable they are. Anyone who thinks he is safe for a minute in the Solomons is daft.'

But my mind was full of the color and motion of the forest. And my ears buzzed with thousands of bird-calls and the droning undertone of bees and insects and the deep-throated chant of native dancers. The throbbing rhythms of the hills haunted me, and the swaying movement of bronzed bodies with their flashing spears and tinkling anklets of shell.

8 wwwwww

... perfect life of leisure

SEND ME those cannibal portraits,' said Mr. Harding as he put us aboard the schooner. 'I may need them for the Governor next time we have an uprising here. Hope I'll see the movies in Sydney some day.'

There was genuine regret in his voice as he said good-bye to us. He held our hands tightly in his for a long time and as though he were struggling with a sense of loneliness. 'I haven't enjoyed a visit so much in many years,' he said quietly and with great feeling.

Over two weeks at Penduffryn had slipped by in a flash. Daily trips into the jungle had given us valuable pictures and information and we had both enjoyed ourselves so much that we could have remained indefinitely. But Mr. Creswell, who had been politely indulging our stay, had to be off. He must make a number of trading stops along the coast of Guadalcanal and would then go on to Savo and Tulagi. And days were important to a trader even in this timeless part of the world.

His little ship had been scrubbed from bow to stern and was trim and fresh, and actually smelled clean. She seemed eager to be out to sea and almost to pick her own way through the tortuous channel. She leaped into the wind as we hoisted sail.

We turned northwest and followed the coastline at a safe distance throughout the morning. The air was brisk and clean after the soggy air on land. I was glad to get away from all the mosquitoes and flies and buzzing pests. This was ideal for the Solomons — a home on board ship, with occasional visits ashore that one could terminate at will, taking the beauty of the jungles in small doses, and retreating to the open water where there were always health and refreshment and protection and escape.

In the early afternoon we pulled into the calm of a bay, behind a jutting point of land. A village sprawled among the coconut trees along the shore. Here the skipper hoped to find tortoise-shell and mother-of-pearl, so we loaded the dinghy with a supply of trade knives, beads, tobacco, and calico and rowed ashore. The natives must have been saving shell for him for months, for they all had something to sell. But along the beach there were scores of fishermen, and these Martin and I went to photograph, while Mr. Creswell plied his trade.

The fishermen used large square nets of coconut fibre. Suspended from an umbrella-frame of three or four shafts of bamboo, the net was held out over the water on a long bamboo pole, then dipped and held deep under the surface. Along came mackerel, rounding up whitebait for their dinner, shooing the smaller fish inshore, over the net — and the fisherman had his catch. Mullet were also caught, and bonita, snapper, and even the mackerel themselves.

When they finished, the fishermen, helped by the young boys, carried their catch back to the village and there on the beach divided it among the families. The chief took his choice — the biggest and best of the fish. Then the assistant chief and medicine men helped themselves. The rest of the supply was divided equally among the women. There was no fighting or disagreement over the food and no bickering. The whole proceeding went off like a sort of picnic, with everyone happy and chattering.

'A pretty ideal social system,' said Martin as we rowed back
to the schooner, 'if you could only like fish enough to live on it.
They really have something there — and a big improvement
over the savage struggle for existence back home.'

During the next several days we put in at village after village along the coast of Guadalcanal. Some were merely a
few huts housing a single family and relatives; others com-
prised a dozen or more fine buildings and made quite a
community. Living on their coconuts and fish and trade,
these coast people seemed to be a different breed from the
hill folk. They were supposed to have come here from other
islands and to have taken the beaches by storm, driving the
original inhabitants back into the bush. They seemed to be
more sophisticated, but were just as primitive in the way they
lived.

'You can say they live on their wits,' said the skipper.
'Fishing is a high art in any place and these people are artists
at it in all its forms.'

They all fished, from the merest tots to the old men and
women. I was sure they fished for sport as much as food, for
they were always working at it, and if it were only food they
wanted, they could have caught all they wished in just a few
minutes a day.

They seldom used bait, but they had an infinite variety of
cleverly made lures. Most of these were of mother-of-pearl,
carved in the shape of a fish with hooks of tortoise-shell
attached. The favorites were imitations of whitebait, on
which many of the larger fish fed.

Sometimes a man made a long cast with a coiled line, doing this very smoothly. If there was not a quick strike, he
jerked his line as he drew it in, so as to give the lure plenty of
action. Others tossed coconut crumbs on the surface to
attract the fish. Some fishermen used a conical basket to
land their catch. But those who were too lazy to make baskets
merely flopped their fish into the canoe and hit them over
the head with a paddle.

The youngsters used bamboo poles and sometimes merely a bamboo twig, with a lure and a hook of tortoise-shell or bone attached. When gulls began circling overhead and plummeting into the sea, a school of fish was obviously out there, and the boys would immediately scoot out in their canoes to take advantage of the run. Since the hooks were not barbed, landing any fish with them took genuine skill and speed. But the boys were every bit as clever as their elders.

While Martin made pictures of the natives and their canoe-houses, where I was forbidden to go, I fished by the hour. With a line of coconut or pandanus fibre or of a creeper called 'lawa,' a tortoise-shell hook and shell spinner, I soon found I could catch more fish here than I ever did at home with flies or night crawlers.

At last I was right in my element. Fishing had been a favorite sport from my girlhood, when I went with my dad down to the river at home in Kansas to catch croppies and perch out of the muddy water. The taboos were now going to be of some use to me, for I would rather fish than see all the headhouses in the South Seas.

My eyes nearly popped at the strange things I pulled out of the deep. Sea-bass, swordfish, snapper, mackerel, and rock cod were all exciting enough, but there were scores of other queer-looking things I had never seen or heard of. One was black-and-white with zebra stripes. Another was scarlet, but the moment he left the water, the color faded to a dead white, and I learned that he was poisonous. One of the most beautiful was a small silver fish, as gleaming as polished sterling, and marked with coral stripes. There was an attractive beige creature, with aquamarine markings, and others with orange and brown and beige polka dots and glossy amber fins.

When I landed a small shark and then a whip ray, I was glad I had a youngster with me armed with a knife, to take care of them. But when I drew in an octopus, spewing his murky black fluid, I was ready to give up.

Most curious of all was the blowfish, small and flat with a loose prickly skin which inflated like a balloon the moment I landed him. I saw that the teeth in his small mouth were just like a baby's. He glared at me and then began to grate his teeth angrily. My little canoe-boy scratched the fish's stomach, whereupon it grew larger and larger until I was sure it would burst. Then, to my astonishment, I saw that it was clearly marked with the stars and stripes. That seemed to warrant his freedom, so I tossed him back into the water. He bounced along on the surface for a few moments, then suddenly deflated, flipped over and dove out of sight.

The little blue-and-silver flying fish would break water and fly almost across our bow, sometimes gliding hundreds of yards. I was told that they were almost impossible to catch, but made excellent food, something like herring. Some natives did hook them with bait of robber crabs and prawns.

Mullet abounded everywhere and were liked by the islanders. When these were smoked, they were every bit as good as kippers. The favorites for food were the crevallés, large and firm and very tasty, along with sea-bass and snapper. There was also a curious goatfish, with a skull rounding down like a Roman nose and with two barbels at the chin, like goat's whiskers. It was much prized by the fishermen for eating.

A scorpion fish gave me a painful wound. It was reddish in color, with light and dark cross-markings. Its long sharp spines and the rays of its fins were also marked with light and dark bands. The fins were almost half as long as the fish itself, and it looked so queer that I picked it up to examine it closely. One of its spines stuck into my hand, and the poison it injected gave me such a swelling and pain that I hurried ashore and gave myself a stiff treatment of ammonia and then hot water and permanganate of potash. The skipper told me that these stings were extremely dangerous.

In spite of my wound, I paddled about the coral reefs for the next several days at every stop we made, and spent long hours drifting and watching the fascinating movement and color in the waters below. Over the clear white sandy bottom and among the rocks and undulating coral fans and spines, thousands of bright-hued creatures swam in and out of the crevices and shadows. Butterfly fishes in vivid yellow, marked with black bands and eye-dots; trigger-fish in the most bizarre of colors; blue jellyfish trailing long tentacles; parrot fish flashing their greens and reds in the shafts of sunlight; and beautiful wrasses, in blues, reds, greens, yellows, blacks, and rainbow shades, gave living color to the depths.

At low tide the shore and rocks were strewn with almost equal color and interest. Among the coral and the seaweed were sea anemones in golden hues, starfish in varied shades, blue and red crabs, big and little, spiny lobsters and mussels, sea urchins with bristling golden spikes, and thousands of colorful shells from tiny periwinkles to giant conchs.

The natives were epicures in their simple fashion. If one has to live on fish, he needs a change of cookery occasionally. I had seen some of the natives eating fish raw, which seemed a very lazy habit, and the skipper told me that was the cause of elephantiasis. Others boiled them or simply tossed them into the coals and roasted them until the skin was black and then peeled the skin away and ate the flesh. Crabs and shrimps thus roasted were delicious. It was more appetizing to rub the fish over with coconut oil, wrap them in succulent leaves, and bake them in the coals. I saw one old woman place salt water in a wooden bowl and then drop hot stones into the water and the fish on top of those. The stones made the water steam and boil and the fish bleached and cooked in no time, the salt of the water giving it a fine flavor.

I cooked fish in the way the islanders did and also made fish and clam chowders, all of which were a great relief from canned foods.

Whatever they were doing, the natives carried their tomahawks or spears and wicker shields. They acted as though always on guard or ready for a raid from some quarter.

Whether they actually expected a raid any moment or whether this was some survival from earlier times or merely a badge of masculine authority, I could not tell. But the equipment all looked very businesslike, so I kept my revolvers strapped on and carried my rifle, to be prepared for whatever might happen. Otherwise, I was friendly with them all and paid no apparent attention to their warlike regalia.

One day I let a native shoot my rifle. He handled it awkwardly and seemed to know nothing about firearms. I braced it properly against his shoulder and put his finger on the trigger. As he pulled the trigger, he lifted the gun against his cheek and shot into the trees. The gun gave him quite a kick. He put his hand to his jaw and looked after the bullet and then at me, scared almost white, and finally he said, 'My word, strong fellah too much.' He handed the gun back to me, as gingerly as though he thought it were going to bite him or explode in his hand.

The natives were expert with bow and arrow, especially at shooting pigeons. The arrows were made of the midrib of a palm leaf. And since most of their tips were dipped in poison, I was careful not to touch them. If the arrow missed its mark, but scratched the bird or animal, the poison still took effect, and it was then only a matter of trailing the prey until it fell. In spite of the poison, the flesh would be good to eat.

Wild pigs were plentiful in the bush and these the hunters caught in nets or speared on the run. Sometimes they used their mangy little native dogs to run the pigs down and hold them at bay. As everywhere among primitive people, the pig was a favorite food, and here especially, for these fish-eating natives had a well-developed taste for fats.

Watching a hunt one day, I saw the natives string up the pig and clean him and at once begin collecting wood for a fire. It took them only a minute to strike fire in the primitive American Indian fashion. A man took a piece of soft palm-wood and made a groove in it. Then he sharpened a harder stick to a point and rubbed this up and down the groove of the other. Small shavings collected at the end of the groove and the heat of the rubbing soon made the sawdust begin to smoke. He then blew on the smoking bits and the shavings burst into a tiny flame. This he transferred to leaves and twigs and soon had a roaring fire and glowing coals.

The pig was roasted and we sat down to one of the best feasts I have ever had. The men gave me bits of the crisp skin, which they seemed to prize, and coconut milk in a freshly hollowed shell. They gorged themselves for an hour. There was very little of the pig to take home to the village when we had finished.

One afternoon, as I sauntered along a bush trail looking for pigeons for our dinner, I heard a grunt and saw a mother pig standing in the path eyeing me fiercely. I froze to the spot and gripped my rifle, for I expected her to charge. Then, calmly as you please, six little pigs walked out of the under-growth and into the trail. Seeing me, they huddled around their mother, looking very scared and very appealing. The mother glared and grunted at me bravely, as though she would tear me to ribbons if I touched her precious family, and then they all dove into the bush on the other side of the trail and disappeared. Immediately, the father, a big fellow, ap-peared in the same spot. He grunted and made several false charges toward me, but thought better of it and also dis-appeared, crashing away through the jungle.

With their every want provided for, these coast natives seemed to live the perfect life of leisure. There were pigs and fish on every hand, and coconuts literally fell from heaven. Their youngsters did most of the tortoise hunting and much of the fishing — for fun. They had clean beaches and plenty of water for bathing and cooking and no gardens to tend. No wonder the hill people envied them and tended to move down to the coast when they learned of its advantages. Instead of the sages whispering, 'Go West, young man,' they probably advised their youths, 'Go down to the beach, get rich and loaf.'

Our skipper had completed his trading and had a rich load

of tortoise and other commercial shell. The tortoise-shell, which had been rudely torn from the backs of the big turtles, was nothing much to look at in this form. But I learned that the natives had a great regard for its value even before the traders came. In addition to making it into fishhooks and other articles of use, they made all sorts of ornaments for their noses, ears, hair, and arms from the carved and polished shell, as well as decorations for their canoes and canoe-houses.

The amount of Hawksbill tortoise-shell we had was worth a small fortune by the time it reached the retail counters at home in the form of toilet articles, vanity cases, and jewelry, the skipper explained. And the mother-of-pearl, golden pearl, and black-lip pearl, of which we also had a considerable quantity, would represent a large sum when cut into pins, earrings, knife-handles, and a thousand other articles, including buttons for garments.

'A good haul this trip,' the skipper said, as he rubbed his hands with a satisfied air. 'The best I've ever had except when I picked up two beautiful pearls several years ago. Get this down to Sydney and I'll have a few hundred pounds. At least enough to pay up all my debts and buy a few Tom and Jerry's. With what we take on at Savo, we will do very well. I think you've brought me luck this trip.'

We were heading toward Savo, which looked like a single peak against the horizon as it jutted out of the sea and the morning haze. Martin pumped questions at Mr. Creswell about the island, its reputed volcano and buccaneering inhabitants.

'For some reason Guadalcanal has been a great temptation to the Savo natives,' the skipper replied. 'They have been fighting each other for centuries, with the same old canoes and the same spears and arrows, with about every kind of stratagem and cunning known to man, and with the ignorance and hate that make all wars. As far as I know, the score is about even. They are both tough fighters, but the men of Savo are as bad as they come down here. They will trade and carry on, as offhand as a bunch of country boys back home, but when their blood is up, and they go after heads, they are devils of the worst kind. No holy missions or other discipline has ever been able to cure or calm them.'

He went on to confirm what we had already been told, that Savo was full of 'bad blood.' Evidently they had elevated headhunting to a high art, and by their constant attacks had driven many of the people of Guadalcanal out of their villages back into the hills for peace and protection. They had ranged as far as Florida, Ysabel, and other islands. But on Malaita they had apparently met their match, for the only known and recent expedition to that island had cost the invaders most of their own heads.

The skipper's explanation for this gangsterism was that the island population was a polyglot of outcast persons and tribes from other islands and that they were almost an outlaw people by now, with little of the pure Savo blood left in them. To make them more of a menace, some of the Savo men had recently obtained better arms than most natives possessed. With Snider rifles, steel tomahawks and knives, the old spears and arrows would be no competition.

'They're getting too smart and overbearing,' he said. 'If this goes on, Government will have to give the place a good cleaning-up and a lesson in decency, in the only language they understand.'

9 〰〰〰〰

... mendacity ... and strength

*S*AVO WAS AN ATTRACTIVE ISLE for one with
so troubled a reputation. But I had learned by now that al-
luring beaches and slumbering jungle were no token of what
to expect from any part of the Solomons. Almost round in
shape, the little island was actually a volcanic cone pushed
up from the sea. Heavy clouds overhung the peak and made
it look as though it were in eruption. The volcano was dead,
the skipper assured us, though smoke and steam still issued
from fumaroles on its sides. Its slopes down to the beach were
heavily covered with scrub timber and coconut palms.

Canoes raced out to us as we neared the shore. The paddlers eyed us curiously, but said little except to chatter among
themselves. They swung into our wake and followed us with
a speed that was surprising.

'You can be sure they have something to sell, if only a
scrubby old yam,' grunted the skipper.

The moment we anchored, we were surrounded by canoes,
pressing up close to us. Alongside was a little boy in a canoe
not much larger than he was. He was bailing out water with
his two hands, but when he saw me, he quickly held up two
yams and began jabbering in a language I hadn't yet heard.
I gave him a stick of tobacco and he handed me both the

yams, as seriously as a big businessman. The tobacco he stuck through a hole in the lobe of his ear.

The youngster waited a moment, and then, as though he had just had a bright idea, dove into a pile of leaves in the stern of the canoe and produced two other yams. These were much larger and finer than the first. He held them out to me. I nodded that it was a deal and offered another stick of tobacco, but he shook his head and held up two fingers. I was outbargained, and gave him two sticks of tobacco. These he stuck through a hole in his other ear. He paddled away without a smile, though I am sure he was laughing all over at how he had swindled the missus, and would be complimented by his father for the fine tobacco.

As soon as we landed and the skipper had begun his trading, I asked him if he would mind our climbing to the crater. He thought it was too far away and asked the natives how long it would take. They all began jabbering about the devil-devils who lived up there and swore that we would surely die if we looked inside the volcano. So we compromised on seeing the hot springs. The skipper gave us several of the boatboys, and, with a dozen villagers to carry our cameras and equipment, Martin and I started off.

We followed a thin trail that led up a ravine alongside a small stream. The forest had been cut away in many places to make room for the gardens, which the natives changed every year so as to have virgin soil. But otherwise there was a mass of jungle growth and the boys had to use knives every now and then to cut our way.

Half a mile or more up the ravine, we came to the first hot spring. It was a bubbling pool, from the surface of which came little puffs and wisps of steam. It was overgrown with green scum and surrounded by soft, reeking mire that smelled of rot and decay. While we sat down to rest, the natives stuck their yams into the mud and cooked them.

'More easy living,' said Martin. 'If they just piped this natural heater down to the beach, they would give life on Savo its last perfect touch.'

As we climbed, we found other hot springs along the stream. Our curiosity was now so piqued that we couldn't resist going on to the top. But the villagers refused to accompany us. Finally, we persuaded one stout boy to guide us and brave the devil-devils and told him we would protect him whatever happened.

As we neared the summit, the undergrowth became so heavy that we had to hack our way through, but we finally came out on the rim. Below us was a large crater, silent as a tomb, and completely overgrown with scrubby trees and bush and creepers. Masses of stone were strewn over the floor.

'If there are any devil-devils in there, they have a rough time of it,' Martin said.

We poked about the débris and watched the native boy, who was speechless with fear. But there was nothing worth photographing, so we hurried back down the mountainside to take advantage of the light. We decided that native legends were better left unexplored.

The skipper was furious and gave us a lecture on obeying his orders. We couldn't be trusted out of his sight, he grumbled, and he had promised Mr. Bell to be responsible for our safety. But he finally calmed down and seemed proud of what he called our Yankee disregard of the consequences.

'I see you'll get what you are after, if they don't get you first,' he said.

Standing around him were thirty or more naked savages who had just brought in their shells and copra to trade. Every one had a sliver of bone or wood through his nose, and most of them had wooden disks or shell ornaments in their ear lobes, and cowrie shells in their bushy hair. Every man had some vicious-looking weapon. Several had spears with barbed points of fishbone attached to long palmwood shafts. Some had bows and arrows with barbed heads. Others had heavy warclubs or tomahawks made of hardwood.

'Are the spears and arrows poisoned?' I asked.

'Nine times out of ten,' said the skipper. 'And better not

touch them. They have an easy way of poisoning their spear-points down here. They thrust the point into a decomposing corpse and leave it there for several days. When the process is finished, the weapon will finish off anything it strikes. To kill a man they usually throw the spear into his abdomen, where the barbed point makes a deep and ragged wound, and the poison does the rest.'

I looked at the men around us. They were sturdy, but their mouths turned down weakly and their eyes were the shiftiest I had seen. They seemed to combine the mendacity of the Malaitans with the strength of the Guadalcanal natives. They had probably sprung from both people, and they were constantly at war with both. Martin was busily making pictures and I could see that he was happy to get these faces.

Among the natives was an old man with a Snider rifle thrown over his shoulder and a small cartridge pouch on his belt. He seemed reasonably friendly and harmless, and I asked the skipper if I could see the rifle.

'Go ask him,' the skipper said.

I walked forward and gave the old man a stick of tobacco. Then I admired the gun and saw that he understood and appreciated the attention. I held out my hand and asked him to see the piece. To my surprise, he handed it to me. It was a clumsy old weapon that looked as rusty and corroded as though it had been buried for years. I held it up and looked through the barrel. There was only a small gleam of light, for the inside was a mass of rust and dirt. I would have been scared to death to shoot the gun and was sure it would do no damage except to the person who fired it.

The other natives were eyeing me with sour looks. Carrying out my act, I asked to see one of the tomahawks, and handed its owner a stick of tobacco. He let me have the hatchet. It was made of hardwood and reminded me of the tomahawks of the early American Indians, but the head was larger, and it had a beautifully carved handle.

A row of notches behind the head of the tomahawk caught my eye, as I handed it back to the owner.

'How many heads have you got with this?' I asked. Then, turning to *bêche-de-mer*, I repeated, 'How many head belong this one fellah akkus belong you, you ketchum?'

The native rolled his eyes with savage innocence and made-believe he did not understand. But I saw him wink at one of the others, as much as to say, 'If this Mary pushes me, I will tell her that I cut only yams and taro, but she needn't think I will talk about heads.'

But now my eyes popped. In the fuzzy hair of the next man was an orange cowrie shell. I had been told that these were extremely rare and that only a few were known to exist, one of them being on display at the British Museum. I called the attention of Mr. Creswell.

'It's genuine, all right,' the skipper said. 'But he wouldn't part with it for anything. That is his claim to distinction and he knows that his shell makes all the women look at him. And, besides, it is worth several wives. Watch me. I'll offer him my ship for it and see what he does.'

The skipper proceeded to trade for the cowrie shell. First, he offered a case of tobacco, then two cases, and then three. The native only stared. Then the skipper offered him a pipe. Then a fine knife and a wrist watch. But the native's face was impassive.

With a flourish, the skipper motioned to his ship and said, 'My word, Boy. Me givum you boat belong me. You sailo sea belong you. You lookum plenty chief belong you. You givem me shell belong you. Hah?'

'Me likum this one fellah; no wantum boat belong you,' mumbled the savage, without expression, but with complete finality.

Dusk was falling. The cook-fires had been started, and we smelled the delicious odor of roasting almonds, yams, and taro.

We walked to the nearest fire, around which two women were bustling, and watched the dinner being made. With bamboo tongs the women turned the food over and over on the coals and finally lifted out the charred pieces and scraped off the burned skin. Then they mashed the pulp and mixed in burnt almonds and wild ginger. This 'pudding' they wrapped in wild fig leaves to serve.

The men, hungry from their hard day's work of doing nothing, ate with a relish. They seemed to pay little or no attention to us and offered us no food. This was a relief. I was glad we did not have to stay and eat with these people.

After dinner on the schooner, we moved down the coast, for the curiosity of the natives might lead them to some mischief during the night. I tossed out a line, hoping to catch our breakfast, and sat in the balmy air, watching the clear stars and the rippling water.

Fish leaped and splashed and made phosphorescent streaks across the surface. Thousands of fireflies flashed among the trees along the shore and gave the place a touch of fairyland. And crickets set up such a claque and clatter that I could scarcely hear the skipper's voice.

'You'll probably catch nothing but sharks here, young lady,' he said. 'The place is full of them. If you fell in here, you wouldn't last a second. Savo sharks dote on young girls.'

'Why the Savo sharks?' I asked. 'Aren't they the same sharks we had at Guadalcanal?'

'A special brand,' he said. 'Over here the natives feed their dead to the sharks. It's a ritual and has gone on for so long that the sharks have a real taste for human blood. With infanticide and the population as crazy as it is, the fish are pretty well fed. Burial ground is scarce on Savo, so I suppose there is some sense in the practice. It's as reasonable as cremation, and easier.'

He pointed to the water. I saw several large fins cut the surface, swim past and then return. The great fish were apparently curious about our ship.

'When the natives bury someone at sea, they have a great ceremony,' the skipper continued. 'The medicine men take the body out in a large canoe, and the relatives and mourners follow in other canoes, wailing and carrying on. The medicine men do a series of incantations, committing the soul of the deceased to the deep. They believe that when the body is disposed of, the soul enters a shark and the shark thereby becomes sacred.'

A monster shark broke beside us.

'That was the ghost of some Savo man or woman, looking you over,' he said. 'The place is full of Savo ancestors, and if they fight down there in the deep, the way they do in real life, they must have a merry time. The natives wouldn't kill a shark here for anything.'

'What if a native fisherman caught a shark?' I asked.

'He would feel as though he had caught his grandfather, and let him go, quick! Why, they are so fanatical that if a man is bitten by a shark and is saved, they will throw him back in to be devoured, so as not to anger the spirits. They even make sacrifices to the sharks of their most precious belongings, like beads and shell money and porpoise teeth. Some families have their own shark images in the headhouse and their own private houses for shark worship. There are shark temples in some of the islands, with medicine men to guard the sacred images and do daily rituals on the beach. When a chief dies, they make a big hollow receptacle of wood, in the form of a shark, and put his body and his most valuable trinkets into it, and let him rot in the sacred image.'

'How do I tell a man-eating shark, from the others?' I asked.

'They are so horrible-looking you will almost know them by instinct,' he replied. 'They have a blunt head and broad, triangular, saw-edged teeth. They run up to thirty feet in length and are fast. But if you see any shark down here, just figure it's a man-eater and get out of his way.'

He explained that there were plenty of sharks in all warm waters. The ground sharks were harmless, running about twelve feet long and feeding on fish, which seemed to satisfy their appetite.

'If you catch the long, slender blue shark, cut him up for steaks,' the skipper added. 'And the mako isn't bad. He is a strong, fast swimmer and looks like a man-eater, but has a tuna's crescent-shaped fin to remember him by. Baby mako steak is fine eating.'

He could have his shark steaks, I told him. I would stick to bully-beef.

'We probably exaggerate the whole shark business,' he said. 'But just as well, for they aren't nice playmates in any water. I have lost two boys to them and the sight of their agony is something I won't forget. Some people like to swim in the sea, but I'll take mine in a teacup, and stay out of a shark's belly, whether I am snow-white or not. I am going to make all my mistakes with sharks on the safe side.'

He then told us a wild sea-serpent story. The creature was supposed to appear every now and then off Savo.

'Probably a combination of all the sharks they have seen,' he said. 'Twenty fathoms long, with sharp eighteen-inch teeth. It feeds on baby sharks and other sea creatures, scooping up huge mouthfuls at each gulp. The incarnation of a devilish and brutal chief of the olden days, the natives say, a kind of Savo Satan. But nobody I can find has ever seen the beast. And if anyone did see it, that person would fall dead or go insane, they tell me.'

That night, my dreams were full of sharks. I rode them bareback, fought them off while swimming, and found myself being taken out to sea by Savo natives in a great war-canoe to be fed to the sharks. I woke up yelling for Martin.

For several days we moved from village to village, collecting copra and shell. Martin was very pleased with his pictures. These would make a fine rogues' gallery, I thought, for the people were more depraved-looking than the best we had seen on Malaita. The old men especially were grizzled and hairy and altogether an ugly lot.

The faces of the young men were smooth-shaven, and this surprised me, for I knew they had no razors. One morning I saw a youngster squatting outside a hut, while another boy with small clam shells plucked out his whiskers, one by one. The sitter patiently endured the pain, which went on for a long time, for the beards of these men were heavy. This, I found, was also the way in which they 'cut' their mustaches into fancy patterns, and sometimes also the hair on their heads.

Here, for the first time, I noticed several bald men. The natives all had such abundant hair that these old fellows were conspicuous. And others were quite gray with age. The women cut their hair short. It was probably too much to bother with at their heavy work in the gardens. Many of them were entirely smooth on top.

'Look at those beads and gewgaws,' said Martin, pointing to a group of women. They were young girls and very attractive, but were loaded down with necklaces, bracelets, and anklets of teeth, seeds, and shell.

'Now do you see why I think jewelry is barbaric?' he said. 'That's why I can't stand these South Sea women.'

I was glad he couldn't stand their jewelry, for sometimes I felt pretty jealous as he photographed these young girls, all of them without a stitch of clothing.

The chiefs here on Savo were very pompous and arrogant. They reminded me of the school bullies we had back home, except they were grown-up and much more terrible to look at. Each village had its chief, but some were more aggressive than others and by bluff and energy had extended their influence over other villages. If their manner proved anything, they were a warlike breed. But they were all so sullen that I wondered if they ever had a happy moment in their lives. Probably only when they were at war, which was ample proof of their stupidity.

'They aren't stupid when it comes to trade,' said the skipper.

He told me how cunningly they bargained and tricked him if he didn't watch their every move.

'They are supposed to string their miserable little smoked copra kernels in rows of ten,' he said. 'They know what ten is, all right. But if I don't count every one, they will short-change me every time. Especially if the meats are larger and look like a full string. I've had them offer me seven and even six for ten, and when I catch them at their mischief, their eyes laugh and they seem to have almost as much fun as though they had got away with their little game.'

The skipper paid the natives a stick of tobacco for each string of ten half-nuts. The tobacco sticks cost him about a cent apiece, so that for a ton of copra, roughly a thousand strings, he would pay forty pounds of tobacco or about fifteen dollars. Adding freight and brokerage, he would have a cost on delivery at Sydney of about thirty dollars and would sell the copra for about thirty-five dollars, with a profit of five dollars or more a ton. The skipper said that if he collected five hundred tons per year, he was doing well, and he some-times had less.

Even the children smoked tobacco. There never seemed to be enough for all the needs, and the craving for it, along with its scarcity, gave it an exaggerated value. A small piece of tobacco twist would buy several fishhooks of tortoise-shell which had taken the natives months to make, while a few sticks would buy a man's most prized possessions. A home-grown 'bru-brush' leaf was rolled into twists to resemble to-bacco. It was a poor imitation, but they stuffed it into their pipes and seemed to enjoy it when they had nothing better.

'Tomorrow, I'm going to give you a real treat,' confided the skipper one evening. 'I'll show you one of the wonders of the Solomons, and one of the wonders of the world for that matter. The megapodes.'

'Who are they?' I asked.

'Birds, not people,' he said, with some impatience. 'And the queerest birds you ever saw. They are nothing much to look at — something like a guinea fowl but larger. The traders call them brush turkey. They mate and lay their eggs with great ceremony, something like the rare argus pheasant. This is their laying season, and if we have luck we will see a great show. One of their favorite laying-grounds is on the beach down below and if we are there at dawn we should see them.'

He told us how the birds dug great pits, sometimes as deep as three and four feet and as broad as fifteen feet, scratching out the earth with their claws and their overpowerful legs. They deposited their eggs and filled in the loose soil, twigs and leaves, and made a mound above.

Apparently each bird laid one egg, buried it, and went off without further concern, leaving it for the sun to hatch and for the little chick to burrow his own way to the surface. The eggs looked like ducks' eggs and were highly prized by the natives, who used them, regardless of their age, for eating and for ceremonials.

'As a matter of fact, I have seen natives digging and the birds laying their eggs, only a few yards apart, and the birds not seeming to tumble to what was going on or not to care,' the skipper added. 'The natives catch the little chicks too, and save them for the pot. But they never kill nor molest the grown birds, which they respect and revere. In the old days it was an offense punishable by death to kill a megapode, and even today a native is thrown out of a village or otherwise punished if he is caught killing one of the hens.'

Next morning, we landed at a little after seven and followed the skipper through the bush to the laying-grounds. There, on the beach and in the forest, were hundreds of the birds on every side, scratching away at the sand and digging or covering their pits. They worked with breathless speed, as though their lives depended upon it and there were not a moment to lose.

When the pit was completed, the egg deposited, and the hole filled in and covered over with earth and twigs, the bird would walk about in a satisfied way, something like a chicken in a farmyard that had just finished laying, and would probably have cackled if it could. Instead, it made a low raucous sound and then flew away, to leave its offspring to fate and the hungry natives.

Native dogs went after the megapode hens and killed them indiscriminately, Mr. Creswell said, but the natives speared any dog they found doing it. Monitor lizards also dug up the eggs and even ate the young chicks if they could. The natives protected the birds in every possible way, just as we protect barnyard fowl from marauders.

'They seem to think the birds were put here for their express benefit,' he said. 'And digging for those eggs is probably the hardest work the men on Savo ever do.'

Always curious, I wanted to taste one of the eggs. Martin helped me dig it up and I took it back to the ship, and made it into an omelette. It was exactly like a hen's egg and not at all strong or offensive. But I was skeptical about the hardy little chicks that could dig themselves out of such a grave at birth and I still thought the skipper was jollying me.

'It's true,' he said. 'More than that, the little things are born with their feathers on, and they can fly right off after hatching. It's the only bird in the world that can do that. I've seen them do it. A friend gave me some of the eggs and I had them in my kitchen at Tulagi, and the chicks pecked their way out of the shells and flew against the window, trying to get out.'

That seemed too much, and I told him so.

'Reasonable or not, they do it,' he said seriously. 'A chick hatched on a trader's yacht and flew about forty feet out over the water and back again into the rigging. It's the most extraordinary bird in all the world, in my opinion, and one of the principal freaks of these queer islands.'

We had hoped to see the salt fields and the fishing rituals about which the skipper had told us, but his schooner was heavily loaded and we knew he had given us all the time he could afford. Without further delay, we put off for Tulagi.

'Wish I could go exploring with you two,' he said. 'It must be great to have nothing to do but make pictures. I've got a living to make. Furthermore, the Governor is going to take you in tow at Tulagi.'

10 〰〰〰

. . . they call him Marco

COMING INTO THE HARBOR at Tulagi after our several weeks in the jungles, the sight of a sailing ship and of the docks and the small boats gave me a decided thrill. The neat white houses along the shore and banked against the hill made the place look almost like a metropolis.

I tidied up as best I could in the only outfit I had left: a clean blouse and battered white hat, riding-breeches and puttees. By now I had learned that a few clothes went a long way in these outposts. The white population did its best to keep up appearances and their self-respect, but being away from the stores and the fashion magazines soon led everyone to relax into whatever he had or what was most comfortable. The native servants did the rest, for the constant punishment they gave all clothing in the wash, beating them with sticks and stones, soon reduced the best of wardrobes to mere odds and ends. The most one could hope for was to be clean and tidy even if a little tattered.

Standing on the wharf, waiting for us to come ashore, were the Governor and his boys. I was glad I had thought to put on fresh clothes, but one look at the Governor made me feel quite all right about my appearance. His white suit had shrunk noticeably and, although the shorts were severely creased, their color was on the jaundiced side and they were considerably the worse for wear. The coat was short at the sleeves and looked as though the houseboy had stopped pressing after he finished the lapels. His white helmet was scruffed, but freshly whitened. He wore brown brogues, highly polished, and heavy brown socks that had obviously been mended several times. His starched collar and polka-dotted tie, done into a fixed knot, and his neatly cropped mustache were thoroughly respectable. And his malacca cane, with a beautiful tortoise-shell handle, was the last official touch.

He shook our hands warmly. 'Thank God you are back,' he said. 'When you left for Malaita, I expected I would soon have a call from Mr. Bell for a punitive expedition. It wasn't just the fact of your going there but you *look* reckless. And besides, we have never before permitted a woman to go to Malaita, let alone going into the interior.'

We assured him that everything had been very tame, thanks to his and Mr. Bell's precautions, and we had not even had a spear thrown at us. There would be no more cause to worry on our account, for we could now take care of ourselves. I added that Martin was sorry, but he hadn't got one really exciting picture.

The Governor glared at me. 'Your cocksureness is probably your best protection,' he said crisply and a little sarcastically. 'I hope you don't lose it down here, or that it isn't the end of you, as it may well be. In any case, I am not going to depend on your American nerve to take care of my responsibility. And I don't want your country declaring war on mine just because I overlooked my duty.'

The Governor greeted Mr. Creswell and complimented him. Then he invited us all to Government House for dinner and to give him a full report.

'Meantime, I have a nice house for you.' He pointed to a white bungalow halfway up the hill, reached by a long flight of steps. 'Two hundred steps by actual count,' he said. 'But the air is splendid.'

As we strolled up the wharf, he told us that he was keeping his promise, and threat, to turn us over to a 'bodyguard' for the rest of our stay in the Solomons.

'One of my best friends, Harold Markham,' he said, 'is due here any time now. He has just the ship you need and knows more about the islands than any of us. And he has more personality than any man I know. We all love him and so will you.'

All this attention, whether from friendship or duty, was very pleasant. The Governor had even engaged the servants we would need. 'They are a little raw,' he said, 'but they will help you along until Markham arrives.'

Within a few hours we had taken our belongings from the ship and the storehouse and had installed ourselves in the cool and pleasant little house. It was scantily furnished and very plain, but it seemed almost palatial after the cramped quarters of the schooner and the jungle huts. From the verandah I could see out over the entire harbor and the little town. And all around us was a luxuriant garden filled with creepers, shrubs, and flowers of every imaginable color.

That evening we went to the Governor's for dinner. I had managed to find a cotton dress which I had brought from home and hurriedly ironed it into partial respectability. Martin got out a white suit that was a bit yellowed but presentable. We resolved that however much we needed clothes, we would buy only essentials and save our money, for we might need every last penny before we left the Solomons.

Despite our shabby appearance, the Governor received us as cordially as though we had come straight from London in the latest vogue. We both felt a new affection for him. Mr. Creswell had completely shed his rough clothes and wore a mess jacket and black trousers and cummerbund. He looked more than ever like an aristocrat, and Martin jollied him about this the rest of the evening.

The Governor was extremely interested in all that we had seen and done, and he showed new and unexpected sympathy with our ambitious plans.

'Of course, what you want is impracticable. You won't see cannibals in action, as you put it. And if you do get that close to a cannibal feast, your biggest job will be getting away without a spear in your backs. Nobody sees these feasts and comes away to tell about them. Furthermore, they are becoming very infrequent and I hope we have actually seen the last of them.'

Evidently it was the policy of the Government to minimize cannibalism, either out of pride in what they were doing to stamp it out or because they did not want to be criticized by the world for not keeping perfect control. Or they were 'holding the thought,' as a means of bringing better times to pass.

As the Governor talked we could see that he wanted us to think that everything was in good order, probably to discourage us as much as anything else. We appreciated his earnestness and friendship, but it was clear that the sooner we got away from Tulagi, the better for our success.

I hoped that Markham would not be some pompous moralist or 'straw boss' for the Governor.

'If he should be,' said Martin as we walked out to the verandah, 'we will cut loose from the whole crowd and go native. I'm not going to let anybody stop us till we get what we are after.'

This sounded very brave, but I knew Martin's enthusiasms. And I knew that the only practical way for us to get on here was to do as the Governor said, to be diplomatic and understanding, and to have his every help instead of his opposition. We would have to play the game with the authorities or go back home empty-handed.

We sat in the dark looking out over the harbor, calm under the arching stars, and watching the moon sail down the sky toward Savo and Guadalcanal. The din of the crickets shut out other sounds and brought the jungle close. Except for the comfort about us, we might easily have been in the hills of Malaita, instead of at Tulagi and Government House. In the Governor I could see much the same tension of responsibility and the same idealism as we had found in Mr. Bell.

'We patrol the big islands as best we can,' he was saying. 'But there are hundreds of small islands — more than nine hundred in the Solomons alone. Worse than a needle in the proverbial haystack if you got out there and were lost. Many a man has disappeared in a few hours and never a trace of him has been found.'

I could see that Martin was impressed.

'Even if you had the finest ship made, you couldn't prowl around these islands alone,' the Governor went on. 'The rocks and coral reefs stick up everywhere and in a heavy sea or a storm, you would be cracked to bits. But with Markham, I will know you are all right — he knows every nook in the islands, almost every rock in the sea, and all the treacherous channels.'

'Tell us about Markham,' Martin said. 'Judging from all this enthusiasm, he sounds made to order.'

'They call him Marco,' the Governor replied, 'Marco Polo of the Sea. He married a native girl, has two little children, and can be at one and the same time the most generous and the toughest man imaginable.'

He explained that Markham had a fine education, had traveled widely, and knew almost everything about the Solomons. He had a fine capacity for management, and would some day be very rich.

'The natives love him,' the Governor went on. 'Along with being the best navigator in the Solomons, he has enormous luck and rides through adversities that would kill any other human being. We are just sure that he has been lost, when there he is, sailing into the harbor, as calmly as you please, ready for the next calamity.'

Mr. Creswell warmly agreed. 'Don't mind Marco's rough talk,' he said. 'It may shock you, for he can curse worse than any sailor, but when he swears, it is so expressive that it's almost poetry. He is an absolute genius afloat and you will be grateful for the Governor's advice on this.'

They were full of Markham reminiscences.

'I have seen him in Sydney spend a year's income in a week,' said the skipper. 'He took me to dinner at the Australia Hotel and ordered food and wines like a Parisian connoisseur. He drank bottles of champagne and was still as sober as an owl. He was the most perfect and natural host I've ever seen. Then he tipped the waitress with a pair of tickets to the theatre and gave the captain a five-pound note. He must have had plenty of money in his youth, for he can spend it like a veteran.'

The Governor thought Markham had come from a wealthy family. He had lived in London and on the Continent and in America.

'On one of our Australian trips,' he said, 'Marco gave one of my friends exquisite Goura and Bird of Paradise feathers, just because she admired them. He said he wanted people to have things they appreciated and was proud to see a woman wear something that made her happy. Yet on one spending spree down there, he bought his wife, Lily, a diamond ring, which, of course, she couldn't appreciate — a pearl shell would have meant more to her — and silks galore, which she couldn't possibly wear out here in the jungle. He is always bringing home a cargo of garden seeds, comforts and gadgets of all kinds. He's another wonder of the Solomons.'

This interlude of waiting for Markham to arrive gave me a chance to enjoy being domestic. Before I had married Martin and had been whisked off to an exploring career, I had dreamed of having a little home in Kansas and a garden such as my father had at Chanute and a houseful of children. Now, I started cooking the dishes Martin liked back home and had not tasted for over a year, such as fried chicken and lamb stew with dumplings and floating island pudding. I baked cakes, and experimented with the native foods I had seen on our recent trip. And I made the house look presentable enough to have the Governor and others in to dinner.

There was a great deal of work to be done. Martin had all

his still negatives to develop and print and his motion-picture film to test and seal and ship to Australia, where it would be cared for by our friend, Ernie Higgins. Our jungle wardrobe had to be replenished. I budgeted our food and supplies for the next six months and checked over our accounts.

Languages came to me easily and the servants helped me finish out my *bêche-de-mer* vocabulary. With the thirty-nine basic words and a few extra English words and pantomimic gestures thrown in, I could now make myself understood to the houseboy and the natives of Tulagi. But our second boy, who seemed too stupid to comprehend anything, never could understand me. He was always doing the opposite of what I wanted, and I struggled to find a way to make myself clear to him.

One morning Martin wanted some things packed in a wooden box, and I said to the boy, 'You go along, one fellah boat belong Master. You ketchum one fellah saw belong me. You bringum two fellah.'

I waited for a long time and no saw arrived. After more than an hour, the boy came back with one of the Governor's personal servants, who was evidently to act as interpreter.

'What name, Missus, you askum this one fellah boy belong you?' the newcomer asked.

So I told the Governor's boy that I wanted a saw which he would find in our little cutter down at the dock. He clicked his bare heels and saluted and turned to my boy, with a great show of authority.

'You go along one fellah boat,' he said. 'You ketchum one fellah, he brother belong hammer. You push him he go; you pull him, he come.'

'Ah, savvy,' said my boy with a bright grin, and off he ran for the implement.

Nearly all my trading was with the Chinese store, which had everything from fish and vegetables to drygoods and hardware. The owner was a jovial old man who would rather talk pidgin English with me than to sell me his goods.

But, like all the others here, he was probably so lonely that he made the most of every visitor from abroad to catch up on the world he had practically abandoned. He prospered despite the smallness of the community and was said to make a real fortune from the traders, who were profligate with their money when they had it.

Martin and I both needed trousers, jumpers, and shirts, and, although I begrudged the expense at this time, I ordered them of a Japanese sea-captain's tailor, named Ishimoto, who had recently come to the island. He was extremely polite and very able as a shirtmaker.

When Ishimoto found that we were making motion pictures, he was very interested and said that he took amateur photographs. He plied Martin with a thousand questions. One day he brought two of his cameras for Martin to see. They proved to be the latest thing; an Eastman kodak and the other a fine German camera, with a ground-glass focusing plate.

He spent a great deal of time at the house thereafter, taking pointers from Martin on how to get the best results from exposures and timing, and also developing, which he said he did for himself in his own darkroom. He went over our prints at great length with both of us, admiring Martin's prize shots and getting our criticism on his own work.

Later, we learned that he had a boat — an unpretentious little whaleboat with a sail — and that he was often seen sailing up and down the harbor and among the islands near-by.

Suddenly, Martin came down with malaria and I rushed him to the hospital. It was the worst attack he had ever had and, except for the doctor and nurse, it would probably have been fatal.

'Isn't there any escape from this fever?' I asked the nurse. 'Is he going to have these spells all his life?'

'He is young and he looks lucky,' she answered. 'But if he goes to London and the cold, damp fog hits him, he will probably have malaria. If he has a sudden change of temperature, although he may be feeling at the top of his energy, he will probably have malaria. It may get him at high altitudes. And it may strike him if he is out in a cold night. When he least expects it, that is when it will probably attack. The worst attacks of all will be upon going home from the tropics — the change is so great. There is no accounting for this fickle fever. It may come on at any moment, or he may go for years without having it. Otherwise, he looks as though he were going to have a most healthy life and live to be a hundred.'

Martin's work was the most important thing in the world in my eyes, and I prayed daily for his success and his health. In addition to being the handsomest and the kindest man I knew, he was an idealist and he would go far in the world if he could keep his stride.

Realizing that I would have to take care of Martin and myself for this and many other ailments we were likely to have, I asked the nurse and the hospital doctor to help me. They were glad to do so and began letting me visit the patients with them and gave me a quick first-aid course. Soon, they permitted me to assist them with dressings and treatments, so that I became an unofficial nurse and spent hours each day with them. The doctor made up a complete kit of medicines, splints, and bandages for me to take along.

'You will do,' he said finally. 'I see you have the nerve and the stomach for medicine. You will probably need plenty of both.'

But he cautioned me not to play doctor with the natives.

'The natives have some frightful afflictions,' he said. 'They are always having accidents and wounds, and they will be asking you for help. Give it to them, but be careful. They are regular babies when they are ill — think the evil spirits are after them and won't put up a fight. But they aren't accustomed to drugs, so they have different reactions from ours to some treatments. Take no chances. Give them nothing but simple first-aid.'

Real medicine was for the doctors, he explained.

'If anything goes wrong, they will be sure you are using magic on them. And if someone you treat should die, they may take your head for your pains.'

I learned how to detect the most common maladies and so to protect ourselves from infection. These were several kinds of ringworm, leprosy, elephantiasis, smallpox, venereal diseases, influenza, lung diseases, abscesses, and a variety of skin infections.

'Stick to those puttees,' said the doctor. 'They are almost unbearably hot, but they protect you from scratches.'

I had been trying to persuade Martin to wear puttees or high boots, but he would not. He insisted on wearing shorts. His legs were badly cut by thorns and brush and had developed ulcers which refused to heal in this climate. These we now treated with permanganate of potash. It was a painful treatment to take, and almost equally agonizing to see him suffer from it, but it did the trick and made him well.

I learned that ringworm had to be treated with the strongest thing available and stocked up with tincture of iodine for that. Coral cuts would be poisonous and needed blue vitriol. Some of the poison vines and vegetation would be worse than poison ivy at home and they required salves and lotions. I was bulging with don'ts and other information and I began to feel equal to anything that could happen. We now had only to be careful and sensible to keep our health.

We were down at the dock with the Governor one day, watching the unloading of a fine cargo of tortoise-shell, when we saw a ketch coming down the harbor. She looked streamlined and fleet as a yacht as she sped along in the fresh breeze.

'It's Markham!' said the Governor suddenly, looking very pleased. 'And his famous *Lily*, named after his wife. Isn't she a handsome little ship? The best there is in the Solomons.'

The ketch came gracefully up to the dock and moored, and Markham stepped ashore. He was all that the Governor had predicted — a fine, big, bronzed figure. He wore a white cotton shirt, open at the throat, gray felt hat, white slacks, and canvas shoes. He walked with the pitch of a sailor, but with an air of great self-confidence.

He came up to the Governor, saluted and shook hands.

'Nice to see you, sir,' he said.

The Governor chatted with him for a moment. Then he took Markham by the arm and said, 'I have some people for you to meet.'

'What have I done now?' said Markham.

He came over to us, took off his hat and smiled as though sure we were going to like him, and we did, on sight. He took Martin's hand and gave it a quick sharp grip.

'Yankees, I'll wager,' he said.

'Will you rent us your boat and yourself?' Martin blurted out.

'Why, sure, if you keep her fed and pay the gasoline. That kicker is a hungry old bird. Where do you want to go anyway?'

The Governor explained what we wanted and why he had determined to put us in Markham's hands.

Everything was soon arranged. When Markham's copra cargo was unloaded, we would set off in the *Lily*. He must first go home to the Island of Lord Howe in the Leueneua Lagoon. Then we would go on to the other islands that we wanted to visit.

'But on one condition,' Markham said, as he looked at me. 'That you will help me do my shopping. That needs a woman's hand.'

. . . King of an island principality

*O*NE WHO HAS NEVER SEEN the South Seas from
a small ship has never seen them at all. From the deck of a
passenger steamer, he may glimpse occasional bonita or whale
or a school of porpoise, but the rest escapes his eye. Now, as
we cut through the waves on Markham's swift little vessel, so
close to the water that it often swept over us, I felt a new
comradeship with the sea, and became aware of the great
abundance and variety and beauty of the fish in these warm
waters.

My favorite perch was to straddle the jib boom over the
bow, when the waves were not too rough. This was exciting,
for the boom dipped and rose out of the choppy water, and I
had to hold on for dear life. It was cool and fresh and gave
me a sense of flying.

Porpoise swam ahead of us, and as they thrust out of the
water and dove again they were almost close enough to touch.
Schools of bonita seemed to think we were a great fish trying
to catch them. Swift, streamlined flying fish broke water and
skimmed along beside me like little flashes of blue light. And
gray-blue sharks showed their white bellies as they swept close
to look us over and turned up their ugly mouths to seize
frightened bonita almost under my feet.

Martin objected to my being so reckless, but Markham indulged me, probably seeing that there was no use to do anything else. 'Hi, Mate,' Markham would finally shout to me, 'I think you've had enough adventure today.' And he would then haul me in.

Every day I took my turn at the wheel. Markham showed me how to box the compass, handle the rudder, manage the sails, and I began to feel that I could captain the ship if I had to. Martin was very clever at handling a ship, probably a throwback to his Viking ancestry.

The ship's food was atrocious. When I finally found weevils in the crackers I was eating, I complained. Markham only jollied me about being squeamish.

'Just brush 'em off and forget it,' he said. 'I've eaten thousands and they're perfectly harmless.'

He said he thought the jungles helped to dispose of a lot of useless niceties of civilization. I was sure he didn't mean it and was only trying to help me get adjusted to the place.

Good food was important to our health and I knew that my husband's success depended upon it, and probably our married happiness. My grandmother's chief advice had been, 'If he has good nourishing food, everything will be all right.'

I watched Markham's cook-boy struggle in the tiny galley to produce something edible out of the tinned stores. It was hopeless. After two days of bully-beef in different forms, for breakfast, lunch, and dinner, I rebelled.

'Would you like me to make you some hot biscuits for breakfast?' I asked, approaching the subject as diplomatically as possible.

'You're appointed cook right now,' said Markham, as though he had been hoping I would make the proposal.

The stores were discouraging to an American appetite. Even though we had had little else for months, we had not yet learned to like the sailor's staples. Canned beef, tea, condensed milk, sugar, hardtack, 'salmon' which was really dogfish, a few potatoes and onions, and a little flour, were all that I could find, and I was glad that I had laid in a generous supply of necessities. Markham explained that he took with him only food enough for his boys, for back home he would have enough of everything we needed.

'I guess you have got used to bully-beef by now,' he said defensively. 'For me, it's as good as any steak you get in Sydney. Bully-beef and tea are a feast in the Solomons.'

Markham's wants were evidently very simple; he had adapted himself to his life here and had learned to live on the land.

We could have fish for a change, I thought. I got out a hand line and in a few minutes was trolling. Markham said he could improve my technique and gave me a large hook and a native spinner made of mother-of-pearl. It was a kind of home-made 'Hawaiian wiggler,' now a favorite among sportsmen, and it worked magic.

As the ship sped ahead, the white spinner threshed about in the water and a maddened kingfish struck at it. In no time at all I had a haul of fish large enough for several days.

Then, to cap my excitement, I hooked a marlin, which gave me a fine fight. He was the first marlin I had ever caught. I tried to draw him in, but he leaped and shook himself and did acrobatics in the air and then sped away, nearly taking me with him. Here was a new kind of adventure.

Markham showed me how to play the fish and had his boys stand by. Having no rod and reel, my hands were soon burned and cut by the line, so the boys' tough hands were a great help. I refused to let go. Markham managed the ship like a professional fisher captain. After an hour, we landed the fish, to find that I had a great seventy-five-pounder.

The boys were so excited with this catch that they could hardly wait for their share. All took a hand and quickly cleaned the fish. They completely neglected the ship for the moment, but Markham did not complain and let them have their holiday. He cursed with excitement, but not at the boys. They threw the entrails overboard and these attracted masses of fish and sharks until we had hundreds of fins flashing all around us.

Now we at least had a variation on our menu and I went into the galley and made a fish chowder. As the men ate it, they swore that it was the best food that they had had in months, and so it seemed even to me.

'Do you know how bully-beef got its Solomons name of "bullamacow"?' asked Markham. 'The first Governor here had a houseboy who asked him what that animal was on the wrapper of a tin. He answered that it was a bull. Several days later, the boy asked again and the Governor absently told him that it was a cow. Thoroughly confused and taking no chances of making a mistake, the boy thereafter called the tins "bullamacow." And the name has stuck to them ever since.'

Markham was a thorough gentleman in every respect and was always amusing and entertaining company. But the moment he became excited, he could swear longer and louder than anybody I had ever heard. He paid no attention whatever to me, except to apologize, by an ashamed smile in my direction, when the explosion was over.

I wouldn't have missed one of those displays for the world. They were a high art. Nothing seemed to impress the crew as much as one of these eloquent diatribes. But, although the boys trembled at Markham's tongue-lashing, I could see that they actually obeyed him more from affection than fear. They knew where his heart was, however meanly he cursed them.

Obviously Markham's loss of temper was no habit, for he was usually sweet-dispositioned. And it was no lack of good words, for he had a fine vocabulary. The crew boys would have tried anybody's patience. At times they were so incredibly stupid or lazy or indifferent that no normal human being could resist blowing up at them. And Markham was one of those perfectionists who believed in doing nothing unless he did it well.

Furthermore, he never laid a hand on a native, which seemed to me the essence of breeding, self-discipline, and good judgment. If he administered a thrashing, it was verbal. He used such perfect English between the curses that the boys probably couldn't understand what he said, but they knew well enough what he meant, and no one on board had the slightest doubt about who was boss.

I asked him if he had ever had any serious trouble with his crew or help.

'Nothing to last very long,' he said, with a twinkle in his blue eyes. 'If they ever got cheeky, they know I'd knock seven bells out of them. I'm always kind until kindness doesn't work any longer. But I've seldom had to use direct action.'

He said there had been brutal whites in the islands and they had done no end of harm. He tried to show the natives that as long as they behaved they would be treated with extreme justice and even gentleness. But that if they wanted trouble, they would get plenty of it.

He told me about a native who had come at him not long ago with a drawn knife. He had turned just in time to see the fellow coming.

'I gave him a good kick in the stomach,' Markham said. 'And while he was reeling from that, I hit him one in the jaw and shut him straight up. He will be a good boy for a long time.'

I was sure Markham actually enjoyed danger. He knew he was superior to all the people around him and was willing to prove it at any minute. And I could see that he was afraid of nothing.

Markham told us that he was born in England, had lumbered in Nova Scotia, had been a cowboy, a P. & O. ship's officer, a resident of South Africa, and a trooper in the Boer War. Disappointed in love, he had gone to sea again and had wound up in the Solomons, where he had fallen in love with a native girl and settled down to plantation life for keeps.

'When Lily was young, she was beautiful,' he said reflectively about his wife, and as though warning us not to be disappointed in her. 'She is deaf now, though she's only twenty,' Markham continued. And then, with a chuckle, 'But that's a great help, for she can't hear my twaddle and my bad language — and she doesn't talk back! The youngsters are as fine and sweet as she is and they are going to have the best of education and comfort that hard work and money can buy.'

He told us his plans for sending the children to Australia and, whether they married or not, for setting them up wherever they wanted to live, with the best of everything. I could detect in his voice a tone of resentment and supposed he had suffered some personal hurt in his past that he was going to even up in his children's happiness.

'But if they are really smart,' he added, 'they will come back here and live in simplicity, for that is the greatest luxury of all, in my opinion.'

I asked him about his wife and whether she liked the settlements or the plantation.

'It's probably conceit to say this,' he said, 'but I think she likes best to be where I am. She doesn't look like much, but she means a lot to me and is very sweet and she loves me and is loyal. And there are a lot of white women that aren't that.'

Here was probably the clue to Markham's running away to the Solomons.

Martin had also run away from home. In his case, it was school and a school-teacher he did not like. I could see that he and Markham would be bosom friends with their independence and rebel blood and their love of the unspoiled and unsettled out-of-doors.

Marco, as he had become affectionately known to all the Solomons, had become virtual King of an island principality some two hundred miles north of the Solomons proper, but within the British administration. He had been given his plantation on the Island of Lord Howe, also known as Ong

Tong Java, and a trading concession embracing several small adjoining coral islands and the vast lagoon which they rimmed. The lagoon extended for more than eighteen miles across and over forty miles long, Markham told us, and was as close to Heaven as he ever hoped to be.

He had no interest in money, he said, except that it gave him an occasional trip to civilization, and meant a future capital for those he loved. When copra was going well, he could make ten to twelve thousand dollars per year, and that was more than he could spend even if he were living in Sydney.

I remembered the skipper's stories of Markham's profligate visits to Australia. His spending sprees and his generosity were probably just fits of boredom. Or the touch of the artist in him that made him want to do everything perfectly and to the limit.

He suddenly pointed out to sea.

'There was a neat little island in here, a few years ago,' he said. 'It seemed to pop right up out of the ocean during an earthquake, and stood there as securely as you please. I charted it. Now it's gone. Probably just couldn't stand all the headhunting and murder around here. You never know what's going to happen in the Solomons. The natives tell me of having seen islands blown to bits and disappear in a mass of stones and ashes. They have a right to be superstitious.'

Markham seemed always to be in motion. He was continuously going forward to talk to his boys, back to the stern to take over the wheel for a stretch, down into the engine room, or up into the rigging to see what he could see over our low horizon. He seemed to be moving even when he was standing still, so intense was his energy and so lively his mind. He had to be doing something, if only smoking a pipe.

Most of all he seemed to like the engine room. This was a tiny compartment in the center of the ship, covered by a hatch, in which the little kicker labored and puffed and threw out foul odors of burned gasoline. I took one look into it and found it so full of old rags, grease cans, and old tools that my curiosity was at once satisfied and I decided to stick to the comparative order and cleanliness of the deck.

Small holds fore and aft usually carried coconuts, but these were now stuffed with burlap-wrapped bundles, most of them pasted up with Australian labels. With a little planning and discipline the boys could have got in twice as much material. But the bundles were dumped with the natives' usual sense of disorder.

The deck was piled high with cargo covered with tarpaulins, except for a clear space for walking around the edge. Markham was taking back everything his people would require for their own use during the coming six months as well as stocks for his little store and goods for his copra-trading. Calico in every conceivable color and design, large quantities of tobacco, pipes, fishhooks and line, mouth-organs, earrings and other cheap jewelry, knives, beads, biscuits, singlets, belts, whistles, masks, Coney-Island toy gadgets, wrist watches, clocks, and other trinkets.

'They want everything a child wants,' he said. 'And very little makes them happy for a long time.'

There was no cabin, so we had to sleep anywhere we could find room to stretch. The boys crawled into the forward hold, where they somehow wriggled into the openings between cargo. Martin and I slept on deck. Martin found a depression on top of the cargo. I tried this, but the ship tossed about so and the place was so full of sharp edges of crates that I decided to sleep on the hatch. There they tied me each night, so that I shouldn't be washed overboard. Marco slept on a bunk below deck beside his precious engine. I wondered how he could stand the stench of gas and oil, but I suppose it was like attar of roses to him after all these years at sea.

Throughout the day we kept the little engine going, even when there was smooth water, for we wanted to make all possible speed. And there was no telling when a squall might come up, for these little storms struck from nowhere and any-

Convicted cannibal. A Solomon Islander tried and convicted by the British at Tulagi. He had killed and eaten two enemy tribesmen.

Markham and the crew of the 'Lily.'   The crewboys, stupid, lazy and indifferent, would have exhausted anybody's patience.

La La, one of Markham's daughters. His native wife, Lily, wore beautiful lava-lavas; his children nothing but beads.

Tattooing a boy on Ong Tong Java. Boys are first tattooed when they are between nine and twelve years old. A two-inch strip of tiny dots is then run down their backs and arms.

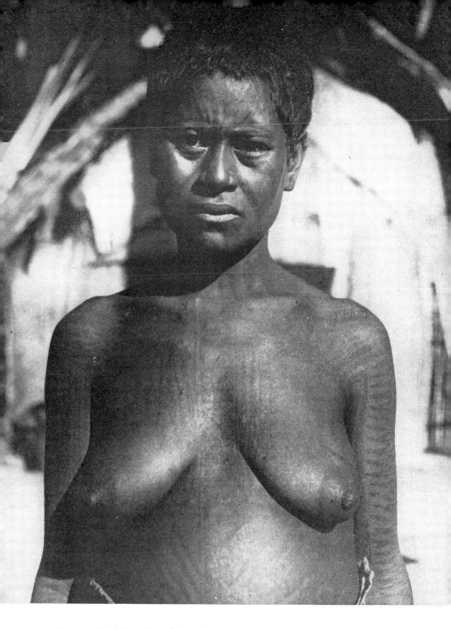

A tattooed girl at Ong Tong Java. Girls are first tattooed when they are seven, but the artwork is not completed until just before marriage.

The pleasantest cemetery in the world. The headstones at Ong Tong Java are coral, sometimes carved in fish patterns or dyed black, indigo or red. The white sand is always clean swept.

where. There was seldom a dull moment for the skipper, either in minding his sails or the wheel, or in attending to the speed and whims of the engine, or in managing the boys, who apparently waited for him to do the thinking at all times.

'When that squall hits us, we're going to roll,' Marco would shout. 'You're going to feel as if the ship were turning over. And your stomach probably will.'

Martin was usually sure to be ill even without this suggestion. And he would sometimes lie for hours, looking ghostly pale and very miserable. I had the good luck never to be seasick, though it made me ill to see Martin suffer in that way and I did my best to make him comfortable.

'It's no use,' he would argue. 'I wasn't made to be a sailor. The sea is no place for taking pictures, anyway.'

Cooking amidst all this crowding cargo and on such a bouncing little shell was quite a chore. The 'galley' was a little sheet-iron, home-made brazier for wood coals, covered over with a flat sheet of iron to hold the pots and pans. It was set in the stern and was protected by a shield of tin with two side 'wings' in the shape of a dressing-table mirror, and braced against the breeze.

If the sea were rough, the pots and pans bounced and slid about, and I once came within an inch of being scalded. I then simply gave up trying to cook and opened a tin of bully-beef which we ate with hardtack or biscuits. The storm often lasted for days and warm food, even tea, became a luxury. I was glad when things calmed down and I could make something decent. I knew the men both needed good meals.

Properly prepared, even bully-beef became palatable. It was very good when stewed or made into hash or sliced with potato salad. One day we caught a turtle and had delicious steaks. Next day I made a turtle soup which seemed even better.

We never tired of the many kinds of fish. These I boiled, steamed, creamed, stewed, and fried. And I made chowders with the few potatoes and onions Markham provided. From our own boxes we had pineapples, bananas, dried fruits, chocolate, and coffee.

With the aid of my baking powder I made muffins and biscuits. My first batch of dropped spoon-biscuits were coming along nicely when a squall hit us and the rain drenched them, but they were better than hardtack.

The galley smoke was as bad as the squalls. Markham protested and said I'd better give it all up as a bad job.

'You can be skipper, but I am cook,' I told him. 'And I have just as bad a temper as you have.'

Whether or not he took this seriously, he let me have my way thereafter. He seemed to know nothing about cookery and not to care.

Every day at noon, Marco 'took the sun' and made elaborate calculations. I was never sure whether he did this seriously or for show. He seemed to know everything there was to know about the practical side of sailing and probably knew just where he was in these waters, with or without calculations. He managed the ship so expertly, and with so little effort, that we both felt completely at ease with him and would have sailed with him anywhere.

'All of a sudden, Ong Tong Java will pop right out of the sea and we will be home,' he said. 'The land is so low in the water, the highest point only sixteen feet above high tide, that the boy in the mast up there will see it before we do.'

Then we would be among the reefs, he explained.

'I wouldn't care to come in at midnight,' he continued. 'That's how the place was discovered — two ships coming from opposite directions wrecked on the reefs on the same night. A fellow named Tasman sighted the island, away back in 1643, and named it after an island he knew in Java. That seemed to be enough of it for him. There isn't much to invite anyone to stop.'

'How do you keep from washing off in a hurricane?' I asked.

'God is just good to us and that seems the way it should be

in a place so close to Heaven,' he replied. 'Nobody on the island has ever lost his life through storm, except from capsizing out in a boat, and the natives have been here a long time. One reason for that is the natural protection of the reefs. You'll see for yourself. The place is actually a string of bead-like islands built up by coral from the rim of an enormous submerged volcano. Inside the rim is a great lagoon of smooth water, so peaceful that you will forget all about hurricanes. But getting in there is one of the trickiest jobs there is — a single narrow entrance and plenty of rock.'

He had scarcely stopped speaking when there was a shout and a great commotion aboard.

'Land ho!' shouted the boy in the mast.

I picked up the glasses, but could see only billowing sea. Markham had leaped to the wheel and was intently watching ahead as though he could see beneath the surface. He was actually finding his channel by the color of the water and the nature of the waves.

For what seemed hours we crept along with little sail and a throttled engine while the boys took soundings and Markham shouted orders and cursed at his best. The surf became heavy and the ship plunged and rocked. Then, through the glasses, we saw the palms of his island and the white beach of powdered coral.

'The tin roof will be my house,' he said eagerly. 'And the first woman on the beach will be my Lily!'

We skimmed through the last reefs and on into a calm lagoon, now reflecting the sunset sky and making a great lake of opal and gold.

All the population seemed to be on the beach to welcome us. Before we could anchor, a score of canoes were paddling madly toward us and we were soon surrounded by shouting children and young men.

'It's just like getting out the band, back in Kansas,' said Martin. 'And Marco looks just as pleased.'

Two husky men leaped aboard, carrying palm leaves.

They walked solemnly from the bow of the ship to the stern, passing the broad leaves over every object on board, including us and the crew, and then tying the leaves to the stern. Now I knew the meaning of that bunch of dead palms, which Markham had carried at the stern throughout the journey. Either he was yielding to the native superstition or had become a believer. I asked him which it was.

'Both,' he said. 'I wouldn't want to worry any of them, least of all Lily. They tie a bunch of palms to the stern of my boat every time I go anywhere, just to be sure I am clear of the evil spirits and will be taken care of. It's something like people at home wearing charms, isn't it? But with these people, superstitions are their whole life. And you can't live with them long without respecting them; you will see for yourself.'

I was wearing some striped pajamas that I had found to be cool and comfortable, and a soft slouch hat. Martin and Marco were still wearing lava-lavas that they seemed to like. And in these we went ashore. We seemed almost overdressed among the natives. A few of the women wore lava-lavas. The others, men, women, and children, were entirely nude or wore only brief loincloths.

As we landed, a lovely girl dressed in a lava-lava pushed through the crowd and shouted to us. It was Lily.

Marco hopped out into the water and waded ashore.

They embraced, but did not kiss. Marco stood for several minutes looking down at her and talking to her softly. And she eyed him with that radiance which only one who loves deeply can ever display, or understand.

12 ~~~~~~~~

... nicest people in the Solomons

*T*HE MEN OF LEUENEUA were handsome beyond any we had seen in the Solomons. Tall, athletic, and clean, they hardly seemed to belong to the benighted people of Malaita and the other islands, but they definitely belonged to the beauty of this place.

They walked with a poise and dignity and grace that suggested hauteur, but they were obviously simple and unaffected and friendly. They smiled easily, especially if they had our attention, and with the disarming manner of children.

Their skin was bronzed and, when rubbed with coconut oil, had the texture and gloss of satin. They also rubbed themselves with a yellow oil from a certain leaf. This left a green color in abrasions, tattoo marks, and crevices of the skin, like a sort of patina, and heightened the bronzed effect.

Their features were sharp and bold and well defined, and decidedly Polynesian. Well-developed heads, high foreheads, and strong chins showed intelligence, and their mouths had firmness and character. The eyes were large and soft brown, and the lashes long enough to make most women envious. The lips were thin and shapely and the noses well modeled, and not flat.

Their long hair was naturally curly, rather than kinky as

in the other islands, and was tied up on their heads or into a knot or combed long down the back.

Their hands were long and slender and their gestures deliberate and graceful. They did everything with such notable ease and grace that they had an altogether aristocratic air.

'Probably came from Hawaii,' Marco answered to my question about them. 'One theory is that they drifted down from the Gilberts and Ellice Islands. But, of course, nobody knows. Some of their idols are of hardwood that isn't found here or anywhere around, and this supports the Hawaii theory. They are certainly Polynesians and as fine as they come.'

The young women had all the beauty of the men, but had spoiled it by close-cropping their hair, which gave their faces a pudgy look. They went completely nude, except that they wore tattooing all over their bodies. The delicate patterns, done in indigo dye, made them look as though they were wearing black lace tights.

When the women wore decorations, they wore them around the waist. But above and below the waist they were always completely nude. Some of the old women with no figures wore wampum belts, and some wore a kind of apron made of strings of mother-of-pearl or other shell. Their noses and ears were pierced and sometimes carried a shell ornament, but they seemed to feel that their tattooing was enough to wear. After all, they had to spend most of their waking time in a garden, so adornments were of little use.

The mothers petted and fussed over their small sons and treated them like dolls. Little girls were almost ignored, except that they had their heads shaved and were prepared from the cradle for the drudgery of life. The boys were adorned with bracelets, anklets, and necklaces, had their hair done up in all kinds of patterns, had their bodies rubbed with coconut oil and their noses pierced to carry ornaments at a later age.

Choicest decorations of the men were tortoise-shell nose

ornaments, worn by the chief and all the devil-devil men. These were intricate figures, carved in fantastic human shapes and other forms, probably ritualistic, and so large that they often covered the mouth. When a man with a nose-ring ate or drank, he had to hold up the ornament with one hand. This seemed to me a great price to pay for charm, although I suppose it was no worse than a man wearing a walrus mustache. I wondered what a man with a nose-ring did when he sneezed or blew his nose.

Since the women did all the work, this ease of living made the men very lazy, but they had such nice dispositions and were so friendly and gay that one couldn't quarrel with them. They never seemed to quarrel among themselves, although I knew they must. They would gather on the beach or in a clearing and sing and dance on the slightest provocation. Dancing seemed, in fact, to be their only ambition.

At night, groups of men and women would go to the beaches and dance together for hours under the swishing palms and the bright moon and stars, or sit in clusters chanting and singing, without ever seeming to tire. The men would duck each other, or the women, in the surf, and splash about hilariously like youngsters.

They seemed to have nothing whatever to worry about and to have found the simplest and most satisfying kind of happiness.

Their songs and dances were endless in variety. I counted over twenty, but every now and then I heard a new one and stole up to watch and listen. They often improvised. A man or woman would leap into the center of a cluster and do a solo performance while the others sat and watched with great interest, clapping with their hands or chanting. Every now and then a girl or boy would hop in beside the dancer, do a few steps or wriggles and retire. Even the old people joined in, sometimes very coquettishly, though they were able only to shuffle about and imagine the fancy steps they would like to do if they were agile enough.

The men excelled at dancing and were always showing off to the women. A handsome young Adonis would do all sorts of acrobatics before the girls, giving special attention to one, and the girls would applaud wildly and beg for more. Every night on Leueneua we fell asleep to the soft lullaby of natives singing.

While Marco overhauled his ship for our forthcoming journey, Lily acted as our guide and interpreter. At all other times she was waiting on her Master, whom she adored, or caring for their two tiny daughters. Lily wore only a lava-lava, but she always seemed to have a different one. Marco had brought her a large assortment of them in the most vivid and gay patterns. The children toddled about in nothing at all, like two beautiful little brown dolls, and I played with them by the hour.

Although the island enjoyed a perfect peace, it was actually divided into two parts and held under rigid taboos. At our end of the island was one clan or village and at the other end another. These two groups lived apart and were forbidden to mingle except on matters of state or trade. Wisely, they were permitted and even encouraged to intermarry, but all such matters were arranged by the chiefs and the devil-devil men, and if girls and boys of the two villages were found together otherwise, they were severely punished.

The island was only three quarters of a mile wide at its widest point and about four and a half miles long, but it did not seem to be overcrowded, although there were over twenty-five hundred persons in the two settlements. The population was shrinking rapidly according to Markham and had been reduced from five thousand in only a few years.

Intramarriage, together with pneumonia and other diseases, was weakening the stock, and what had once been a strong and thriving colony was likely to be reduced to a mere handful if the death-rate continued. Marco talked sadly of this and seemed very bewildered, not knowing what to do about it. The natives either paid no attention to the problem or looked upon whatever happened as the will of the Gods.

No mission station had ever been able to establish itself here. 'A missionary once landed,' said Markham, 'but he was given no comfort. He made the mistake of abusing the chief. Then he went berserk and tried to chop up the two big idols with a hatchet. I saved his life, but they literally kicked him off the island. Nobody seems to know what became of him. If he had only been a doctor and had had some sense, he could have accomplished wonders.'

Marco's sentiments about missionaries were mixed, but he seemed to feel more impatience than affection for them. He argued with Martin and me, for we greatly admired the missionary courage and self-sacrifice and believed in the good of their ardent work. He seemed to feel that their evangelizing was a futility and a failure, but that their medical and social services were really accomplishing something — the settler's traditional outlook.

'As to the natives' morals, the missionaries will be the ruination of them,' he said heatedly. 'Nobody has any business dressing up natives when they get along so well in the nude. They only develop diseases through wearing restrictive and unwashed clothing, in which they look terrible anyway.'

Lily was no typical native in this respect. She loved soap, and not only scrubbed her lava-lavas, but took long and lathery baths in the improvised shower which Marco had rigged up behind the house.

'Whenever I miss her,' he said, 'I am sure to find her in the shower, soaping herself all over. I bring her cases of soap — all the scents I can find — and I'm never sure whether it is the scent or the bath she likes most. I'm mighty glad to find anything to make her happy; there isn't much in our civilization she cares for.'

We were walking through the forest one morning when we heard muffled screams, as though someone were being tortured or perhaps murdered. Hurrying in that direction we found two old women bending over a child who lay on the ground. We stole up and found that a little girl was being tattooed. The old women looked at us, grinned, and went on with their work, as though very proud of themselves. Since they did not seem to mind, Martin quickly set up his cameras and began making pictures.

The little girl was probably ten or eleven years old. She lay on her back, with her arms over her eyes, and gripped her shoulders to bear the pain. Across her forehead were the older tattoo marks she had received as a child of seven. But now she was being covered from the knees to the waist with the lacework which would be the first part of her 'dress.' This would be completed at the time of her marriage.

The tattooing instrument was a short piece of wood into which were set several needle-sharp fish bones. The points were placed against the skin and the wood block was given a quick tap-tap with a small mallet. Little red dots at once appeared on the flesh, some of them bleeding heavily. Then indigo dye was rubbed into the punctured skin, while the poor child screamed and wailed. Up over the tender portions of her abdomen they etched the pattern, and I knew what agony this must mean. The whole idea made me ill. Just then, either to cleanse or to revive the child, the old women lifted her and carried her to the beach, where they dipped her limp body and washed the wounds in the salt water.

This work sometimes required a week to complete, Markham told us. And often the child died from poisoning. I wondered how any of them lived through it.

'But when she has her tattooing done, that girl will be as proud as a peacock,' he said. 'Of course, the real art-work is done when she is married — usually when she is pregnant. Then the patterns are extended up over her breasts and back and arms and face, so that she is covered from head to foot. The girls don't look like much when it is all over. They look about ten years older and pretty mutilated. But they seem to think it's great, and the men rave over them.'

Boys received their first tattooing at about sixteen. Then,

a two-inch strip of tiny tattoo dots was run down the back from their shoulders to the buttocks and a similar ribbon down each arm from the shoulder. Certain boys gave themselves special decorations on their chests or backs or arms.

At eighteen, or thereabouts, they had their noses pierced by tortoise-shell rings, cut and clipped on each nostril so as to press through the flesh in time. The holes thus made were filled with pieces of wood which they wore for months. Ultimately they would be permitted to wear nose ornaments of tortoise-shell for special occasions.

The natives were so curious that they were always crowding around to watch us, as though we were strange animals. The children never gave us any privacy. If we were taking pictures, they were always in the way. If Martin lit a cigar, they stood and gaped and watched every puff he took, just as though something exciting were about to happen. They watched us eat and dress and, unless Martin stood guard, I couldn't even bathe without some peeping Toms spying on me.

'They think you are from some other island far away,' said Markham, 'and are probably a freak. After all, this island and the lagoon are the entire world to them. A map wouldn't mean a thing and, even if you explained it to them, they couldn't or wouldn't believe you. You're just as fascinating to them as lions and gorillas in a zoo are to us. Since everything they do is right, by their standards, everything you do is a little crazy, and they are getting a lot of amusement out of you. They haven't met even the usual traders out here and haven't been abused, so they aren't afraid.'

They were having a circus over our visit, he thought.

'And when you go away,' he said, 'they will tell a lot of wild stories about what this or that one saw you do and you will become a legend with all kinds of variations. They will probably even cook up some dances, imitating the way you walk and talk, and will tell the children they have to be good or they will grow up to be queer like the white idiots that visited them years ago.'

Walking up the beach one morning, Markham stopped and led us up the slope into a coconut grove.

'The nicest cemetery you have ever seen,' he said.

The grove was filled with gleaming headstones of pink and white coral. Some had been dyed a solid color, black or indigo or red. Many were carved, principally in fish patterns. Some of the carvings were so realistic that a bonita or small shark seemed actually to be hanging there. Others of the stones were covered with matting to protect the coral from weathering.

The pure white sand looked as though it had just been clean swept, for there were no leaves or twigs to be seen and not even a footprint. The graves were fashioned in little mounds, much like our own, and many were marked with a border of coral stones. Markham was right. This was the most orderly and immaculate burying place we had ever seen.

I was just about to say that people who could take such care of their dead and be so kind to their old people and their children must be very superior, when we saw at the far end of the cemetery a woman, seated on a grave, wearing a large grass hat and a kind of shawl of black trade-cotton. She was swaying back and forth, and as we came up to her we could hear her low moaning.

'Mourning for her husband,' said Markham. 'She will have to stay there as long as the chief decrees, maybe weeks, maybe months. Sometimes they do a stretch on the grave each day; sometimes she has to live right there for the entire period of mourning, her food and water being brought to her. Depends on how whimsical the chief happens to be just then. It's a cruel custom, but they have had it for centuries, and it's no crazier than some of our own.'

He told us about the simple funeral ceremony. The body was buried as soon as possible. Immediately the devil-devil men pronounced a person dead, the whole family went into mourning, the women wailing continuously. The body was wrapped in a fine mat and carried in a procession, with the devil-devil men leading, to the grave. All the dead person's jewelry and trinkets were buried with him, especially his tortoise-shell nose-ring and his weapons if he were a man.

'For some reason, they are careless about the length of the grave,' Markham added. 'If it doesn't happen to be long enough, they don't bother to enlarge it, they just lay the torso in it and push the legs in afterward, in any position. The men get off easily on the mourning. But I suppose the chief settles some old scores that way, for I've seen men sentenced to mourn on a grave the same as the women, though rarely.'

Since the shark was the God of these people, all this care of the body seemed contradictory. The people of Savo were consistent when they threw a body to their shark Gods to be eaten, but here they evidently had some lingering personal sentiment, or other reservations.

'The only trouble with these natives is their superstitions,' Markham went on. 'They are a fearless people in everything, but, like all the other islanders, they are scared to death of devil-devils. I have seen them go right in and swim among the sharks and seldom get clipped, but if I lit a match in the forest on a dark night and they didn't know who I was or what I was doing, they would all run like hares. They would be sure that little flare of light was an evil spirit. Just an unfamiliar sound will sometimes panic them. Like all the rest of us, I suppose they fear only what they don't know, but they make themselves rather miserable. And of course the devil-devil men keep such things going, for they believe in the hocus-pocus. If there weren't superstitions, they would be out of a job.'

The devil-devil men made good picture subjects, for they had alert features, even if they were somewhat wild. They were stalwart fellows, and looked very well fed. All wore tortoise-shell nose ornaments dangling over their mouths. And they seemed the most self-confident and arrogant men on the island.

'Back home they would be politicians and tax collectors,' said Martin.

At dawn one morning, we were on our way to the lagoon for a dip when we saw a procession coming toward the beach. There were at least twenty men, walking rapidly and carrying on their shoulders large objects that looked like logs. They were devil-devil men and they carried great idols, carved with human figures and fish, much like totem poles. We stepped behind a tree and watched.

At the water's edge, they stopped and placed the idols upright, facing toward the water. Then they dipped the images with great ceremony and low chanting, toward the sea, several times. One of them made a sort of speech toward the water. Then they shouldered the idols again and marched away.

This ceremony, we learned, was performed each morning just before sunrise and again at sunset. The idea seemed to be to assure the shark God that the proper obeisances were being made in his honor and also to recognize the souls of the departed in their shark incarnation. This also worked a kind of blessing on the fishing for the day, according to Markham. The shark spirits were guardians of the fishing and their help was absolutely necessary to a good catch.

Martin was very eager to photograph the ceremony and got me up repeatedly at the crack of day to help with the cameras and the film. Despite the bad light, he finally managed to make some excellent motion pictures. He was delighted.

'The best action we've got, up to now,' he said.

The Parade of the Virgins would be especially worth waiting for, Markham had told us. This was a field-day for the devil-devil men, for they would choose from among the girls brides for the young men just coming of age. It was a show of their authority over the lives of the people.

For days in advance, both villages prepared for the event. The ceremonial ground, a large clearing in the heart of the island, was cleaned and swept daily. Devil-devil men bustled about from family to family, pompous and important, making preparations for the presentation of the daughters. The women put each girl through a series of rituals, rubbing her body with yellow ochre and with coconut oil. The chief and the old men instructed the boys on their new duties as full-grown men and 'citizens,' and on their behavior toward their wives after marriage. Dancing and singing went on day and night, but in a very serious and solemn tone.

On the morning of the ceremony, Martin and I were on the ground with our cameras ready, immediately after sunrise.

Already, the preliminaries were under way. Devil-devil men were seated in a long row at hollowed bamboo logs and were beating on these with bamboo sticks, making the sound of drums and zylophones. A group of a dozen men sat in a circle near-by, blowing on conch shells from time to time, and making a most agreeable soft and mellow interlude.

Every now and then young men, their bodies thoroughly oiled, would come up and go through a dance. Then older men, wearing nose-rings and bracelets and anklets of shell, took their places and went through intricate steps. The devil-devil men relieved each other from time to time, but the music and dancing never stopped until well past noon.

Gradually, the crowd began to collect, and we became aware of the size of the island's population. Everyone must have been there, all twenty-five hundred of them. They crowded around the clearing and made a long avenue, leading off into the forest in one direction and down to the lagoon in the other.

Devil-devil men now strutted up and down the lines of spectators, fanning themselves theatrically with woven palm leaves.

Finally, there was a great stir and chattering and then a hush. At the far end of the forest lane we saw two devil-devil men leading between them the first of the virgins. She was hardly more than a child, slight and timid. She walked with a very stilted and uncertain step, as though dazed by all this attention and the staring of so many eyes. She was entirely nude, except for a coconut leaf band around her waist, and a few coconut leaves in her hair, evidently more as a protection against evil spirits than as a covering.

The audience remained awesomely silent throughout. There was only the occasional sensuous sound of the conch shells and the swish of palms overhead.

Other girls followed, singly or in pairs, accompanied always by devil-devil men strutting along importantly beside them. The sunlight glistened on the girls' bronzed and oiled bodies and gave them the appearance of animated sculptures. Watching them, one was almost unaware of their nudity, except to appreciate the extreme grace of their lovely figures. And as they turned away toward the lagoon, with the shadows of overhanging palm leaves giving new tones to the sunlit bronze of their skin, I knew that here was a moment of beauty and happiness I should never forget.

Hundreds of pounds of fish had been caught and quantities of yams and taro were on hand, and now the fires were lighted for a grand feast. The work was well organized, for there seemed to be no confusion. The throng divided into small groups, and by five o'clock all were busily eating.

As the dinner wore off, the festivities started all over again. We walked through the groves and along the beach. Everywhere men and women were wildly singing and dancing. The whole island seemed to be lifting its voice in a song of celebration. Surely the young couples were receiving a blessing of music.

'What has become of the girls?' I asked Markham, seeing none of the virgins about.

The devil-devil men were finishing off the ceremony — distributing the girls to the men of their choice, he said. Not the girls' choice, but the devil-devil men's.

'It's all taboo, even to me,' he added, 'so I can't tell you much about it. Lily and I didn't go through all that. I just paid her father ten pounds and took her down to Tulagi and got ourselves properly married.'

The virgins would all have husbands by now, and the devil-

devil men and mothers would soon give them lectures on their wifely behavior.

'Must be quite a temptation to the devil-devil men to take care of the lads they like most in passing around the young girls,' he said. 'Some youngster might come from his own family, you know, or might have brought him nice fish every day, or other presents. Or might have been especially religious. It's just human not to slight a boy like that.'

'It seems pretty hard on the girls. Don't they ever rebel? Suppose they get some beast of a man?' I asked.

'That's where the devil-devil men are really clever. The ritual is that the boy and girl never see each other — for a year. He visits her each night and they live together until dawn, when he gets up and slips away. At least that is the theory. If they happen to meet in the open during the day and recognize each other, they are supposed to cover their faces. Each lives with his and her family through the day for that period. Then, if a baby is born, they are finally married and set up full housekeeping. Otherwise, the boy may cast her aside and ask for another bride, and she is given to another man for another trial marriage of a year. Or the devil-devil men may decide not to give her a chance if they are in a bad mood, and she may live unmarried for the rest of her days.'

He added that she might appeal to the chief, but that he was actually behind the devil-devil men and probably gave the original orders. There would be little difference in her life, in any case, for whether she were married or unmarried, her lot was one of drudgery from morn to night, just as in the other islands. Although the men were far more kind and easygoing here and not nearly as brutal as among the Melanesians, they still maintained a complete male tyranny.

Woman's only choice was to say 'yes,' whatever happened to her.

'There is another funny element in the marriage relation,' Markham continued. 'When the women come to a certain age and grow ill, they are all retired to a segment of the island,

where they have to live through that period in special huts.
Their food and water are brought to them, but they are
otherwise completely quarantined.'

Whatever these natives did, they did with dispatch and
finality.

'The taboos are so heavy that everybody conforms, without
extreme punishment,' he said. 'I haven't seen anyone killed
or mutilated or badly abused for infractions of any kind, since
I've lived here. The taboos do all the restraining necessary.'

I could see that Markham regarded his little Paradise as
almost without fault or blemish. What the natives did was
right, and he was further convinced that what they did was
as good as or better than what foreigners did back home —
better, at least, for his island. He did not want them changed.

'Have you noticed,' he said, 'that you haven't seen spears
and weapons since you've been here? You won't. They
don't even wear them when they dance. And they seldom do
a dance that is warlike, except for effect or rhythm. They use
their spears only for fishing. I don't say it's ideal, but it
shows that they are the nicest people in the Solomons.'

13 ᴡᴡᴡᴡᴡ

... no room for sissies

'Y OU'RE GOING TO SEE SOME FUN,' said Markham excitedly one morning. 'Get out the cameras. A big fish-drive is coming off. This happens only once in a great while. It's a big show. Everybody joins in, and you'll see some fancy spearing that will open your eyes.'

He had told us about these occasional round-ups. Life here was so easy that the men became overlazy and even neglected to fish. So, either through desperation for food or at the command of the chief, a fish-drive developed. This was as much a lark as a labor and everyone welcomed it as a holiday from boredom.

When all was ready, Markham took us out in the *Lily* to give us a close-up of the performance. The men had formed a large semicircle of canoes, well offshore. This was gradually enlarging as new canoes joined them, and spread out against the vast lagoon. Little boys were out in their small skiffs nearer shore. The women ranged along the beach, holding palm leaves in their hands.

'They are after bonita first of all,' he said. 'Bonita is the God of the fish world. There is no competition, of course, with their shark God, which occupies a kind of personal relationship, through their ancestors. They have all kinds of

bonita images around, in their headhouses, on the grave-
stones, and on their canoes. It is a beautiful fish to see, silvery-
green and blue, and is good eating, so I admire their taste.'

But they would sweep up all kinds of other sea food, he
told us. Swordfish, mullet, kingfish, red snapper, rockfish,
dolphin, marlin, sawfish, catfish, mackerel, sea-bass, blowfish,
and even ray and shark. Sometimes they would get as much
as two or three tons in a single drive.

We stood by as the drive began. Again, the devil-devil men
were giving all the orders and pompously directing the
proceedings.

Over the bow of each canoe was lowered a line, carrying a
sinker. Attached to the upper end was a rattle or series of
rattles made of clacking shells, and a bunch of palm leaves
for good luck.

At a signal, the fishermen began to shake the lines to create
an underwater clatter and scare the fish shoreward. The
paddlers slowly propelled the canoes toward the island, in a
tightening and diminishing semicircle.

The little boys joined in with their skiffs at the ends of the
line. Those who did not have skiffs paddled out on logs and
slabs of wood, their arms also trailing rattles under the water.

We hurried ashore and found the women wading into the
lagoon, swishing their palm leaves under the surface.

The circle now closed. When the canoes reached shallow
water, spearsmen leaped overboard, lunging right and left
at their prey with deft, sharp strokes, and bringing up fish on
their blades at almost every thrust. There was order in all
this wild scramble and no one seemed to get in anyone else's
way or be hurt. It was one of our most thrilling experiences,
and we captured the best of it on film.

But the performance was not finished. The women and
children dragged the fish ashore and tossed them into piles
along the sand.

When the work was finally done, the devil-devil men came
ashore and surveyed the haul. First they selected a choice

group of bonita and other fish for the chief. There were several hundred pounds, but this would not be too much for the feast which he must now give. The assistant chief also received a generous share. Then the devil-devil men gave themselves a satisfactory portion. Next, the women were assembled and each family was given what approximated an equal share in poundage and quality.

'Pretty just, don't you think?' said Markham, eyeing all this with interest and pride. 'A nice kind of co-operation. This place is so perfect, it is just a freak. And when I get away from here, I begin to wonder if I'm not daffy and if it really exists at all.'

A few days later we made a fishing expedition of our own. Markham had been wanting to show us how he dynamited fish, for speed and convenience. It was a hazardous business, but was a fine lazy man's device for getting food cheaply. It was much practiced by the traders and settlers, though frowned upon by the Government because of the risks.

'One old blighter blew himself to bits over at Bougainville,' said Markham, with a shake of his head. 'He was an absent-minded bloke and was smoking a cigar. He lit the dynamite fuse with his cigar and threw the cigar into the water, letting the dynamite go right off in his hand. When they brought the boys in to the Governor for questioning, the head boy said, "Him gone fellah too much. Me no seeum again." '

Markham seemed to remember this lesson well. I saw that he handed the dynamite to one of his boys to toss, instead of throwing it himself.

The boy had just sighted a school of fish and pointed to them — a dark patch of water with glints of silver on the surface, where the fins were breaking. He examined the fuse, touched a match, paused for a breathless moment, and then gave the dynamite a heave. As it struck the water, there was a great mushroom of spray and fish.

We rushed to the spot and saw hundreds of fish of all kinds, stunned and floating on the surface. Our boys leaped overboard to gather in the catch, tossing the fish into canoes which we had towed. Before they could finish, many of the fish regained consciousness, flapped about and swam off, but Markham had at least a thousand pounds of food for his dynamite stick. The catch was principally mullet, but there were also bonita and several fine tuna of twelve to fifteen pounds.

Returning home, Markham selected some of the very best fish and sent them off to the chief with his compliments. Then he took a generous supply of tuna and bonita for himself. The rest he left on the beach to be divided among the villagers. Dozens of men and women had already come down to receive the present of food which they knew he would have for them and thus avoid having to work for a living for several days.

I had asked Markham so many questions about pearls and shells that he took me on a full day's trip around the lagoon to see what we could find.

'We'll do a little shell-exploring on our own,' he said. 'You can give up your husband for one day, can't you?'

He stopped to pay his respects to the chief of Palau, another of his islands. Few of the islands of the lagoon were inhabited and those sparsely, but Palau had a sizeable settlement and enough coconuts and shells to make its trade important.

After a brief visit with the chief, Markham gave him a case of tobacco, cotton cloth, and biscuits. The chief wore a pair of the orange cowrie shells that I wanted so much. I begged for them. Markham offered more goods. But the canny old chief knew the value of what he had and only shook his head and grinned.

We set off for the atolls where Markham said the best shells were to be had. The tide was out and we were soon among great beds of the celebrated trochas shells. These were cone-shaped, tapering down to a base, three to five inches across, the outside rough and marked with red and green splashes. Inside was a heavy layer of brilliant mother-of-pearl, the source of our pearl buttons at home. We selected some of the best and the boys took out the snails, a great favorite among them, but which I found to be too tough for any use.

Moving on to other atolls, we found salmon-pink conchs, green snail, and other beautiful shells, until I had a collection of several bushels. The oyster-shaped 'gold-lip,' nearly a foot across, with a center of silver and a rim of gold, was the prize of the lot. From these the natives throughout the Solomons made the crescents I had seen them wear at their throats and across their breasts. Most astonishing were the 'giant' clams, one to three feet across. These were treacherous, for they often snapped shut on a native digger and took off toes or fingers.

When the tide came in, we struggled back over the rugged coral to the *Lily* and made for home with my treasure. I knew I couldn't possibly take the shells with me, but I would at least have the pleasure of looking at them, over and over again, while we remained at Leueneua.

Markham now decided to give his ship a final overhauling so that we could be on our way. He was his own best mechanic and for several days he gave the engine his complete attention. Then, taking advantage of the shallows in the lagoon and of the low tide, he let the vessel lie first on one side and then the other, caulking her seams and holes and cleaning off the barnacles.

'She needs a painting,' said Markham, screwing his face into a scowl. 'She gets the best of care. When I collect the swag from you two, I'll take her into Tulagi and give her a real polish.'

His ketch, his wife Lily, and his two daughters were, without doubt, his only prized possessions and he lavished upon them every tender affection.

While Marco toiled over the ship, Martin worked at his films and I had a chance to fish as much as I wanted. With two little boys for guides I went off daily in a canoe, though Markham made me promise never to get out of his sight, lest we capsize and be eaten by sharks.

There in the calm emerald lagoon, I spent as much of my
time watching the fish as catching them, for they were a con-
tinual riot of color. Peering into the depths, I had the feeling
that I was floating in fantastic patterns of light which swirled
up about me in a dizzying stream. The water was literally
full of rainbows.

In the shallows were forests and gardens of brilliant coral.
Delicate shapes of trees, fans, stems, and tendrils moved
sinuously, as the fish swam in and out, flashing their own deep
and pastel shades into the color compositions: grays, mauves,
pinks, whites, creams, and reds.

When evening came and the sun turned the piled-up
clouds to crimson, amethyst, and gold, I knew that there was
no more beautiful place on earth. Then, the emerald of the
lagoon slowly changed to opal and caught the colors and
cloud masses of the sky one by one. I had gooseflesh from
excitement and happiness.

Here, I dreamed we would some day have a home. Or at
least a ship like Markham's so that we could enjoy all this
and live like gods. Perhaps it was just as well, after all, that
we had not settled down in Independence, Kansas.

In a few days I caught more than thirty kinds of fish. The
lagoon was like a grab-bag. I never knew what I should pull
up next.

My little boys were as full of curiosity and excitement as
I, and perhaps more, for they knew they would carry home
that night a fine load of food to their admiring parents. And
a present of some kind besides. They boldly asked me for my
hat, my scarfs, and even my blouses, but I compromised on
tinned lollypops and hard candies, and in the end I gave
them each a colored handkerchief. Money would have been
useless to them, except to wear as a necklace.

The moment I hooked a fish, their eyes snapped and rolled,
and they flashed me a smile showing their gleaming white
teeth. When I brought him to the surface, they were both
overboard in a big splash to help me land him. Sometimes a

shark would rush in and almost take the fish out of their hands, but they showed no fear. This worried and astonished me. Markham assured me that they not only knew their sharks, but apparently enjoyed a kind of immunity through courage.

'Every now and then a shark gets one of them, and he is either a goner or a life cripple,' he said. 'And often a shark will brush the skin and sandpaper a piece of hide right off. It makes an ugly wound that takes forever to heal and is hard to treat, but they figure it is one chance in a thousand.'

I was equally amazed at the way they could walk on coral with their bare feet. Whenever I went walking or wading along the shore, I wore boots with the thickest soles I had, for the cut of razor-sharp coral is vicious and makes ugly sores, and often results in fatal poisoning. But the native feet, even of these youngsters, seemed to grow a specially callous under-covering that was as good as any shoe leather. When they swam about under water, I noticed that the bottoms of their feet always showed white in the green depths.

The men and boys were expert swimmers. They were al-most literally cradled in the lagoon. When a boy passed five and began to show some curiosity and self-reliance, the father took him fishing one day and deliberately threw him over-board. There was no choice for the child but to sink or swim, so swim he did. Of course, the father stood by, ready to come to his aid if he sank, but with centuries of living in the water behind him, one good ducking was usually enough. Having mastered the shallows of the lagoon, the boy would be taken to deep water and later on to the reefs and to the open sea. There was no room for sissies among these people and where the shark was God.

While I was fishing one day, I saw two young men splash-ing in deep water not far away. They seemed to be struggling with something. Fearing that a shark might be attacking them, I paddled over to them as quickly as I could. But there was no shark. The boys had captured two turtles and were towing them to shore!

One of the young men was swimming with his turtle in tow. He had a noose of coconut rope around the turtle's neck, and the turtle was swimming along on his own power. The turtle had no choice, since he couldn't go down and didn't want to be strangled. The boy would take a stroke with his one free hand and give a scissors kick of his feet, and the turtle would flap his flippers in unison. I paddled along enjoying the comedy.

The other boy was having a battle. His turtle was not so agreeable, for they had lassooed his flipper and he had drawn in his head and was putting up a fight. He was a huge fellow, at least three feet across, but in the water he looked even larger. Yard by yard the boy yanked him forward, and slowly got him to land. Several men came out to help.

I expected to see the turtles killed and cut into steaks and soup meat, but something quite different happened. The boys dragged their prey down the beach and threw them into a large pit dug in the sand, and covered over with bamboo poles. I peered into the enclosure and saw that there were several other turtles confined there. It was a kind of stockyard.

Some of the turtles were the queerest I had ever seen. They had no shells and their backs showed nude and brown.

'The boys have ripped off their shells — it's very good quality tortoise,' said Markham when I asked him what it was all about. 'Seems cruel, but the turtles live, and these boys are making quite a business of it. They are very kind to the poor things — feed them small fish and crabs — and the turtle slowly grows another shell. If the fishing is very good, the boys let the old-timers go. Mighty enterprising!'

Next day he had one of his boys show me a stretch of beach where the turtles habitually came to lay their eggs. Here the natives had another thriving 'industry.' They would encourage the turtles by digging little pits for them and leaving soft sand for covering. As soon as the turtle had deposited her eggs, the natives dug them up. But the patient turtles apparently kept right on laying and continued to return season after season.

Other natives had trapped and imprisoned turtles here, in little enclosures, keeping them and taking care of them with food until their laying was completed. And this seemed also to work like a charm, though it was a great deal of labor. If I were here, I thought, I would raise chickens and feed them on plenty of insects and coconut meat, and have more and better eggs.

Turtle eggs never appealed to me for food. They were round, rubbery and soft-shelled, and were all yolk. Although the yolk tasted much like that of a hen's egg, it was tough when boiled for long. When scrambled, the eggs were quite tasty and were a nice relief from having no eggs at all.

These free days enabled me to explore the island on my own, and with my two little pickaninnies, who now stuck to me like glue, I took long trips until I had covered most of the area.

The men were now gathering the coconut crop. The nuts were permitted to ripen and fall to the ground, and were then stacked in great piles. These were carried in strings on the backs of the men or floated in great rafts to the drying ground. Here, the husks were removed by striking them downward against the sharp upright points of sticks driven into the ground. Then, with an axe, the meats were removed and cut in half. These were laid on racks of bamboo poles and cured for half a day or longer over smouldering and smudgy fires made of coconut husks.

Markham explained that sun-drying would not be practicable in this climate because of the sudden rains, although the smoke-dried article would be worth much less than sun-dried or kiln-dried copra. Some day he meant to have his own kilns, when he was richer and had a proper plantation of his own.

As soon as the copra meats were dried, the natives tied them together in long strings of twenty halves. These were

usually sold in groups of ten strings, which would be one
hundred complete nuts or 'one hundred copra,' and would
sell to Markham for five dollars or for goods in that amount.
One hundred copra thus became the native unit of exchange
and this was true throughout the islands. But here in Leueneua, copra was their only money, and the shell and tooth
money of the southern Solomons seemed to be unknown.

Markham had now refurbished his ship. With his usual
dispatch, he announced that we would leave in a few hours.

Martin was, of course, impatient to be off. He felt he had
already spent too much film on devil-devil men, cemeteries
and virgins, and cloud effects were not in his catalogue just
now. If we were going to get on with our cannibal pictures,
we had no more time to lose.

We asked Markham to help us make all speed and to stand
by us until we found what we were looking for, even if it took
six months.

'I'll take you around all right,' he said, with a chuckle.
'But I'm not promising you the impossible.'

Lily and the youngsters were so saddened by our leaving
that I felt very guilty, although I knew that this restless sailor
of hers would be going somewhere and leaving her here alone,
whether we were the excuse or not.

Our luggage had gone out to the ship and we all stood on
the beach in the afternoon sun ready to step into the dinghy.
Martin and I shook hands with Lily and I gave the two little
girls a hug and kiss.

Markham stood for a moment holding Lily by the hand,
and gazing out toward the sea.

She looked up at him worshipfully. If he had been King
of all the South Seas, she could not have been more proud of
him.

I watched to see what his farewell would be. He turned,
took her chin in his hand and looked quietly into her eyes
for a moment.

'Good girl!' was all he said, giving her a brisk pat on the shoulder.

Markham stood in the stern of the dinghy and waved to her until we touched the ship. Then suddenly all his affection and attention shifted to the *Lily*. In a matter of minutes we were moving across the opalescent lagoon toward the reefs under great banks of billowing cloud.

14 wwwwww

. . . a taste for human brains

*I*F YOU WANT A PICTURE of the best cannibal in the Solomons, there he is,' said Markham.

He pointed to his boy Mauki, who stood at the wheel, solemnly steering the ship and shouting orders to the crew as though he were Master. Mauki was small but strong. His hair was close-cropped and black and kinky. His features, small and on the delicate side, were made stern by deep lines in his weatherbeaten face.

Mauki had been much in evidence since we left Leueneua. He had often piloted the ship. He had taken care of the engine, minded the sails, and helped me with the cooking. He seldom spoke, but he seemed to understand at the slightest word and to be quick and efficient about everything. There was not a lazy bone in his body.

'He has a great record,' Markham said. 'Son of a big chief on Malaita. His father was killed when he was a boy and he was taken into slavery by another tribe. Ultimately, he was sold on a recruiting contract to a plantation, and was then sent by the company to Ong Tong Java, my island, as cook to a German trader.'

The trader was a brute and half crazy, Markham said. He had such terrible outbursts of temper and fury that he became an outcast among the whites and was regarded as a devil-devil by the Islanders.

'The wretch had a mitten made of the hide of a sting ray, which is used by the natives as a wood file and is rough as a rasp,' Markham continued. 'This he used for discipline. He would give anyone he didn't like a swipe with it. One day he took a piece of hide off Mauki's back for some trivial offense. He had killed two wives and was abusing a third.'

Markham spat into the sea, as though he were spitting in the villain's eye.

'When the mad trader finally became ill,' Markham went on, 'Mauki took the rasp and dehided him. He got so worked up that he cut off the fellow's head. Then he fled. But Mauki had only begun. He went back to Malaita, with the rage still on him. There, he finished off the chief who had killed his father, and took the heads of a dozen of the tribesmen, before he cooled off. That takes a man of parts! Of course, the Government got him when the story leaked out. But he proved to the officials just what had happened to him at the hands of the mad German, and they let him off with a suspended sentence. For some time now, I've been his guardian and employer. Get *his* picture and you have the best man that ever came off Malaita.'

I saw Martin look at Mauki appreciatively.

Since leaving Leueneua, we had been coasting briskly along under the gentle persuasion of the trade wind. The balmy days in the clear sun were so relaxing that we lolled about the deck in lava-lavas and did little but dream and listen to Markham's endless and colorful stories about himself and the islands. These I did my best to provoke.

'This place is bound to get you sooner or later,' he drawled. 'If it isn't the fever or the yaws, it is the lassitude. All white men want to go to the tropics where the blood runs warm, but the tropics weren't made for them. Their skulls and skin aren't tough enough, or they abuse themselves with rum and neglect. Stay down here for ten years and you are sure to be a little queer in the head. Something happens to you that you can't explain. And it's like opium, for you can't give it up.'

He lay back in his chair, watching the clouds bank up against the horizon, and puffed reflectively at a giant briar pipe.

'Take Tom Butler, for example,' he continued. 'One of the finest Irishmen I ever met. Big and strong and ruddy when I first met him in Sydney, twenty years ago, and the biggest-hearted creature God ever made. A fine trader. Always kept his word — never struck or abused a native in his life — easygoing good company anywhere — everybody loved him. I still love him, but he's finished. Lives like a pig and is just wasting away. Native girl takes care of him, but he is too gone to work. Just dying on his feet, if he's still able to stand. I must go and see Tom — we will try to stop on the way down, if you can stand it — one of the saddest sights you'll ever see. It gets them all in time. Right as rain!'

Markham told us of other derelicts, men who had come out from home to make their fortunes or to run away from some intolerable hurt or pressure. Some came with fortunes and soon squandered them, to retreat to some tiny island, go native and shun all white company, moping and melancholy and bitter. And others who came with nothing but health and their wits and ambitions made sizeable fortunes, only to succumb to gambling and easy living or merely to indolence and drink.

'It takes character to succeed out here,' he said. 'More than anywhere on earth, I suppose. If a man has it, he can have a fine time and make a good thing for himself. Good character will shine wherever you lay it down. But it takes sterling will-power to resist all the corrosions of the tropics. They sneak up on you from all sides. And if a man is weak and hasn't character, here is where he will show up to be a rotter quicker than any place, with no restraints, all the advantages on his side, and every man a law to himself. In a

few years a lad will be either a beachcomber or a squire.
And I am sorry to say that the majority of them are beachcombers, especially the French and the Germans. I pity their
kids most of all.'

He shook himself and stood up, swaying on his practiced
sea legs, and ran his fingers through his thick red hair.

'Say, I'm getting morbid,' he said defensively. Then his
Irish eyes lit up with one of his come-hither smiles. 'You
know, I'm going to show you people my new home. I've
got it all staked out. I'm going to take over one of these fair
days, and settle down. I've had my eye on this place since I
first saw it years ago — one more good crop and she's mine.'

Markham grew more enthusiastic than I had ever seen him,
telling us about New Georgia, where he had found a perfect
little harbor and an alluvial plain at the mouth of a small
stream, with a background of wooded hills for scenic beauty.
Here he would have the best coconut plantation in the
Solomons, perhaps not so large as the biggest, but enough to
make him a generous income for the rest of his days.

'I'm just as sick of living out of a tin as you are,' he said,
'and here I'm going to have all the fruits and vegetables that
will grow. Almost anything will grow in that soil: avocados,
Hawaiian pineapple, mango, papaya, melons, oranges,
pomegranates, pomelo, kumquats, Brazil cherries, lichis,
bananas, figs. And what vegetables I'll have to make the
Tulagi blighters envious: Golden Bantam corn, squash, lettuce, tomatoes, peppers, beans, peas, carrots, potatoes,
onions ——'

He was almost out of breath in his enthusiasm and I began
to see a new and domestic Markham, whom we had not yet
discovered. The Solomons were evidently not going to get
Markham, or he was at least going to have his little Empire
all in order when the 'corrosions' overtook him, and be ready
to spend his last days as a beachcomber de luxe.

'Every farmer wants to be a sailor and every sailor a
farmer,' said Martin. 'A plantation takes a lot of care and

time and I can't imagine an old sea-hand like you ever settling down. Leueneua is the most beautiful spot I've ever seen, but you admit you don't stay there for more than a few winks.'

I knew that Martin was thinking about Lily and the children. So was I. Was Markham's move some new emancipation he was looking for?

'Who said I would give up trading?' Markham shot back. 'But trading is just for money-making, and not too much at that. What I want is a home, for pleasure and peace and the leisure that money is supposed to buy. I want a proper home for Lily and the girls, where they can live like human beings, and like the best of them. Lily is my wife, not just a convenience, and she's the best wife I've ever seen; it's time she had a place that amounted to something. And she is a fine boss; there was never a better one. With me to plan and Lily to run things, we will make Penduffryn look like a farthing!'

He went on to tell us how many hundred acres he would have in coconuts in a year's time, and how they would be up and bearing in a few years more. He would have a real kiln for drying copra. He would go to Sydney, but spend all his money for machinery this time instead of fun. Mauki would be his overseer. With a staff of the best boys to be found in Malaita, Mauki would show them all what a chief's son was made of.

'But the New Georgia natives are cannibals, aren't they?' I asked.

'They aren't any angels,' Markham replied. 'But from so many years of trading, they know me pretty well by now, and they haven't given me any trouble yet. I have a theory that if the natives have an ounce of sense in them, and these fellows are a lot better than they are on Guadalcanal and Malaita, they will respect a white man who minds his trade and keeps his word. You have to be on the watch for one of those ceremonial outbursts, but Mauki and his Malaita boys will put the fear of God in them.'

He gave Mauki, at the wheel, an approving and confident look. And I hoped that his trust was warranted.

'The trouble with New Georgia,' Markham added with a scowl, 'is the missionaries. They have quite a foothold there and are ruining the natives, in my opinion. Attach a bunch of natives to a mission station for a while and they get too smart. I don't mean intelligent, which everybody would welcome, but just mean. I don't know what happens to them. Just too abrupt a change from their old ways probably or it may be resentment that builds up against the whites' overlordship or they mistake the missionary kindness for weakness. But they are the cheekiest and most treacherous natives we have and I don't like them a little bit.'

Here was the old grouch again. I saw that Martin was about to challenge him and this would mean another of the interminable arguments about missionaries, so I did my best to change the subject.

'Speaking of all those nice fruits and vegetables on your new plantation, how would you like your bully-beef cooked tonight, Marco?' I asked.

In a short time I had a surprise ready for them, in clam chowder with potatoes and onions, and hot biscuits.

We finished our dinner under one of the most serene and brilliant and most golden of Pacific sunsets. I got out my ukelele and we all sang soft Hawaiian songs until the stars came out in thousands and gave an immensity to the universe about us which made even missionary problems seem trivial.

Next morning we were moving through a channel between far islands of considerable size. Markham pointed out Santa Ysabel to the south and said that he would like to stop there briefly to inquire of a chief about copra, which he would pick up in a few months.

Within two hours we were passing through the reefs, which Markham always seemed to know and to negotiate as though they did not exist.

Coming close to shore, I looked through the binoculars.

There was a crowd of natives on the beach. We anchored
and rowed ashore in the dinghy. Drawn up to the beach was
a whaleboat, and standing in the stern was a black boy
excitedly talking to the natives, who were squatted on the
sand about him.

'It's a native missionary,' said Markham. 'One of the converts sent out from the missionary stations to preach the
Gospel to the backward ones. They are pretty good sometimes, but they have a hard time getting hold of the Bible
ideas. We'll go up and listen. Have a look at the getup he's
wearing.'

The boy wore a blue coat, white shorts, white shirt and
stiff collar. He was barefooted. In one hand, he held a
large Bible from which he seemed to be reading.

He paid no apparent attention to us and went straight on
with his sermon, which was a native version of the Garden of
Eden episode, all in *bêche-de-mer*, something as follows:

'One time God, he big fellah belong white mastah, he
makum one fellah man. He callum this one fellah man
Adam. He name belong him.

'God he watchum this one fellah man Adam; he walk about
too much.

'God he speakum, "What name this one fellah Adam,
he wantum?" God he scratchum head belong him. He
speakum, "Ah, me savvy. This one fellah man; wantum one
fellah woman."

'God he makum one fellah man Adam sleepum long fellah
too much. God he takum bone, belong one fellah man Adam;
he makum one fellah woman. He callum one fellah woman
Mary. She name belong him.

'God he speakum, "Adam — Mary, me plantum one fellah
garden belong you two fellah. Me plantum yam, me plantum
taro, me plantum banana. One tree belong one fellah garden
belong you two fellah, me plantum; he name belong him
apple. You two fellah no eatum one fellah apple."

'Adam, Mary he walk along one fellah garden. He eatum
plenty fruit belong one fellah garden.

'Mary she speakum, "Adam, he one fellah fruit, God he speakum no eatum."

'Mary, she talk, talk, talk all same girl talk along boy along Queensland makum trouble along boy.

'Adam he speakum, "Mary, we eatum one fellah."

'They eatum. When finish, my Christ, they fright like hell.

'God he walkum along garden. He lookum two fellah.

'He speakum, "Adam, me plantum one fellah garden belong you two fellah. Me plantum one fellah tree, fruit he name belong apple. Me speakum you two fellah, you no eatum. You eatum one fellah apple?"

'"No, God, me no eatum," Adam speakum.

'God he say, "Mary, you eatum one fellah apple?"

'Mary she look along God big eye belong her. She speakum, "No, God, me no eatum."

'God he speakum, "What name you two fellah, you gamman belong me?"' (meaning lie).

'Adam he speakum, "No, God, me no gamman belong you."

'Mary speakum, "Me no gamman."

'God he cross fellah too much. He scratchum head belong him.

'He speakum, "You two fellah, you ketchum bokkus belong bell; you gettum hell along scrub"' (meaning they must scrub hell for life).

Martin made pictures of the missionary and the natives while Markham disposed of his trade.

I tried to make up to the youngsters, but they ran like hares and seemed unwilling even to take the gifts I offered them.

Then I tried the women and found them almost equally shy. Finally, with temptations of tobacco and beads, I lured a small group of them and began trying to talk in mixed English, *bêche-de-mer*, and pantomime. They stared at me, as though half-amused, and entirely uncomprehending.

Suddenly one of them mumbled, 'Where father belong you he stop?'

'Oh, he no father belong me; he husband belong me,' I replied with a smile.

'How long you stop along this one man belong you?' she asked.

'Oh, about two years,' I said.

'My word! He long fellah too much. Me think close-up you die finish,' she exclaimed.

Two years, in that polygamous place, seemed just too long for anyone to live with one spouse.

But their woman's curiosity was now aroused, and another, to whom I had just handed a bead bracelet, timidly said, 'Where pickaninny belong he stop?'

By this she meant, where were my children.

'I no got,' said I.

Her eyes grew wide with incredulity and pity. 'What's matter,' she asked, 'devil-devil he cross along you?'

Having concluded his business favorably, Markham reappeared and motioned us to the boat. The chief had come with him, a very black and very fat, bushy-haired native, clad in a singlet and G-string. He seemed jovial enough, but was more interested in the case of tobacco which Markham handed him than in us or our cameras.

'He would gladly kill you for two sticks of the stuff,' said Markham as we pushed off, and this I was willing to believe.

Late the following afternoon we reached Markham's idyll, New Georgia, in time to watch the flaming sun sink behind distant purple mountains and turn the lagoon into a pool of amethyst. Whatever the natives here might be like, and none could equal those of Leueneua in friendliness and charm, Markham would evidently lose nothing in beauty. Rough as he was, I knew that it meant more to him than he would admit; the Irish in him would alone be assurance of that.

After breakfast next day, we moved along the coast, as picturesque as any we had seen at Malaita, and presently came to his 'plantation.' The approach and the land itself were perfectly suited to his plans.

He was beside himself with excitement as we landed to do a hurried inspection. He showed us about as though he owned the place and were already established there.

'You want a home in the Solomons, Osa,' said he. 'Here it is! When I have my plantation going, there will be a place for both of you here. Send me the plans and I'll build you just the kind of a house you wish. You can come and stay with Lily and me as long as you can stand the Solomons, or forever.'

Markham proposed that we go back into the hills to visit the chief who would one day be his neighbor, and also see his expected property from above. Three fishermen whom we found on the beach agreed to lead the way and Markham assured us that they could be trusted, he thought. Mauki and two of our boys carried the guns and cameras, and we made our way along a thin trail across the grassy plain and were soon climbing gentle brush-covered slopes.

As we climbed, Markham paused to point out again and again the fine expanse of lowland below and told us how he would have his gardens here and his boathouse there and his house facing the bay with a broad expanse of real lawn and gardens of flowers. He thought he would even surprise the Tulagi people and have a golf course when he had time, for he liked golf and wanted to make up for twenty years of lost time. There was no doubt in our minds that he would outdo Penduffryn when he really began, and with his determination he would surely make all his plans come true.

As we entered the forest, the undergrowth became exceptionally heavy and the going was rough. Often we had to cut our way through with big knives. Overhead the trees shut out the sun and gave the jungle a chill and clammy air, especially among the swamps and bogs. The earth was sometimes so soft, it sucked in our feet, and rotting logs and roots cut our boots. Some of the shrubs and vines had long thorns. On one vine the thorns were hooked and very sharp. These cut our clothing and scratched the skin, and Markham told me to take care of the scratches or they would become little ulcers.

I was glad to have the birds again. They were as plentiful as on Malaita and Guadalcanal. The jungle was full of them. They were not easy to see in the dense bush, but their calls made a din everywhere. Their color and sound and excitement made everything seem normal and cheerful, and in this depressing place I felt much less afraid.

Markham said our chances of being taken and eaten if we went into the deep interior of New Georgia would probably be about ten to one, unless we had some well-armed troops.

'They may be as bad or worse on Malaita,' he said, 'but these fellows can be terrible killers. The new generation is better behaved, but Government has had to come in and destroy whole villages and punish the chief and smash and scatter his skulls and canoes and paraphernalia, and generally put the fear of God into them. The missionaries have got along quite well, though, and parts of the coast are rather tame.'

I wondered whether he thought the natives were this treacherous. If so, he could not seriously intend to live here.

By noon we had come to the settlement. Judging from the numerous pigs, the tribe was prosperous enough. The men who came to meet us wore few ornaments and nothing else. They had long bushy uncombed hair and stolid faces and cut ears that reminded me uncomfortably of the natives of Malaita. Markham evidently had a 'way' with them, but I wondered if he were not relying on this too much and would not do better to buy a lot at Tulagi and call it a day.

While we waited for the chief, Markham pointed out his headhouse, a long structure with a high sloping roof, well built and heavily thatched. Behind was a similar house with a lower roof, which he explained was the men's clubhouse and where he had been entertained on previous visits. He remembered especially a feast of roast pig in his honor, one of the most friendly and impressive of ceremonies.

'All these people are the chief's close relatives,' Markham said. 'They feel they can trust their immediate families and it makes better discipline.'

We strolled down the clearing, gathering a company of big-eyed and curious children, some of whom were terribly broken out with ringworm. I fished into my pocket, took out a red bead necklace and gave it to a little girl who toddled along behind the others. She took the trinket and began to cry, which made all the others laugh and seemed to thaw out the up-to-now cool greeting.

One of the children was gnawing on something that looked like a piece of earth. I asked him to let me see it and he held out his hand. There was a lump of clay. I couldn't believe my eyes.

'It's earth, all right,' said Markham. 'I've seen that before. Perhaps they get some minerals they like or a taste of salt which they crave or are just trying to stave off hunger. And they are so ignorant or degenerate they don't know any better.'

From the edge of the forest we heard a thin wailing chant and I asked about it. Markham led the way in that direction. Three old men were shuffling about a fire, into which they threw leaves and sticks of wood from time to time. They were evidently conducting some kind of ceremony.

'Making rain,' said Markham. 'Must have a drought, for they usually get plenty of showers around here.'

'Does it work?' asked Martin, who was preparing to get a picture.

'They all believe it. But I've seen rain hold off for a month after all the hocus-pocus,' Markham replied.

I asked Martin to inquire of the men who followed us if the old men would make rain.

'Yes, they *have* made the rain, but it has not yet fallen,' the leader said with a solemn face.

Markham was careful not to smile at this remark and watched the dance very earnestly. But I could see that he was bursting with something to say.

'If I had to be a Solomons native, I'd want to be one of those fellows,' he finally said, as we moved away. 'The best of everything to eat and nothing to do but play around and dance. The chief has the head medicine man watch his head-house, which is about the greatest responsibility any of them has. And whatever they do is right, for even the chief believes in them. They acquire enormous power and importance, advising the tribe on every blessed thing. If a pig is born, the medicine man whispers into his ear and he grows fat. He whispers into a baby's ear and the boy becomes big and strong. He waves his hand over the garden and it prospers. And if any of the rites fail, like that rain ceremony, the evil spirits make a perfect alibi. Most boys grow up, most marriages succeed, most crops in this fertile place thrive anyway, so the law of averages makes enough success to keep the medicine men going strong.'

There seemed to be no tattooing here. But I saw one man with abrasions over his face and another with a pattern of these over his shoulders.

'The hill people do that in some islands,' said Markham. They burn the skin with hot stones to make the scars, or cut the skin with a knife or piece of flint or shell. Then they dust earth into the wound, to keep it from healing and raise a welt. Sometimes they insert a lump of clay or piece of wood in the wound, to make the scar larger. Must be very painful.'

The welts on the man's face gave him a very fierce expression.

'The women are ugly when done up that way,' Markham added. 'Their husbands encourage them to disfigure themselves, though. Probably to make them less attractive to other men.'

I saw that both the men and women carried little gourds in their waistbands or attached to their armlets. One of the men dipped a stick into the gourd and rubbed it on his teeth. He did this again and again. I went closer and saw that his teeth were black and his lips crimson. Betel nut, I thought.

'No, that is lime,' said Markham. 'They pulverize it and dote on it. They think it makes them beautiful and gives them protection and power all at once. Betel-nut crimsons the lips and teeth, but it rots the teeth, so they become black. They usually chew a combination of betel nut, betel-pepper leaf, and lime. They would scorn white teeth like yours, except to wear around their necks as a decoration, or tell their friends about as a curiosity from a far-off land.'

Some of the men had a lime paste on their hair.

'They leave it on for months,' Markham said. 'When they wash it out, the hair is straw blond! But the lime kills the cooties.'

I asked for a betel nut to taste. I was willing to risk having red lips. It tasted just like alum — unpleasantly puckery. Then I added some lime and tried again. I gagged and immediately spit it out. My mouth was on fire — as though I had taken a spoonful of cayenne pepper. I must have made a horrible face, for everyone laughed, especially the natives.

That would satisfy my curiosity about local customs, Martin remarked. But Markham was sorry I hadn't stuck it out.

'First time I've seen anything stop you,' he said. 'That would have given you the same effect as a shot of grog. Lights you up — makes you feel very important. But if you kept at it you would have nightmares and a very bad head.'

One of the warriors had a striking hat, a small, bright pancake cocked on one side of his head. It was made of tightly woven grass and dyed purple, with a pattern of black and yellow. He wore it rakishly over his forehead and down over one eye. Against his lime-bleached hair, it was very colorful and fetching. But he carried a businesslike spear and his face and eyes were strong and fierce, and he certainly did not look effeminate.

Another had his nose literally inlaid with shell. Around the base of his nostrils he had pierced small holes in which he had inserted shell disks like little buttons, in different sizes and colors. Martin went up to him and counted eighteen of these.

One man had through his nose a human shinbone nearly a foot long, the longest I had seen. From his ears hung a jingling mass of small red shells. In the fleshy tip of his nose was a piece of pearl shell carved in the figure of a bird in flight. I wondered how he balanced the bird there and if it ever fell out, but the ornament looked as though it had been there for a long time.

Presently the chief came out of his house and Mauki handed him Markham's usual generous gift of tobacco and biscuits. The chief was a huge black fellow, heavily decorated with shell necklaces and a large clam-shell breastplate and a tiara of cowrie shells. He wore a piece of banana leaf for a G-string and carried in his hand a spear made of barbed fish bone mounted on a smooth round shaft of wood. He was solemn with self-importance and authority, but seemed friendly enough, and Markham was soon rattling off *bêche-de-mer* at such a rate that we could scarcely follow him.

The chief became chatty and amiable, and asked us to remain for a feast. There was to be a wedding the next day. But Markham begged off, and we took our leave, with most of the village following us.

'I wouldn't mind a good bit of roast pork tonight,' said Markham as we moved on down the trail. 'But they like their pork "high" on New Georgia. Sometimes they bury the pig in the earth for several days and then dig it up and turn it over the fire. Has quite a tang, to say the least. And I've seen them eat pigs almost raw — hit them over the head to keep the blood inside — warm them over the fire, and then distribute to the men, some of whom eat the flesh the way it is.'

'I wouldn't touch their pork, even if I cooked it myself,' I said. 'One look at those filthy houses and the filthier pigs and I've lost all my appetite.'

But by the time we reached the bay, I had an appetite for something fresh, so I took my tackle from the dinghy and with the help of Mauki and the boys, went back to fish the stream for my dinner. Before dark, I had twenty pounds of rock cod. Our dinner was late, but a fine fish chowder and those delicious fresh-water fish were as good, Markham agreed, as a chief's feast anywhere on New Georgia.

Markham continued through the evening to talk of his plantation-to-be and what he would be able to do to make himself completely independent in the next decade, but the thought of thousands of those natives so close at hand had cooled my enthusiasm. I asked him if he thought it wise to spend so much precious capital and energy on this wild place. He merely chuckled and said that he liked to have he-men around. He wouldn't want to live on an island with a bunch of sissies. He wanted excitement and color and the New Georgia natives were a good compromise between vitality and restraint.

'You mustn't take me too seriously about the missionaries,' he said. 'They have done their part here. And they have been awfully nice to me. I think they ought to drop their evangelizing and preach through their hospitals and medicine, but I know that isn't going to happen. Government is as much to blame as they are for not having made things better, faster.'

He lapsed into stories of the heroism of some of the early mission leaders on New Georgia and how they had fearlessly risked their lives and suffered every kind of privation, illness, and discomfort, for no gain whatever except to see their work progress and to make year-by-year inroads upon violence and disease.

They had done surprisingly well on New Georgia, he thought. The natives were vital and good seamen and were hard to contain. Although they had never got very far at Malaita, where they found more fight than they wanted, they had overrun Ysabel and Guadalcanal.

'New Georgia warriors on the loose make the worst of our beachcombers look like white lilies,' he said. 'That fellow we saw up in the hills today probably has some of his father's and grandfather's headhunting trophies from Ysabel right there under his roof-tree, and no doubt plenty of his own.'

He told us how the chief would plan the headhunting. Sometimes the victims would be in the next village or right in his own. The man or men chosen to do the deed considered themselves highly honored and would be looked up to in the tribe after that. They might not stage a raid — might actually go and befriend the victims — wait until their confidence was won and they were completely off guard — then spring on them and make the kill.

'New Georgians carried headhunting so far,' he continued, 'that some of them got to be real epicures and developed quite a taste for human brains. They still have it.'

I was about to say, 'Why do you tempt them then by building a palace for a target?' But he anticipated the question.

'They don't like British gunboats,' he said, 'but there was one old chief Paravo here not so long ago, who was very fierce and wanted to kill a white for his collection. He made suspicious passes at several traders, but, somehow, he never seemed to get up nerve. Finally, he took several canoe-loads of his men over to Guadalcanal on a foray against some shore villages. His luck was out and, instead of getting heads, his party was attacked and fled, losing quite a number of warriors. Bad weather caught them and washed them up on a small uninhabited island. They were soon starving. The chief died. His men ate him! When the weather cleared, the stragglers got back to New Georgia. Later on, a white trader came along and they meekly asked him if he would take his ship and go over to the little island and bring the chief's head back to them. I don't think he did. There haven't been any naval expeditions that I have heard about since that one.'

15 ~~~~~~~

. . . happy-go-lucky Heaven

*T*HIS is going to be a social call,' said Markham.

We were sailing into another delightful little bay fringed with coconut palms, beyond which rose hills covered with dense jungle. Along the shore several small huts were visible, but there seemed to be no life. It was one of those heavy and hazy tropical mornings when the beating sun makes air, water, and earth so hot that everything, including one's blood, seems to boil, and torpidity is the only protection left to man and beast.

'I told you about Tom Butler, my beachcomber friend. We'll pay him a little visit,' Markham said. 'Probably the last time I'll see him.'

We made our way down the beach to a rise of ground among the palms. Here there was a dilapidated hut of mat walls and thatched roof, but still no sign of life except a thin wisp of smoke issuing from the doorway. Markham shouted. There was no reply. We went to the door and peered in.

On a bamboo bed lay an emaciated man, covered with a ragged and dirty blanket. Beside him squatted a middle-aged native woman, who rose and stared as we entered. She had a mop of heavy, fuzzy hair, wore large wooden ear-plugs, and a string of shell money around her neck. About her waist was another string of shells, but she wore no clothing.

The man on the couch looked as though he were dead. His eyes were closed and he lay completely motionless. He seemed not even to breathe. A tangled mat of heavy red hair and a shaggy red beard gave his gaunt face a ghastly pallor. His hands, which lay on the dirty coverlet, were shrunken and covered with parched skin.

In the far end of the dark, smoke-filled interior, three other women huddled over a smouldering fire. They were younger than the first, but equally indifferent, or frightened. They stared and did not move.

A large jug of rum stood on the floor near the man's head. Refuse was strewn about, which the women were evidently too lazy to remove. Among the litter were several used tins of bully-beef. From these huge cockroaches were feeding. Lizards scuttled about and one fell from the wall onto the bed. It scampered off along with a huge spider. The entire place seemed full of crawling things and was unspeakably filthy.

Markham walked to the bed.

'Tom, this is Marco,' he said softly.

The man's eyes opened, but he stared as though he saw nothing. Markham continued to speak to him. There was a flicker of life in his face, his lips moved and he mumbled something, but what he said was unintelligible.

Markham picked up a tin cup and poured some water from a stone rum-jug which the woman handed him, then propped the man up and gave him a drink. As the blanket fell from him, we saw that he was naked and a mere skin and bones. He drank a little and fell back on a gunny-sack pillow, too weak even to say thanks.

The woman was now fanning him with a palm leaf. She had still said not a word.

'Poor devil,' said Markham. 'It's beri-beri — they just waste away and pass off into a coma.' I saw that his eyes were full of tears.

The stench and misery of the place gave me nausea and I

New Georgia natives with a small inlaid canoe. The bow sweeps upward and is encrusted with white cowrie shells and mother of pearl.

The native preacher of Santa Ysabel. Reading aloud a bêche-de-mer version of the Garden of Eden episode, he began, 'One time God, he big fellah belong white mastah, makum one fellah man.'

A native missionary, fully clothed but still with the wild eyes of the jungle. He will wear the sweater and trousers until they rot, a good reason for not putting clothes on natives.

The son of New Georgia's chief. Like his elders he has lime paste on his hair to make him blond, protect him from evil, and kill the lice.

Dancers on San Christobal. Each wears a head-band of white cowrie shells and a coronet and skirt of split coconut leaves.

San Christobal warriors in dance regalia. They carry spears and beautifully carved hard wood clubs with large flaring blades.

Three Solomon Island landlords, probably in their fifties. One stick of tobacco was gratefully received for a month's rent.

Osa's home in the San Christobal jungle, where Martin said, 'I hope that Heaven is half as nice.'

went out into the air. If one had a nightmare of death in its most awful form, it could not be worse than this, I thought.

I made for the beach. Even the coconut palms were shabby and neglected. In a few moments Martin and Markham joined me and we walked slowly toward the dinghy.

'He has probably been mad for years,' said Markham, as though talking to himself, 'from loneliness and self-punishment. Got the idea that he owned all the Solomons. One of the nicest fellows in the world, but he always acted as though he were getting even with someone over some silly thing back home.'

For twenty years the big powerful Irishman had traded and run this plantation, Markham told us. He had bought and lived with the woman who was taking care of him now and had a dozen or more children. But instead of keeping his dignity and exploiting his opportunities, he had degenerated to worse than the native level and had squandered all he had on rum. Death was coming almost too late.

'He asked for what he got — it was his choice — he didn't have to live that way,' said Markham. 'Some fellows would make a cesspool out of any heaven you led them into.'

'I'm beginning to think it's the dry rot of the islands,' Martin put in with disgust. 'With the exception of Marco, it seems to have got everything. A kind of degeneracy in beauty. Perfection to the eye and decay right down to the heart. Natives, whites, animal life, even the coconuts go to pot, like these of Butler's, if left to themselves. Creeping jungles, covering and suffocating and deteriorating everything alive. I hope you get out of it, Marco, before it gets *you*.'

Marco did not reply. He only smiled, one of his dreamy, faraway smiles, as we climbed into the dinghy and paddled away.

Nearly four more months had gone by since we had left Tulagi and Martin was getting into his fidgety state again. I knew that our finances were secure enough, but the pictures we were making were not what he wanted. The approaching

monsoons would soon make the weather a problem and time
was becoming increasingly important.

'We're surely getting nowhere fast,' he grumbled. 'I hope
this San Christobal that Marco is taking us to has some excitement. We came for cannibals and all we have is a lot of
fierce-looking natives to make people shudder and say "Why
didn't you get them eating each other?" Can't *you* get some
inspiration, Osa?'

All I could do was to encourage him — we would soon find
the unexpected — it was only a question of keeping in circula-
tion and keeping our eyes open. I felt that almost anywhere
here, in some hair-trigger moment, the natives would break
out, and we would have more than we wanted of cannibals
in action. I hoped only that we would be ready and able to
get the precious film that meant success or failure. As for me,
every day was inspiration. The beauty of the islands and the
excitement of living in this faraway land with the man I loved
was all I wanted and all the happiness and success I required.

San Christobal, which we were now approaching, would
be different and colorful, Markham assured us, and might
have the excitement we were looking for. His plan was to
coast along the shore, to see what we could see of the jungles
and go on to Santa Ana, the principal native settlement.

'That bay has its stories,' he said, pointing out a great in-
dentation of rugged land.

The place looked like just the spot for colonists with its
peaceful shelter for vessels and broad tablelands for cultivation.

'Some traders came in here on a schooner with seven white
men aboard. They had a fine load of tobacco and trade goods
and were shopping for tortoise and pearl shell. They anchored offshore for the night and started moving slowly inland at sunrise. When they turned into the bay there and
anchored, they were surprised to see a thousand natives
coming out to meet them in canoes. The natives came from
all sides, blowing their conch shells and beating their paddles

against their canoes. That meant war. Before the schooner could put about, it was surrounded and boarded.'

Markham became very animated as he described the fierce battle.

'The white men shot it out,' he said, 'but what could seven men, even with good rifles, do against a thousand blacks? The more natives they shot, the more natives swarmed aboard, and the wilder they were. The whites were soon killed. For once, the chief now had all the tobacco and biscuits and calico he wanted, and it hadn't cost him a shell. Ultimately, of course, plenty of natives were strung up, and the rest driven back into the jungle. Something for both sides to remember.'

Martin looked very solemn, but I knew he was enjoying the adventure as though it were his own. I supposed he was even imagining himself shooting it out with the natives. I knew, at least in this respect, he would never grow up.

'The women are very good-looking and dress only in a smile,' Markham continued. 'So the Malaita and Guadalcanal and New Georgia braves used to raid the island and take off the women every now and then. Probably a good idea from the standpoint of the race. The women all have bushy hair, unlike the shaven-headed beauties you have been seeing in other places. Nice dispositions, too. You may lose your husband down here, Osa.'

A cluster of men and boys waited for us as we pulled up in the dinghy. All were unarmed and seemed friendly.

'The chief knows me here, so just stand by while I start things,' Markham said. 'Don't be too forward. These men are real cannibals and you never know what they are up to. Just stick to me for the present and don't turn your back on anybody until we smooth them out, and even then keep your eyes peeled.'

He asked for the chief and put out a stick of tobacco to everyone in sight. The men were eyeing Martin's cameras suspiciously and kept staring at me as though I were the funniest freak they had ever seen.

Soon the chief emerged. He was a big, handsome speci-
men, with coal-black bushy hair and strong, intelligent features, much younger than most of the leaders we had seen and
as muscular as an athlete in his prime. He wore a bandeau
of white cowrie shells across his forehead from temple to
temple, and armbands of wampum, and carried a long spear
with a beautifully carved fishbone blade.

'They say that when he became chief and built his new
headhouse here he had quite a feast of "long-pig" (human
flesh),' Markham said. 'The men eat the men and the
women eat the women. A man believes that if he eats a man
he acquires his fighting power, but if he eats a woman he
becomes weak and insignificant.'

Of course, they would deny it, but it was good old San
Christobal custom. They didn't discriminate. They might
go out and get an enemy or take some unsuspecting infant,
or even one of the workmen who is building the headhouse.

'Anyway, the chief has as fine a collection of heads as I
have seen,' Markham added.

The chief and his men seemed quite superior. There was
not the usual grunting and evident stupidity, but everyone
was alert and alive, much like the natives back at Ong Tong
Java. They were healthy, and had luxuriant black bushy
hair. Their skins were not black, but chocolate brown.

The chief's son, a boy in his teens, was dressed up like a
real dandy. He wore a headband of cowrie shells and clusters
of porpoise teeth in each ear. Another large cluster of porpoise teeth was suspended from his nose and over his mouth.
From ear to ear and down under his chin was still another
strand of porpoise teeth. Around his neck hung strand after
strand of teeth and small colored shells, drooping one beneath
the other, so that they made almost a coat of mail over his
chest and hung nearly to his waist. Around his waist and
around each arm were bands of small shells.

Then, I saw something horrible. From the boy's throat
down to his waist hung a string of human teeth, all white.

I supposed they were white men's teeth, but I soon noticed that the teeth of all the natives here were white.

Young girls had come forward and were all staring at me. I looked at them and they smiled. Then they began to giggle like schoolgirls.

Their nude figures were beautiful, the skin seeming lighter than that of the men, almost a light brown. This was probably an illusion, but it gave them a cleaner look. Several had scars, but not one a sore. Their kinky and bushy black hair was well combed. Some had flowers in their hair or behind their ears, and most of them wore in their slightly distended ear lobes small blocks of wood or clusters of shell. Several had armbands with flowers or areca leaves, and one carried a briar pipe thrust through her shell armlet. Some had anklets of small shells, which seemed prettily feminine and much more appropriate to them than to the warriors.

Encouraged by my smiles, they came up to me and felt of my blouse. Then they touched my skin and began rubbing my arm as though to see whether the color would rub off. They went all over me, in fact, and when one of them pinched me, I yelled.

'Just trying to see if you are made the same as they are,' said Martin. 'You are probably the only white woman they have seen, at least this close.'

With this intimate introduction, we were now all on a very friendly footing. When Martin proposed taking my picture with the girls, they readily assented and showed no fear of the black box. They were as nearly like children as any natives we had yet seen. If their men were cannibals, I couldn't believe that these women had any part in the business.

I saw that the girls had mere strings of porpoise teeth or shell about their waists, and nothing more. The older women wore waistbands with a little apron of beads or grass.

'A badge of marriage,' Markham explained. 'The young girls go absolutely nude until they are married. But that covering doesn't make much difference.'

He added that there were no strict moral taboos here as on Malaita. On the contrary, as soon as the girls came of age, they were any man's property. If a man made advances and the girl demurred, the parents urged her to accept him, especially if they were encouraged with a present. The man also gave the girl an armlet or anklet as a gift and I saw that some of the older girls have quite a collection of these.

'One chief made a large fortune in shells by sending his wives around the island,' Markham said.

This promiscuity did not affect the marriage relation, Markham assured us. Married men and women were quite faithful to each other. And it had not apparently affected the girls, for they were the sweetest and most natural we had encountered anywhere. They were also the healthiest and paid more attention to their persons, and they had surely kept their good looks.

'If a woman has a child, she is married to the man,' Markham continued. 'And I have never seen people more attentive to their youngsters. These women are very affectionate mothers. The little boys especially are spoiled.'

When the boys approached puberty, they were taken by the chief into a special clubhouse, where they remained until they came of age.

'They are given a real Spartan training in hunting, fishing, and war, until they are able to do everything a full-grown man does and equally well. In fact, they do most of the work that is done, while the older men direct them and take things easy.'

For the life they had to live, this was equivalent to a university training, he thought. The idea has been copied on the other islands, but nowhere else was there such good discipline.

Several of the girls plunged into the water and swam about like fish, screaming and laughing and splashing. They came up from a dive, shook their heads and dove again.

They were beckoning and calling to me to come in with

them, so I had Markham cut me a piece of his trade cloth and went into a grass hut near-by and came out in a perfect lava-lava.

The girls flocked around me. Now they were all excited about my feet. They got down and looked at my toes and nails and counted them to see if they had the same number.

Before I knew what had happened, they had picked me up and were carrying me down to the water. They took me out to swimming depth and gently tossed me in. Then they swam about me, ducking and diving like porpoises. Several would dive and come up under me, lifting me almost clear of the water, whereupon I got a good ducking. They had a good joke at this and laughed gleefully. I could not swim too well, but with all these experts around me, I put on the best show I could, until I was utterly exhausted and splashed ashore.

I lay down to rest and dry my hair, and the girls came again and sat around me, chattering and laughing to themselves as though they had discovered a new toy or pet of some kind. Two of the girls ran off and soon came back with a headband of shells which they tied across my forehead, a bracelet of coral and an anklet of small shells. Another brought a flower and stuck it in my wet hair.

Another gave me the waist-string she wore, made of tiny shells. At this I demurred, though I accepted the shells. I would keep my lava-lava dress for the present, I tried to make them understand. They seemed not to mind.

'The chief wants to put on a show for you,' Markham said, 'and you are going to see something worth photographing.'

We all followed the chief and his entourage through the jungle into the village clearing. While the men were preparing for their part in the event, the girls, now decked out in bracelets and anklets of shell and with wild flowers in their hair, began the dance.

Several little boys playing small pan-pipes led the girls around in a wide circle. The pipes were shrill and monotonous, but had a certain exhilaration about them, and the girls soon began to chant and clap their hands in a definite rhythm.

The circle broke and the girls fell into two files, one behind the other, now moving from side to side and stamping their feet for emphasis. They began to sway in a sort of hula-hula, and came up to us, with their hands on their hips and executing a series of beautiful movements and evolutions.

They began a gentle hissing as they came forward again with an undulating sort of rhythm. This was unmistakably a 'snake' dance. They were now moving in a rapid tempo. They leaped and swayed from side to side, hissing in unison and with increasing volume, 'hss-hss-hss; hss-hss-hss; hss-hss-hss.'

The spell of the dance was almost hypnotic. Martin was in his element, making motion pictures, and I was so captivated that I forgot to take my still pictures until he roused me.

Now the men came forward. They were very handsome in a simple but attractive regalia. Each wore a headband of white cowrie shells and above this was a band of fibre from which split coconut leaves protruded outward in wide-sweeping strands, to make a kind of coronet. Each wore a collar of several strands of porpoise teeth. Some wore clam-shell breastplates, others, nose-rings and earrings, and others many strands of small shells. There were armbands and anklets aplenty, and several of the men had flowers and areca leaves in their hair and in their armlets. From their waists hung more strands of coconut leaf, suggesting skirts. They carried large clubs, beautifully carved, with large flaring blades, and some had spears.

A small son of the chief about ten years of age ran forward with a spear in one hand and a wicker shield in the other and began fencing with an imaginary enemy. He danced backward in a lively but not too studied arrangement, while the elders stood approvingly by and clapped their hands and encouraged him. He seemed very proud of himself when he stopped, exhausted.

The men now began as the girls had done and went through a swift series of dances, much more vigorous and far more professional. They took up the snake dance in the same manner, but in faster tempo, and they wound up, lunging with their spears and clubs in a realistic snake-like thrust. While they rested, the girls began again. Then the men came forward with small clubs, similar to boomerangs, and went through a group of hunting dances, all very smooth and impressive.

'That looks like some connection with the Australian bushman,' said Martin.

We examined the boomerangs and found them all beautifully carved, principally with bird figures, and Markham confirmed that these were used in stalking birds and small game.

But now, we had a dramatic piece. A fresh group of dancers came out, entirely nude, except that they had around their throats and arms and legs strands of vine that resembled long hair. They ambled forward on all fours, like apes, grunting loudly. At their appearance the women screamed and ran for their houses. All this was part of the act, we found. The ape-men made for the women, but the first group of dancers intercepted them with their spears and clubs and a mêlée ensued, all in dance rhythm. During the struggle, the warriors overcame the ape-men, who slowly retreated. Finally, pursued by the warriors, the ape-men fled, and one by one took to the trees.

Here it was again, the legend of the apes. There must be something to warrant this folklore and belief, now acted out just as we had heard it rumored on Malaita. Perhaps there would be gorillas or ourangs yet found in the highlands of the Solomons. Or, these people had ancestors who came from Borneo and Malaya, where apes were intimately known.

'If a woman dies at childbirth, they believe the child becomes an ape-man,' Markham said. 'So they throw it into a fire and destroy it with a big ceremony.'

I saw that most of the shells which the chief and his attendants and wives wore were small and red. These were evidently highly prized.

'They are like gold pieces,' supplied Markham. 'The most valuable money they have, along with porpoise teeth. The commoners usually have white shells, you will notice.'

He asked the chief's favorite wife for one of her several bracelets and brought it to show me. It was made up of hundreds of paper-thin shells, each a soft red in color. They were incredibly delicate and dainty and I could see why the women must enjoy them.

'They make the most of them here,' Markham said. 'But the woman's use of anything is subject to her husband's. I've given a woman a bracelet and in a few minutes seen her husband wearing it. Same as with tobacco. They seem to enjoy loading up the Master and it's probably part of their way with their men.

'Of course the cowrie shells are also valuable,' he went on. 'They are probably the first money ever used in the world and that may give you an idea of the age of these races. At any rate, everyone in the islands has a sentiment for cowrie shells, and when they are woven into a man's hair like that, they are about as near to flowers as anything I know.'

I supposed that the chief had some of the orange cowries that I wanted so badly, but I knew there was nothing that I could offer him that he would want but tobacco and I shouldn't have enough of that. He would not be interested in money. Property was only for enjoyment and use with these natives, and our money would be neither decorative nor useful. It would have no investment value, for there were no investments. At death a man's principal wealth would be buried with him and so completely disappear.

'The chief's son will inherit the chiefdom and probably his father's canoe and certain mementoes,' said Markham. 'The chiefdom he will hold, if he is good enough. He will collect his own wives and shells and heads, with very personal ideas of what is decorative and most valuable to have and to keep. The gardens and the beach and the fishing grounds are the property of the village and they go on from generation to generation, so he doesn't worry about them. It's a simple and rational economy, and must be good enough for them, for they have used it a long time.'

Leaving the village at evening, I felt we were leaving a kind of happy-go-lucky Heaven. The girls came down to the beach with us and waded out into the water, throwing at us flowers which they took from their hair, and shouting what I supposed was their good-bye.

'They are glad to see you laugh,' Markham said. 'You have been kinder to them than probably anyone they know and they are fond of you.'

They dove into the surf and swam and splashed us as we pulled away.

For several days we coasted down the shore of San Christobal, stopping occasionally to meet with similar receptions. Most of the natives seemed astonished at our arrival and all regarded me as a very queer creature. Perhaps this was partly because of my striped pajamas, the coolest thing I had to wear.

Invariably the natives came up to feel of me and try to make out what I was. I didn't mind the girls rubbing my skin to see what it was made of, but when one of the old cannibals rubbed his horny raspy hands up my arm, I wanted to scream. Of course, I knew I mustn't, for we needed their friendship and confidence if Martin was to get any pictures.

At one of the villages we decided to stop for a few days to look over the surrounding bush country and get a taste of native life in the raw. There were two new huts just finished near the beach and these Markham arranged to rent, occupying one himself and giving the other to Martin and me. He knew the chief well and with Mauki for guard and minister, he felt that we were secure.

Our landlord stood around and watched us for a long time.

'We haven't paid our rent, Marco,' said Martin. 'What do I give this fellow?'

He handed the old man two sticks of tobacco and waited to see what would happen. The landlord looked at the sticks for a moment, scratched his head, then turned and walked away.

'He's trying to make out whether he overcharged you,' said Markham.

Since we should be here several days, Markham engaged one of the men of the village for a house servant. He was stooped and wrinkled and looked almost crippled, but he was probably not over forty and was full of vitality. He was black as night and he wore a heavy black walrus mustache that drooped down over his mouth and looked as though it were going to drop off. I dubbed him 'Friday.'

First of all, I had Friday bring me plenty of fresh spring water, enough for drinking and cooking and also enough to fill our canvas bathtub. We had scarcely used our bathtub, with all the sea for bathing. But I was going to give my hair a good scrubbing before I did another thing. I almost went mad when I couldn't wash my hair, but water was so precious, and time often more so, that weeks would pass before I could get at it. I wondered how the hill natives could go for years or forever without a shampoo.

Friday stood by and watched me soap and rinse my hair in a kind of stupefied astonishment. When I finished, I took a little compact mirror I was using and gave it to him. He was now thoroughly bewildered. He sat down and stared into the glass and looked at himself from all angles, for fully an hour. Then he caught the sun and went around flashing bright spots of light into the trees and into other natives' eyes.

'You've probably made him the most important man in the village,' said Markham. 'They will think you've put some kind of magic into him. Now he will be yours for life.'

Only a 'bokkus belong bell' would please him more, Markham thought. This was a black tin box with a small bell fastened inside which would tinkle every time the lid was raised. In this he could keep his trinkets. But we had no 'bokkus' with us.

Friday's face was expressionless and his eyes stared stupidly, whatever happened. I never once saw him smile. When I asked him to do something, he was entirely uncomprehending, but by degrees he began to understand my combined *bêche-de-mer* and pantomime. He did work with a will.

Our food stocks were low, so we must now live on what we could find. I promised to keep the men fed if they would leave everything to me. While they made a trip into the bush, I took Mauki and Friday into the village and traded beads and tobacco for yams, taro, bananas, fresh coconuts, and some wild chickens. Then we scoured the beach and dug for small white clams and caught some rock cod and blackfish. By early evening, when the men came in, I had a simple but tasty dinner ready.

'Boy, oh boy, is this delicious!' said Martin as he finished off his first helping. 'Why do you live out of a can when you can live on the fat of the land, Marco? Why, this is better than the Waldorf-Astoria.'

Encouraged by this reception, I decided next day to give Martin a real treat. I had seen crabs among the coconut trees and if I could get one, I knew he would be very pleased. Mauki borrowed a small native fish net and we started off on a still hunt. There were plenty of clues, for the lumbering crab leaves a wide trail in the sand as he propels his body along with his flippers. These trails ended abruptly at coconut trees. The hermit makes his home in the crotches and holes of these trees and feeds on the fresh fruit. He strips off the coconut husk with his powerful claws and punches through the 'eyes' with his long nippers, or actually breaks off pieces of the shell. Then he deftly scoops out the meat. This was for me one of the unbelievables of the Solomons until I saw it done.

Mauki's quick eyes spotted a huge crab just below a crotch,

slowly edging his way down the tree trunk toward the ground. Stealing up behind the tree with his net in one hand, Mauki waited. To my astonishment, instead of hitting the crab, he seized it with his fingers and tossed it neatly into the net. There the crab thrashed about helplessly. Then, to show me the strength of its pincers, Mauki gave it a stick and it angrily bit the stick in two.

'I've even seen them bite a piece out of a knife,' said Markham that night. 'Keep your fingers out of their way. The boys are clever at catching them with their hands, but it's not for me.'

While we enjoyed boiled crab for our dinner, Markham told us that nothing was a greater delicacy for the natives. They were very fond of all fatty foods, but especially the succulent flesh of these coconut-fed monsters. The crabs would eat nothing but coconuts and would die if deprived of that diet. They ate a coconut a day, so no wonder they were full of oil.

Mauki and Friday and our crew boys had made a fire down the beach and I went over to see how they were making out for dinner. On the coals was a large clay bowl covered over with banana leaves. Mauki lifted the leaves for me to see. There was a coconut crab on top of stones which were nearly immersed in boiling water. The crab was getting a perfect and thorough steam cooking and looked very appetizing.

On a hot rock at the edge of the fire was one of our ship's frying pans. In it, slowly frying in coconut oil, were a score of golden-brown tidbits. They looked like small frizzled pieces of fish. I asked for one to taste. It was crisp and rich, something like fried oyster, but more oily.

The boys laughed.

'What name belong him?' I asked.

'He one fellah walkum belong grass. Good fellah too much,' Mauki said, grinning. 'You eatum one fellah, you strong fellah too much.'

Grasshopper! I thought. There was something for the farmers back in Kansas to exploit. But I wouldn't tell my mother I had eaten one, for she would disown me.

As the days passed, the children of the village flocked around my little rickety hut and the mothers came to stare at me by the hour. For the youngsters I trilled like a canary and they asked to see what I had in my mouth, evidently thinking that I had a bird there. I blew on a blade of grass for them and made a shrill sound. They clapped their hands and screamed with laughter, but although I showed them again and again how to do it, they could not catch on.

They all liked noise and were always making plenty of it. Markham said that they preferred whistles and noise-makers to any gadgets he could trade them and would pay any price for these. During our stay we saw many a native with a tin whistle stuck importantly in the distended lobe of his ear, or in his armlet or belt, or walking solemnly along blowing on one with all his lung power.

Martin came in one evening with his face and hands and legs terribly swollen and his eyes nearly closed. He had been stung by hornets. Markham and the boys had been separated from him and had missed the attack.

I hurriedly got out the ammonia and bathed him in it for a long time. This gave him some relief from the pain and gradually reduced the inflammation.

'Those little devils are bad. And they pry into everything,' grumbled Markham. 'They nest in any kind of cover, bring in dead insects for their young to feed on, and make a mess of your place. I've had them get into my teapot and build a nest in the spout overnight. Once they got into the spout of a syphon bottle, and when I tried to give myself a drink, I got an explosion and a squirt of hornets.'

We had a heavy rain one morning and Martin came back to camp drenched to the skin and shivering so that he could not talk. It was another malaria attack. Then came the fever and his temperature shot up to over 104 and lasted for hours. He complained that his head was splitting and went into a long delirium.

I gave him a double dose of quinine, and by next day had

him comfortable again, but too weak to move and too nause-
ated to eat anything. It was maddening to watch his suffering, but I knew the attack would have to burn itself out.

'When malaria strikes a native,' Markham said, 'he simply
lies down, wherever he is, even if the earth is wet, and waits
until it is over. They have the same symptoms, but seem to
shake less than the whites, so perhaps the chills aren't so
severe. Thousands of them die with it. It takes even the
strongest. It is the scourge of the Solomons and has been for
centuries.'

While Martin and Markham continued their trips into the
interior, I foraged for new foods.

One day I found some wild honey in a tree trunk near
camp. It was watery stuff, not thick like our domestic honey
at home, but it smelled like the mixed scents of several flowers
and was very pleasant to taste. The bees had made little
bags of wax, about the size of a walnut and brown in color.
Mauki said the natives drank the honey like water and used
the wax for caulking their canoes.

I wanted some baking-powder biscuits, but was out of
baking powder. I tried to forget about them, but they kept
coming to my mind. Martin was always talking about wanting an ice-cream soda, but now I wanted biscuits, and they
haunted me. Suddenly I remembered our Eno Fruit Salts.
They would be effervescent. I tried them and, sure enough,
they did the trick. The biscuits were just as good as any I
had made with real baking powder. But I knew that Fruit
Salts would be harder to get than baking powder when that
bottle was gone.

Guided into the forest one day by Mauki, I found flocks of
green pigeons. One tree must have had five hundred little
birds in it. I shot two, and the others vanished so quickly
that I scarcely heard their wings. They were very plump-
breasted, much like our grouse, and two would make an ample
dinner for us.

As I picked up my birds, I saw at the foot of the tree from
which they had fallen a number of partially eaten purple

The mud huts at Vao. Each has a single doorway so low one must stoop to enter, and no other opening except a tiny vent at the top.

Bamboo and thatch houses at Vao. The fences keep out pigs and marauders.

Vao natives and the 'little black bokkus.' Martin had to let them inspect the camera before daring to take their pictures.

New Hebrides chief, decorated with wild boar tusks. The tusks are highly valued, are hung on boo-boos and in the chief's headhouse, and are given to medicine men as presents.

One of Father Prin's converts. A christianized woman at Vao.

Father Prin's first convert on the island of Vao.

fruits, shaped much like a mango, but about two and one half inches long. The birds had picked away most of the flesh, leaving a nut similar to an almond in size and shape.

These nuts, Mauki told me, were very good to eat, especially when roasted, and with two stones he cracked the tough shell and I tasted the meat. It was delicious, very much like our almond, but even richer in flavor. The flesh was also pleasant, with a unique taste, but I preferred the nuts. We collected some of the fresh fruit and many of the nuts to take home.

Farther on, beside the trail, I spied what seemed to be wild sugar cane. Mauki cut the stalk and sure enough it was cane. Some of the natives had it in their gardens, he said. We took along a supply, for often I craved something sweet.

Near-by, attached to long trailing ground vines, were small squashes, much like vegetable marrow. Mauki called them 'Peop,' and I added some to the bag which our man Friday carried. Then I saw in the underbrush what looked like a Kansas pumpkin. This had apparently also escaped at some time from a native garden. After adding some of these and some fern fronds for spinach to our collection, Friday was completely loaded and I sent him back to camp.

We left the trail to go into the forest and I noticed that Mauki was breaking twigs. This was evidently to 'blaze' our way back to the trail. I was always impressed by the sureness and perfect sense of direction with which he and all the natives went through strange country. I carried a compass but seldom used it and, when I did, I found the natives always to be going in the right way.

I asked Mauki if he ever got lost.

He shook his head. 'Me savvy,' he said, with a grin.

As the afternoon drew on and we were about to turn homeward, I saw in the branches of a wild nutmeg tree something that looked like an animal. We rushed for it, and I found that it was a cuscus or opossum hanging by his tail. He roused and drew himself up to the branch, but was very sluggish and seemed to resent our having disturbed his slumber. While he eyed us, Mauki began to shout at him and run about the tree like mad.

The opossum regarded Mauki with astonishment and curiosity for a time, then moved out to the end of a limb. Surveying the ground for an escape, he swung down by his long prehensile tail and tested a lower and longer limb. Now he was thoroughly frightened and he leaped to the connecting branch of an adjoining tree. This seemed quite a feat for such an animal, but I was equally surprised to see him run along the branch almost as quickly as a squirrel. He swung along, half-concealed by the foliage overhead, and we had difficulty in not losing him.

Then I saw him exert his best cunning. Hanging by his tail from the end of a branch, he swung like a pendulum, back and forth in an increasing arc, toward the outstretched branch of a huge tree which, with its height and heavy leafage, would be an excellent hiding-place. Suddenly his tail uncoiled and he sailed across the few intervening feet of space as neatly as any acrobat, and I saw him scurry down the great limb and gain the trunk. I had been hoping to have him for tomorrow's dinner, but I felt that clever little fellow had a right to survive.

'Holy smoke!' yelled Martin when I returned. 'Are we going to have a banquet?'

He seemed more excited over the food than over his films this evening.

'You know,' he said to Markham, 'if Osa and I were really bright, we would chuck the whole of civilization and stay right out here with you!'

He thrust his hands in his pockets and walked up and down beside the fire. He kicked at a rock, stopped and looked up at the sky, and drew in a long, appreciative breath.

'Look at this,' he said. 'The sea and the earth and the sky are full of food, just waiting to be used. You don't need any clothes; they are in the way, and too hot. You have shelter, merely by tying together a few branches and palm leaves. I think this place was made for human beings, and I hope that Heaven is half as nice.'

16 wwwwww

. . . superstitions . . . and pan-pipes

THERE WERE SEVERAL TRIPS still to be made from our little San Christobal base, for we were getting the best characters and the finest arts and ornamentation of our expedition so far.

This was my opportunity. I asked if I could have a real fishing holiday. Markham assented, but gave me Mauki as a bodyguard. I sent Mauki immediately to look for a canoe. In an hour he came back with a cumbersome but substantial little dugout which he had rented. I could keep it as long as I liked, he said, all for a single stick of tobacco.

Early the next morning we started off, guided by a village boy who was an expert fisherman. The lad had brought his home-made tackle, which was a conglomeration of sticks and twine-like lines. I wondered how on earth he would catch fish with that equipment.

We paddled for some distance until we rounded a point and caught the wind. There, to my surprise, the boy tossed up one of his contraptions and it flew into the air — a jungle kite! He held it by a stout cord, resembling hemp and made from jungle vine, until it was well out and steadied. The kite trailed a line to the water, and to this was attached a small stick which floated upright on the surface and had the effect of holding the kite in place overhead and of acting as a cork for the line below. The action of the kite gave the stick a very lively motion.

The kite hovered overhead, just as a bird would hover over a school of fish. This, I learned, was precisely its object, to create the illusion of a bird scouting for food. Game fish were accustomed to follow hovering birds to schools of small fry. These, in turn, were spotted and pursued by still larger fish, notably kingfish and bonita, who likewise used the birds as guides.

Soon there was a strike, and not only did the stick disappear, but the kite dipped deeply. The boy hauled in kite and all. Dangling from the end of his line was a fine bonita.

He removed the fish. There was no hook nor bait; only a queer mass of strong spider web in which the fish's head had become entangled as in a net. This was fishing with a skill and patience to challenge even the best fly-casters.

He had brought several of the sticks or floats and each was beautifully carved, the tops to resemble birds.

With my own tackle, a hook with white colored cockatoo feathers attached to make a 'wiggler,' I had only moderate success, but my boatboy continued to catch bonita with his strange kite and bobber.

Presently a great school of porpoise appeared not far off. I counted over fifty as they rose and dove again. Our boat-boy quickly drew in his kite and line and started paddling in the opposite direction. There would be no fish with porpoise around, Mauki explained.

Our fisherman now set two long lines made of jungle vine. On the end of each was a beautiful little spinner made of mother-of-pearl, and below that a sharp hook made of bonita bone. These he managed so skillfully that, although the hooks were not barbed, I did not see him lose a single fish that struck. By nightfall he had several times as many fish and far more poundage than I.

'You should see them poison fish here,' said Markham that

evening, as he finished his plate of bonita. 'They do as well as I do with dynamite. The bark of a jungle vine which they call "hue" is chopped up into fine pieces, stripped and tossed into a stream or pool as you do when you are "chumming." The fish become groggy, float to the surface, and are captured.'

I asked how they could eat poisoned fish.

'They eat them, all right,' he said. 'The flesh doesn't seem to be affected. Or so slightly it isn't dangerous. But the poison is potent stuff. It would knock you straight out if you took it directly. They use it to dispose of children they don't want. Infanticide is still quite a curse here, especially among girls. They use several poisonous fruits in the same way.'

But the fishermen in our village were too skillful to resort to poison. On the following day, we paddled up and down the shore, watching them at work with their nets and spears. They were anything but lazy, and were especially attractive to watch as the sun glistened on their wet bronzed bodies. We came inshore to get close-ups, moving carefully so as not to disturb their quarry.

They worked singly and in groups. Alert and with spear ready, a single man would stand on a rock or promontory over a pool which he knew fish frequented. The thrust of his spear was so quick and his muscular control so perfect that it amounted to one smooth forward motion, and almost to sleight-of-hand. When he recovered his spear, he usually pulled out a fish with it. The fish was badly torn by the barbed spear, but he did not seem to mind.

Groups of men, working together, formed semicircles in the shallow water, moving inward toward the center. Sometimes they would stand motionless for minutes, eyes fixed on the water, then creep forward again. Then the spears flashed. Every man seemed to have located his fish by silent communication and agreement with the others. There was no confusion and seldom did a man miss his fish.

The spears were handsomely executed and deftly carved. The head was fashioned from a piece of hard palmwood, tapering to a sharp point and notched to give it a series of barbs. This was fastened to a shaft of bamboo about seven feet in length. Others had, in place of a single point, a bundle of three to five slender points bound together.

While we watched one of these groups at work, there was a shout from one of the men and he hobbled ashore. His leg was lacerated and bleeding. I ran over to him and found that his calf had been badly torn. I made a quick tourniquet with my handkerchief to stop the flow of blood and ordered Mauki to bring him in the men's canoe and follow us to camp, where I could give him first aid.

I was still working on the bandage after having doused the wound with several treatments of permanganate of potash and was applying a boric-acid dressing, when Markham came in. He asked me quietly about the accident, but said little until the man had been taken away.

'That was a garfish wound,' he said finally. 'One of the most savage fish in the deep. The natives have a great fear of them, for such a wound often means death, and this one might have if you hadn't been there. The natives are so superstitious they think the garfish can leap out of the water and strike them in their canoes. Of course that doesn't happen. If they are ever struck, it is probably when they are fishing at night with torches, as they often do, and flying fish are attracted to the light. But I want to give you a warning, Doctor Johnson!'

He was in real earnest and graver than I had ever seen him.

'You did a fine thing there and a good job,' he went on. 'But don't play doctor too much. I don't want to discourage your humanitarian sentiments, but if you want to start something, that is a sure way to do it. In small things, a dose of this or that harmless medicine is all right, but as little of *that* as possible. Leave medicine to the missionary doctors who are real physicians. If you give a dose of something and there is a bad reaction, even one that isn't fatal, they are going to blame you, and the first thing you know they will be gossiping that you are an evil spirit and something will happen. For example, if that man should die, they would swear you poisoned the fellow. They would forget all about Mr. Gar-fish, and before morning they would have our heads just to make up for his. It's too ticklish; let it alone. That's the best advice I ever gave you.'

I was provoked and said that I wasn't going to see a man die just for a white man's superstition, and that I would take a chance with mercy against suffering any day. Markham completely ignored me.

'We will be starting down the coast early in the morning,' was all he said.

While we breakfasted in the morning, Mauki and Friday took our belongings in the dinghy off to the *Lily* and Markham went to present a gift to the chief.

Friday seemed to regret our leaving and his face showed a flicker of expression for the first time. Martin gave him two handfuls of tobacco. Then he took off the battered felt hat he was wearing and gave it to him and I gave him a bandana handkerchief. Friday put the hat on his head and the scarf around his neck and grinned.

As we all pushed off in the dinghy, Friday stood there wearing the hat and kerchief and nothing else. He held his precious tobacco in one hand against his stomach and with the other hand waved to us with real affection.

We had barely reached the ship when Markham pointed to several large canoes heading toward us. They were great war-canoes, with high shell-decked prows, five of them. Each held a score of natives. They were moving swiftly and, as they neared, the natives raised their paddles high in the air above their heads at the end of each stroke, yelled 'Hoi,' and dipped them with a vigorous down-thrust. They made a perfect rhythm and the canoes shot forward with amazing speed.

I saw that Martin's face was stern. Then I thought of the man I had bandaged and of Markham's remark that if the fellow died, they would be after Doctor Johnson. Surely nothing could have happened this soon. Perhaps they were just coming to say good-bye.

The canoes swung toward us; but passed us without stopping and sped on. Not a man gave us the slightest attention. Much relieved, I watched them as they moved across the bay and wondered what they were up to.

'Probably going to a fishing ground,' said Markham, 'or to some feast at another village. Or just showing off, which is more likely.'

For two idyllic weeks we idled along the shore of San Christobal, stopping each day for pictures and almost always getting something unique. Everywhere the natives showed the same health and vigor and the same advanced intelligence, but also the same sharp cunning of features and behavior.

At one settlement, we found a marriage festival in full swing with everyone in a very gay mood. I was struck with the musical instruments carried by the men and young boys. Most conspicuous were flutes made of bamboo. They were about three feet long, closed at each end, with a hole near one end for the mouth. There were smaller holes for the fingers, a few inches apart, down the shaft. The tone was sweet and mellow and very pleasing.

There were also pan-pipes, very attractively made. Five short hollow pieces of bamboo of varying lengths were bound together with jungle vine and carried streamers of vine or decorations of areca leaves. These were used to accompany the dances and chants, but some of the men walked about playing softly to themselves and entirely oblivious of us, as though genuinely fond of music for music's sake.

Jew's-harps were the favorite of the youngsters, but some of the men also played them. They were made of a piece of slit bamboo and string. The humming music reminded me of my school days, but the natives were better players than any I had heard.

Another queer instrument, which Markham called a mouth-fiddle, was a kind of large jew's-harp. Two strings were stretched taut from end to end of a bowed stick. One end of the stick was placed in the mouth between the teeth and the strings were strummed with the fingers and made to vibrate.

In little groups the men were dancing to the music of the flutes and pipes, while the women clapped their hands and shouted applause. The dancers carried shields made of woven wicker and pandanus fibre and covered with designs of birds and fish in gay colors. Each carried a spear, the blades made of hardwood carved in a wide variety of shapes and patterns and elaborately barbed. The spears were beautiful as art objects, but with those vicious barbs they were sinister as weapons.

Martin and I walked over to a group of men who were standing with their backs toward us and laughing as though they were enjoying something very funny. On the ground beyond them was a big rat. Its feet had been cut off and it was hobbling about and bleeding heavily. They poked it with sticks to keep it moving and kicked it back when it tried to escape. I hate rats, but the sight of this deliberate cruelty was revolting, and I was glad to leave.

'Now perhaps you can understand,' said Markham, 'how these people could be as wild as they were before they had Government's restraining hand. There is a story of one of these chiefs, not so long ago, building a new canoe-house and war-canoe. When both were built, he launched the canoe by dragging it over the bodies of the workmen, stretched prone on the beach. Then the bodies were eaten and the heads cured and the new house decorated. And that isn't a patch on some of the things that have happened in the Solomons.'

This aesthetic sense and barbaric morals seemed hardly to go together. Yet I could see that these people possessed real genius. Their wood and shell carvings were superior to anything else we had seen, both for imagery and craftsmanship.

Their music had been an inspiration. They had health and vitality and inventiveness and none of the earmarks of degeneracy. Surely they had more to recommend them than the Tom Butlers.

Markham thought they had originated the shark and fish deities and other religious concepts now common in the islands.

Another stop brought us to a different kind of ceremony. From the wailing and the doleful music it was obviously a funeral. The chief's son had died, and he was putting on a great display.

'You might say these celebrations keep the chiefs poor,' Markham said. 'But their notions as to money are different from ours. It's of no good except to enjoy, so they wear all they can and spend the rest. The chief is expected to put on a great show at every good excuse, and most of the chiefs love to do it. Festivals bolster his vanity and help him keep the village good will.'

Scores of women were sitting in front of the chief's house weeping and wailing, and even the children and some of the men joined in. On conchs and jew's-harps, the men were playing mournful and monotonous airs which seemed to be spontaneous and not a ritual. This went on for several hours without interruption, except when a medicine man came out from time to time to shout something and encourage the mourners to better and louder wails.

At length the body, wrapped in grass mats, was brought from the headhouse and carried by six men high on their shoulders toward the forest. The men and women rose and followed, and so did we.

When we reached the burial ground, we saw a platform, set upon heavy posts about fifteen feet high, on which rested a heavy canoe-like dugout. The wailing continued while the pallbearers lifted the body to the platform, and laid it in the canoe. Then they put into the canoe the young man's ornaments, pipes, drinking cup, eating bowl, bamboo lime-box, a small stool, and other personal possessions. A heavy wooden slab was laid over the top and the men climbed down. Gradually the crowd dispersed and the wailing stopped.

I asked Markham what would happen to the body.

'They will let it rot up there,' he replied. 'Then, after a few weeks, they will cut off the head and clean and dry it. The body will be left to the scavengers, but the head will be taken to the canoe-house to occupy a small "canoe" and the principal place of importance, since it belongs to the chief's son. Usually, here on San Christobal, the body is buried in the ground and the head is later dug up. The canoe where it is finally laid to rest is modeled in the form of a shark or swordfish or bonita and inlaid with shell and pearl, and makes a very handsome decoration.'

'I think it's gruesome,' I said.

'No, I suppose these heads are quite an inspiration to the old chief,' said Markham. 'He can walk into the headhouse among his ancestors — something like a family portrait gallery. He can look at them and reflect on how he put this or that enemy out of the way and settled this or that wrong. Just as this fellow will recall what a fine son he had.'

He went on to explain that the scarcity of ground and the use of every available patch for gardening at some time or another made their system of destroying the body and keeping only the head a very practical one from their point of view.

'In Bougainville they use cremation, at least for the men of high rank,' he said, 'and that is probably the most practical sense of all. At Rubana Lagoon they bury the bodies in the open, like this one you have just seen, and the smell in that place is something awful. But they all have their little burial whims. On one island they ask the mother of a child that dies, or the nearest of kin, or the medicine man in case of an adult, whether the body belongs to the land or the sea, and they bury it in the earth or the sea accordingly.'

We were just leaving the village when we spied a ketch coming into the bay. We went out to it in our dinghy and found aboard two Frenchmen whom Markham knew. He introduced us and told us that they were recruiting natives for their plantation on Choisel. Markham told them of the funeral and they decided to wait for a day before going ashore, lest they offend the chief or stir native resentment. I thought this very good taste and was glad they had enough judgment to respect the natives' feelings at such a time.

'The trouble with this recruiting business is the abuse of it,' said Markham when we left the ketch for our own ship. 'These men will probably get one to ten men from a village by playing on the trading instincts of the chief, who may be needing tobacco or a knife or calico badly. Sometimes a case of tobacco, some two hundred cheroots, will buy two boys or more for a year's time. Figuring the cheroot as worth a cent, that is cheap enough even with the cost of feeding and maintaining the boy at work and getting him back home again. Sometimes, when the recruiter makes a good deal, he will give a chief a Snider rifle in the bargain and a couple of rounds of ammunition.'

Most of the guns did not work, but enough of them did to make trouble.

'The trouble starts when the recruiter forgets to return the boys,' Markham went on. 'Anyone with the slightest judgment wouldn't do such a thing, but it is done every now and then. Sometimes boys are killed by accident or mischief and do not return. Again, the boys may not like their indenture and run away, leaving the white man innocently helpless. In any case, the natives don't discriminate between the good and the bad white man. And if the boys are not returned, the old chief feels himself privileged to get the head of the first white man he sees. Out comes the old Snider and, if it will shoot, somebody gets damaged.'

For that reason, he said, the Government fined any trader or recruiter heavily if he were caught trading in Snider rifles. Almost invariably the guns became a menace, not only to the natives, but to every white person who might appear.

'Of course, Government has a lot of illusions,' Markham
said. 'They pooh-pooh cannibalism, and sometimes I think
they really believe there isn't any. That's a comfortable idea
as long as you are sure of your own head. But, unfortunately,
it isn't so, and it's not the way to fix things up down here.
But when I think of what Government has accomplished, and
on their thin revenues and the small personnel, I think it's a
miracle.'

Next morning we had rounded the southern end of San
Christobal and stopped at the attractive little island of Santa
Ana.

Here again we had a fine welcome from the girls, which
seemed to please Martin and Markham, even though the
girls did give me almost all the attention. They were especially clean and vivacious and gay, and I could understand
when Markham said that many a trader came here to find his
wife. The girls had the reputation of being the best-looking
in the islands. Many a native chief sent for them, with lavish
presents, Markham said.

Remembering Markham's statement that virginity was
unknown hereabouts, I still wondered at the sweetness of
these girls.

One of the girls seemed especially bright and pretty, so I
sent back to the ship for a dress to give her. It was a checked
gingham that I could no longer wear and it seemed just a fit
for her. She took it with great wonderment. She looked me
over carefully, as though making sure how the thing were
worn. Then she ran off to her hut. She came out wearing
it as gracefully as any manikin. But she could not seem to
understand that I had given her the dress. Soon she ran off
again to the hut and came back to me, entirely nude and
holding out the dress as though to say, 'It was nice of you to
let me put it on.' Upon Markham's advice, I took it back.

'They have no right wearing dresses,' he said. 'They have
no idea about keeping clothes clean. The things get so filthy
and full of disease that they do them more harm than good.

Keep the dress. She will be better off as she is — healthier, happier, and a lot prettier.'

Markham wanted us to see Ulawa, a near-by island where he said he would show us the finest canoes in all the world. So we hurried on, stopping briefly at Ugi and Santa Catalina which had been visited by the early Spaniards. The natives seemed as progressive as at Santa Ana, but here they went only to Malaita for their wives, even ignoring near-by San Christobal with its beautiful women.

He was right about Ulawa. Although the natives were not up to the San Christobal standards of beauty and energy, they were craftsmen par excellence, and the canoes of which he had boasted were works of great skill.

The canoes were made of planks sewn together with vine and caulked with native gum and beeswax. Some were very large, holding thirty or more men. Along the outside edge, they were inlaid with beautiful mother-of-pearl images, chiefly resembling sharks and fish, but also vines and flowers and human figures. Each bow and stern was extended upward into a sweeping elongation. The stern was plain except for the inlay, but the higher bow was encrusted to its tiptop with white cowrie shells and inlaid to the very end with mother-of-pearl. At the top of the bow was attached a cluster of white cockatoo feathers, or the ever-present bunch of areca leaves.

'This canoe-building with only rough tools is no small art,' said Markham, 'and the master canoe-builder is a professional and a privileged character. All the materials are furnished him and the drudgery is performed by others. The canoes are so good that they bring fancy prices from other islands and a master builder is always well off and never out of work.'

Here as at Ugi there were a great many fantastic wood carvings of sharks, bonita, and sea-birds. Not only the chief's house, but others had supports of these elaborately carved posts. Markham thought they were among the best wood-carvers of the world.

Their bowls were extremely original. They were made from a soft wood, cut and turned in all shapes and sizes. They had elaborately carved handles, and were used for cooking as well as serving. One was a great trough, over twelve feet in length.

'That is a ceremonial kai-kai bowl, used for human flesh at a feast,' said Markham. 'Human brains and sago make a fine dish, one of the chiefs here told me.'

Another receptacle, about four feet long and over two feet wide, was large enough for a bathtub. It had handsome broad handles of sharks' head design, and almost every inch of its exterior was carved in a reticulated pattern, with interwoven leaves and flowers. It was clearly a highly prized bowl and was also made for ceremonial purposes.

The island abounded in bananas, papaya, breadfruit, sago, taro, and other foods, and the natives were all well stuffed. Because the Government had once made them build fences to keep the pigs out, they had killed their pigs, but now had them again, for, although vegetarian, they felt that no feast was a feast without roast pig, if 'long-pig' or human flesh were not available.

I watched a mother piercing her son's ears. She used a sharp bonita-bone hook and took her time. The little fellow, who was about ten years old, tried to be brave, but he squirmed and winced and big tears rolled down his cheeks.

In the holes she inserted little rolls of grass. These would act as springs to help distend the holes, and the grass rolls would be increased in size from time to time as the holes grew larger. Ultimately, the mother would replace the grass rolls with wooden disks. These the boy might continue to enlarge if he liked the idea of having big ear lobes. Some had lobes large enough to hold a saucer and wrapped them up around the ear stump to keep them out of the way.

Some made holes in the center of the ear as well, I noted. And others pierced the nostrils on both sides of the nose and inserted a piece of the bright and attractive nautilus shell. I saw one young man wearing a ring in each side of his nose and a bone through the center.

Some of the women had nose-pieces, but they were plain slivers of wood. Apparently the men got all the attractive and beautiful decorations.

The boys were segregated at an early age and sent to a clubhouse, where they were taught and disciplined by the medicine men and the chief. Here they lived and had their food brought to them by the women, returning to live with their parents only when they became grown men and before their marriage. They learned to fish, swim, and hunt and take care of themselves in all kinds of emergencies, from war to shipwreck.

'And they are even taught ambition,' said Markham, 'or at least to distinguish themselves. Every young man is supposed to get a head to prove his manhood and they go around creating some wrong or digging up old scores to warrant making a headhunting raid.'

The chiefs always told him they never fought nor permitted a fight without some real cause, he said. But if on the day we had landed or during our visit, the chief had become ill, or if he were already ill and died during our stay, that would be a sure sign that we were devil-devils and they would probably go for us.

'It takes very little to make a wrong in their language,' he added.

When the boys came of age, according to Markham, they were married off by the chief with a unique ceremony. He called the village and friends from near-by villages to attend the feast. Those who came to the party must bring presents which would completely outfit the young couple. The men who came must build the house for the newlyweds, so that upon concluding the ceremony, the bride and groom could move in and start housekeeping, complete down to the first meal. The feast was everyone's reward for all this work and trouble.

The young people were permitted to pick the site for their home. Usually each village consisted of a family — the

New Hebrides woman and child.   She wears a piece of fabric hung from a fibre waistband.

*Martin and two natives of Vao. The men are husky and very black
with uncut bushy hair and matted beards.*

New Hebrides cannibal. He wears a human bone through his nose, a typical belt made from bark, and a cartridge pouch obtained from a trader.

Two young men of Vao, handsome but vicious. The bandanas around their waists are improvements suggested by Father Prin.

The ceremonial ground at Vao, a large clearing in the forest surrounded by boo-boos.

Old woman later buried alive on Vao. Thus the natives dispose of old people who have become senile and useless.

New Hebrides native. His bleached hair is as unwashed as the rest of him.

New Hebrides boo-boos decorated with pigs' tusks. The natives beat out messages and rhythms on these boo-boos.

aunts, uncles, and cousins in an expanding circle — and they combined to give the couple the best of everything the family had, including the best land available.

Some, being fishermen, preferred the beach, and others who liked to garden built in the hills. But because of the heavy rains and the mire of the hillsides, most of them preferred the beach.

Individual taste seemed to stop there, however, for the houses were almost always of about the same size, shape, and construction. Where building a house and moving into another one was so easy, architecture seemed just a waste of time and energy.

We stopped at a little Catholic mission where Markham wanted to pay his respects. It was a mere strip of coconut palms and garden along the shore, but there were several neat frame houses painted white. There were five sisters and nine fathers. A church, a school, and a hospital were all busy attending to the natives' needs and it was a very active and efficient little settlement.

Right away the sisters took our clothes in hand. Martin's were in very bad shape, for I had run out of thread and patching material. In almost no time they had his breeches and shirts neatly mended. They even repaired our shoes.

The mother superior was French, a fine, strong, motherly type of woman, and she treated me as though I were a child. She had been in the Solomons for twelve years, and she kept repeating that I was too young to be exploring. She looked at me and shook her head and said that I ought to be sent home. But she was very sweet, and it was good to have such attentions and affection, although they made me homesick for my mother and grandmother.

We had our meals with the fathers. The sisters dined separately. The food was simple, but so good that it reminded me of Penduffryn, especially the real, home-made bread. After the long months of crackers and hardtack, I knew that bread would always be a luxury to me.

'These people have been wonderful to me,' Markham confided, contradicting himself about missionaries. 'They will give up anything they have to make you comfortable.'

At Ulawa and Ugi the men and women worked in unison. In fact, the entire village worked together in a sort of communal system, especially in the gardens. The young boys did most of the fishing and caught quantities of lobster. Their fishtraps, lined with spikes to prevent the captured fish from getting out, were very neat. Along the beach they had built fences over which the high tide washed the fish and left them trapped at the low tide. Nets were cleverly made of the fibre and the leaves of pandanus and coconut, some light for throwing and others as heavy as baskets for hand-seining. The fisher boys made rich hauls which were shared equally after every catch.

Here was probably the best ordered life in the Solomons. There was more discipline and a system of division of food and labor that seemed very equitable and intelligent. If they had only been as handsome as the Ong Tong Java people, they would have been about perfect, but their stubby frames, overdeveloped shoulders and chests, and their tousled heads and creased faces made them far from handsome.

Their superstitions amounted almost to a curse. No woman could walk down the beach in front of a canoe-house, nor land in certain spots nor walk on certain paths — all reminiscent of Malaita.

I asked a little boy his name, and when my question was interpreted to him, he ran away. To speak his own name would have been equivalent to putting himself in my power.

'The more primitive they are, the more they are afraid of the devil-devils,' said Markham. 'Their world is made up of a few living persons and great multitudes of spirits of their ancestors and ghosts and other vague creatures, good and evil. No wonder they look so wild-eyed.'

The wisi-wisi, a little bird about as harmless as a sparrow, brought death if it should perch on a house and sing, Markham said. The kingfisher brought rain. If a poisonous snake came into a village, someone was sure to die. Fireflies were ghosts and the children killed them. Butterflies entering a house were a favorable sign. Rainbows meant that sea spirits were abroad. A thunderstorm was a good omen and meant that visitors were coming. When a native here went to sleep, he was going on a long adventure into the unknown, but lime on his hair would be a protection and help him find what he wanted.

Markham told us a story of Ugi which described their over-developed fears perfectly. Several little boys, just coming of age and learning to fish, had caught and landed a grunter fish which often grunts for hours after it is taken ashore. One of the boys was carrying the fish in a net over his back and as they frolicked along toward home, the fish began to grunt. The boys listened and thought the sound came from the forest. Probably a devil-devil. They began to run, but the sound of the grunting continued and grew louder and louder. The boys were now certain they were being pursued by a ghost. They detoured through the woods to lose it. Finally, unable to get rid of it and petrified with fear, they plunged into the sea which was then running strong and were dashed against the sharp coral rocks.

'That goes for the grown-ups here just as well,' Markham said, 'only they are more superstitious.'

Martin asked why there were so many women.

'This is probably the most married place in the Solomons,' Markham said. 'Many a chief has fifty to sixty wives, as many as his income will permit and his gardens require.'

As the women aged, the chief would go on adding new ones. Even the commoners could take as many wives as they wished and could afford, but since the wives did all the work, their support was no great problem. A commoner, however, would have trouble finding money enough to buy more than one wife.

'But wait until you get to the New Hebrides,' he said.

'There is the most married man in the world since Solomon. Old Nagapate has at least a hundred wives and probably twice that number — nobody knows.'

He had so many he had to keep them in dormitories!

'That brings me to some bad news,' Markham said. 'I have to leave you. But you go to the New Hebrides. They are certainly the worst part of the South Seas, and if you are going to get those cannibal feasts, that is where you will surely get them.'

We begged him to go with us, but he demurred.

'I'm not helping you find cannibals,' he said. 'I'm a hoodoo, and you can take care of yourselves anyway.'

As we talked of the New Hebrides, I could see a new excitement and eagerness in Martin's eyes. He was dissatisfied and discouraged here, and was beginning to feel a sense of frustration.

That night it was agreed that we should go over to Tulagi with Markham, report to the Governor, and start for the New Hebrides. We would have to go all the way into Sydney again and the expense would be heavy, but we would be able to see the worst of the islands, if Markham was any judge, and have another try for the prize we were after.

'They are so bad,' I heard Markham saying, 'that a British gunboat has to go in and shell the islands every now and then, just to keep them quiet. No whites but a few missionaries will live down there — worse than Malaita. And there is only one French priest who has ever been able to manage what might be called a toehold, on the little island of Vao.'

'We'll be lost without you, Marco,' I said, coaxing him to come along, but he interrupted.

'I promised to stand by you, but I've already given you over three months,' he said. 'I can't stay out here forever with you two. I have to get back to my Lily.'

Bride in the Solomons

17 wwwww

. . . shifty eyes . . . dirty skins

I'LL PUT YOU OFF at Vao, if you insist,' said the Captain of the steamer, as we left Sydney. 'But I won't take you to Malekula; not for any money. You are very foolish young people. Why anyone should want to go to such a place unless he had to is more than I can fathom.'

Did we know there were actually cannibals on those islands? Finally, trying to dissuade us, he brought out his most convincing evidence. It was a little book, *The Pacific Island Pilot*, which Martin read eagerly.

'Although an appearance of friendly confidence will often tend to allay their natural feeling of distrust,' he read aloud, 'strangers would do well to maintain a constant watchfulness and use every precaution against being taken by surprise. . . . They are a wild savage race and have the reputation of being treacherous. . . . Cannibalism is still occasionally practiced. Nearly all are armed with Sniders. The bushmen live entirely among the hills in small villages and are seldom seen. Being practically secure from punishment, they have not the same reasons for good behavior as the shore natives, who are in reach of gunboats and discipline. The hill men in the interior should always be treated with caution.'

Martin's eyes shone.

'Captain, that is just the place I'm looking for.'

Early the next morning we were rowed ashore in one of the steamer's lifeboats with all our equipment and supplies, and landed on the surf-swept beach of the little island of Vao.

'It's not so bad as you think,' Father Prin was saying. The gentle priest in black cassock and white pith helmet stood on the beach among a hundred or more staring and hungry old natives.

Trying to put me at my ease and allay the evident shock I felt at the sight of these peculiar people, he said, 'They will be your friends; I have managed to get along with them happily for twenty-seven years.' But he spoke with no great assurance.

Father Prin's boys carried our belongings to a hut. Next door was his chapel, which he immediately proceeded to show me. I interpreted this as another gesture to make me feel at home.

The chapel was a mud and thatch building, but very trim and neatly kept, set in the midst of croton hedges and flowers. Over it arched palm and breadfruit trees and on it he had evidently lavished affectionate care. Inside were several rows of benches and at the far end a raised dais and a simple altar with a crucifix. The only light came through the bamboo doors which opened out on three sides. Simple as it was, it evidently represented to him a great achievement in this lonely place.

Before I could ask him about his work, he was hurrying me toward our hut and offering me his best servant and any stores we needed. From what I knew of these stations, I was sure he must have very little food with which to be so generous.

The natives who crowded around the hut, and even into it to satisfy their curiosity, seemed friendly, although they probably only wanted to be paid with tobacco to go away. They were husky and muscular though dirty, and many had yaws and other sores, especially on their legs and arms.

They were very black and their uncut bushy hair grew in

mops. The women's hair was shorter and roughly trimmed.
Most of the men had full beards which completely framed
their black faces in matted hair. Several wore sticks thrust
into their hair at rakish angles and some wore combs cut out
of wood. Their ear lobes were natural and not elongated as
in the Solomons, but several men wore small shell rings in
their ears and some had pieces of bone in their noses.

Curious belts of bark were worn by the men.

'They tighten their belts when they get hungry,' said
Father Prin with a smile, and this seemed about the only
possible use the belts could have, for they were certainly not
decorative.

From these belts hung a very slight loincloth of dirty trade-
cotton, evidently an improvement suggested by the Father.
The women wore a similar piece of fabric hung from a fibre
waistband, and nothing more. A few had pieces of grass and
leaves dangling from the waist.

Their bodies were not tattooed, but many were marked
with small scars arranged in rude patterns. They cut the
skin, said Father Prin, and inserted pieces of wood or dirt to
make a welt. Then they picked the scab off again and again,
to enlarge the scar.

'I have not tried to change their customs,' he added. 'They
have a right to these and I have tried to win their hearts
rather than their ways. In fact their so-called idols still stand
here within a stone's throw of my church. I want them to
change voluntarily through understanding and reason rather
than more direct persuasion. I know that is possible.'

He was a very advanced missionary, and the respect which
the natives showed him made his progress evident as far as
their hearts were concerned.

That afternoon Father Prin showed us about his domain.
The island was only two miles in diameter. Across a narrow
channel could be seen the mountainous mass of Malekula,
home of the Big Numbers people, about which Markham and
the Captain had told us. We plied the Father with questions

and learned that Malekula had some forty thousand inhabitants, divided into the very wild Big Numbers and Small Numbers tribes on the north, a nomadic people at the center, and pygmy peoples on the southern shore. The Father was reluctant to say much about their being cannibals, but he began quietly to dissuade us from visiting them.

'That man has no fingers,' I whispered as we passed a native, all of whose fingers were gone and the stumps apparently not healed. His feet were terribly scaled and his nose and ears were covered with open sores. I felt sick to my stomach.

'He has leprosy, my child,' said Father Prin calmly, as though that were an everyday matter. 'But it is not contagious.'

I was terrified and wondered why Markham had not warned us. Father Prin said there had been cases on the island for as long as he could remember.

The worst cases went to a leper island in New Caledonia, he said, but the island was far away and there was no money here for transportation. He had reported them, but the facilities were probably crowded anyway.

'But you will see,' he continued, 'that this is not so dangerous as some other diseases and not as easily caught. I know of the case of a Frenchman who contracted the disease and his wife went with him to the island. They lived together seven years before he died. They had two fine children, as healthy as you please, and the wife did not contract leprosy.'

We passed numerous low circular mud huts in which the natives lived. Each had a single doorway and no opening except a tiny vent at the top. The door was so small that one had to crawl to enter. I peered into a hut. It was barren except for a few sticks of wood beside a smouldering fire. Pungent smoke filled the room. Pigs ran in and out of the houses at will.

'I have tried to teach them to build their roofs high and with proper ventilation, like yours. Every time I see women with sore eyes I tell them it is because of their smoke-filled. rooms. One by one I am persuading them.'

This afternoon I saw only old people and wondered if they were all old. But the priest said the younger women were away on Malekula gathering firewood and their husbands would be guarding them.

Presently we saw a great many canoes coming across the channel. Women were paddling most of them. When they beached the canoes, the women climbed out, shouldered great bundles of firewood, and trundled them off. The men lazily sauntered up the beach, some carrying Snider rifles and others clubs in many sizes and shapes.

The Vao islanders were Malekulans who had a long time ago come away from the larger island to escape the constant warfare and they were always on guard against attack from the bullying Big Numbers. But from their own malevolent faces, shifty eyes, wasted bodies, and dirty skins, I doubted that they were far removed from their degenerate Malekula forebears.

There was no doubt in our minds that we had found the people we were looking for.

As we turned toward home we crossed a long clearing, about twenty-five yards wide, which was cut through the forest. It was the tribe's ceremonial ground, Father Prin explained. At various places along the clearing there were rudely carved, upright hollow logs, each with a slit, about six to ten feet, running down its length. The logs had weird faces carved upon them and some were fashioned at the top so that they seemed to be wearing hats. Each represented the standing figure of a chief who had now become a kind of god. From the nose and mouth of each hung a long string of boars' tusks.

These images were the native 'boo-boos,' which served as both idols and drums. As drums, they were used for ceremonials and for signaling purposes. Their messages carried for miles, depending upon the condition of the atmosphere.

We were soon to hear the boo-boos. That evening there came over to us from the ceremonial ground a low, monotonous, hollow beat. This increased in volume until it filled the air and my head began to throb with it. Our boy, 'Atree,' told us that there was a feast in dedication of a new 'devil-devil' or boo-boo, just added to the collection, so we went with him to watch.

The dancing was as monotonous as the music. The natives lacked the vigor and imagination of those we had seen at San Christobal. They went round and round a central fire, stupidly stamping and yelling until they were tired, and then others took their places and continued the routine. The old men stood still and simply lifted one foot and then the other in a slow and lazy rhythm. The shouting grew wilder and rowdier. Martin took pictures with the aid of radium flares, but we soon grew so bored that we went home. Throughout the night, the yelling and the boom of the boo-boos continued. We slept uneasily and with our guns ready.

I had set up housekeeping in our little hut and, although our tinned stores were ample, I wanted fresh food. The channel was reasonably calm, so I borrowed a canoe and went fishing. Here was a surprise, for of all the variety I had seen in the Solomons, there was nothing to equal what I now saw. The myriads of fish had so many colors and shapes that I called them the Impossible Fish. They were hungry creatures and game, and although I had twice enough, I went on fishing until dark when Martin and the houseboy, Atree, came and called me ashore.

Canoes, loaded with men, were arriving from the direction of Malekula. The canoes were rough dugouts equipped with outriggers. They lacked the grace and fine line and size of the beautiful canoes at New Georgia and San Christobal and had none of the craftsmanship or decorations.

Friendly men from the other island were coming in, said Atree. The feast, now in its third day, was still going on, and many pigs had been brought. It was one of the biggest celebrations he had seen in a long time.

The boo-boos were beginning to boom when we reached home. We hurried through dinner and decided to try for more pictures.

When we arrived at the ceremonial grounds, there were many small fires blazing. Some of the natives were now decorated with stripes of lime over their faces, arms, breasts, and backs. Black as they were, I saw several men smudging their faces with charcoal from the fire.

The dance was dull, but it was having its intoxicating effect on the dancers. The yells increased and became more frenzied and hysterical. The boo-boos echoed through the forest and resounded in a deep undertone. When there was a lull in the music, the heavy sound of shuffling feet went on.

Gradually dancers began to drop out and go to the fires. They were growing hungry. By tribal custom each man was his own cook. Even the chief, to whom we were presented and who paid us little attention, was preparing his private fire. He was unable to accept the cookery of an inferior, so even he must cook his own food. I have often felt that way, too, even safe at home.

Staked out about the clearing were hundreds of pigs and chickens. Yams were piled in heaps. At an order from the chief, the men exchanged pigs and chickens as a sort of friendly formality. Thereupon each man broke the legs of his live chicken and one front and hind leg of each pig, and threw the poor creatures on the ground.

They proceeded to build up the fires and toss yams into the embers. Then they wrung the chickens' necks or beat their heads against a rock, and the squawking added to the din. Meantime, the pigs writhed and kicked about, squealing piteously. It was a brutal experience.

At length the men stripped off the blackened skins of their yams and ate the pulp at the center.

'Too lazy and dumb to cook them properly,' muttered Martin. 'Must taste like charcoal.'

Then they took the pigs, one by one, and beat them over

the head with their war clubs, leaving them to scream and jerk their lives away on the earth. They had a deliberation and casualness about their cruelty.

When the fires died down to glowing coals, the pigs and chickens were cut up and wrapped in leaves and thrust into the embers to roast. Then everyone began gorging upon flesh and fat, with grunts and shouts.

They ate as though they had fasted for a long time, and although there was an abundance of food, the men were apparently determined to down it all as soon as possible. At last some were so upset by overeating that they rolled to the ground in distress. Their companions turned them on their stomachs and rubbed them with a rough massage. The only comfort to us in all this was that the natives would be so groggy with food that they would be harmless for days.

'They are merely children,' said Father Prin the next morning. 'They have just so much excess energy that must be worked off. To restrain them would be a mistake; they would only think up something worse.'

Then he told us a hideous story. These natives buried alive their old people who had become senile and useless. The Father had rescued an old man from this fate and persuaded the natives to let him care for the unfortunate. He took the man to his house and fed and cared for him for several days. One day the natives came to visit him and asked to examine the old fellow. They pinched the old man's arms and legs and face and looked into his mouth. Then they began to laugh loudly. It was all right with them to let him live, they said, but what a joke on the Father, for the old man obviously wasn't worth saving.

'Sometimes, the old one will be strong enough to dig his way out of the grave,' said the priest, 'but the natives take away his belongings and refuse to feed him and soon bury him again. They think nothing whatever of it. In fact they often make a festivity of it and even dance on the grave.'

Later we were to see and photograph one of these gruesome live-burials.

Their idea of death was serene enough to take away the sting, the Father thought. They believed that the spirit moved away through the earth to a dwelling place, 'a long way underground,' where it would be happy forever. However, it must pass through certain stages of trial before coming to rest.

Seritan, a legendary cannibal chief of long ago, presided over this deep Heaven. He was a terrible disciplinarian and put the newcoming spirit through a rigorous questionnaire. If the spirit could not answer satisfactorily, he would have the spirit's tongue cut out, or punish it in other ways. But if the questions were answered correctly and likewise other questions along the journey, the spirit would be permitted to dwell there, and if sufficiently clever it might be given a very important post.

The spirits actually ran the living world from their resting place. Occasionally the tribal medicine man could visit the spirit world and receive instructions, and these orders the tribe must obey to the letter, lest great evil befall. As interpreter of the spirit world, the medicine man therefore became a very important and much-feared figure.

Here was an organized superstition that would mean we must be very careful and on our best behavior.

Sacrifices of boar tusks and other 'money' must be made whenever the medicine man decreed. Even if the sacrifices were untouched, the natives were not in the least disturbed, for the spirit world was invisible and could, after all, be understood only by the medicine men.

These superstitions were complicated by witchcraft, which every native believed the medicine men could practice. In fact they employed the medicine men to do harm to their enemies. Death or disease or other misfortune could be worked upon anyone with the proper preparations. First the medicine man must have a lock of hair of the person to be bewitched, or a piece of clothing, or some of his unused food. For this reason, the natives destroyed their cut hair or leftover food — they could afford to take no chances. Even an image would suffice if nothing else could be obtained. A fire was built and the object burned, while the medicine man did certain incantations and communicated with his friends of the underworld.

Special 'gifts' of pigs or boar tusks or other useful property were paid to the medicine man for these services. But, said Father Prin, if the person bewitched discovered the matter in time, he could make counter-gifts to the medicine man and work counter-spells to protect himself. In our language we should call that a racket.

'But we ourselves are only a few hundred years removed from all this,' Father Prin reflected, 'and these customs will soon pass even from Vao and Malekula.'

I had grown so hungry for bread that I tried making some in a frying pan. For yeast I made a concoction of the juice of two wild limes, a few raisins, a little flour, two tablespoons of sugar, and a cup of warm water. This I put in an empty bottle, shook it well, and let it ferment, which seemed to work all right.

The bread was nothing to boast of, but it tasted to us like the real thing. I gave some to the Father and he was delighted. It was the first bread he had tasted in years. Thus encouraged, I made him some hot cakes, using my familiar Eno's Salts in place of baking powder. The cakes were as light as a feather and very digestible.

Father Prin said that he didn't miss civilization, but I knew that he did, and this made his sacrifices all the greater. He had left home as a boy and had never gone back. Once in a while he had made a visit to Vila, the little settlement which was capital of the New Hebrides, or to Noumea, New Caledonia, but he had been to neither place for years.

Going down to the beach for a swim one morning, we saw a large whaleboat, equipped with mast and sail, pulled high up on the beach. It seemed to be in perfect order. We asked the Father and found that it belonged to a trader who was coming back for it sooner or later. We begged him to let us borrow it. Father Prin was reluctant, but we finally persuaded him on condition that we take a crew of his own trained boys.

'Surely an answer to our prayers,' said Martin. 'At last we can get around among the islands as we wish. And without the "protection" which hasn't helped too much. We'll push off just as soon as we can get things ready.'

In our several days on the island I had not yet seen a native swim, although they seemed to be expert canoemen.

'They avoid the water,' said the Father. 'They seldom even drink it. And they swim in it only when they have to. I have seen them walk quite a distance to get out of wading or swimming a stream. They think bathing makes them lose strength.'

Sanitation was something he had done his best to teach them, he said, but it was hard for them to understand. Some of their villages would be almost unlivable if it were not for the pigs and dogs and the wild life which were scavengers and kept things reasonably clean.

'He's a true saint,' said Martin as we left him for our hut. 'Think of a fine, intelligent, capable man like that, with many an occupation and opportunity open to him at home, giving up everything, even the simplest comforts, to devote his life to these people. That is real godliness.'

Father Prin seemed to us to represent the best in practical Christianity and the ideals of the Western World.

'We wouldn't be here and none of the whites would be here if it weren't for men like that and their sacrifices,' Martin said. 'They aren't just opening up the jungles for trade, as critics at home often hint; they wouldn't do these things for trade. They have a vision — a vision of a better world, in which men will understand each other and be able to live together in peace. And they are willing to die for that vision and Faith. We should be mighty grateful to them.'

... fatten their children like pigs

*W*HAT ON EARTH is happening? Look at the water!'
Martin was shouting.

All around our whaleboat the sea was boiling and seething
like water in a teakettle. Fish came to the surface and floated
there as if stunned and others began to leap high in the air.
The little boat tossed about wildly and the crew boys yelled
with fear. I took Martin's hand and held on.

For what seemed to be half an hour but was probably only
a few minutes, this disturbance continued and we thought
we should capsize. The water that splashed aboard was
warm and I wondered if a volcano were going to burst up
from the ocean. Obviously this was a submarine eruption of
some kind. Anything might happen in this bedeviled place.

There was no disciplining the crew. The momentum of
our boat and the sweep of the upheaval were carrying us into
a bay. At last we came into calm water and we got the boys
back to the oars, but not until they had hauled in some of the
fish that were everywhere about us.

'The natives will have boiled fish for a week,' said Martin.
'Tons and tons of precooked food.'

Just then a great fin bore down on us and a huge shark cut
past, striking at the floating fish. Others followed him, gorg-

A *New Hebrides head dryer, inspecting his work. He has taken off all
the flesh and built up the face in clay to look like the original.*

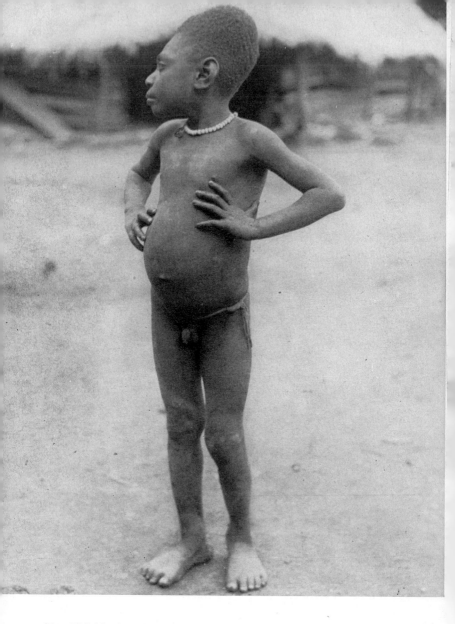

*New Hebrides long-headed child. His head has been bound to distort
it into a queer potato-like shape.*

Native of the long-headed people. They look like imbeciles, but they act like the nicest people in the South Seas.

Chief of the long-heads. Colorful cockatoo feathers stick out from his hair to form a crown.

Malekula native beside a composite figure. The head is a dried tribesman's, the body is of clay, the feet and hands of wooden sticks.

The most powerful of the New Hebrides chiefs. A pompous fellow with a shock of hair, beetle brows and deepset eyes.

ing themselves on this readymade feast. One came right up
to the boat and I couldn't resist letting go at him with my
revolver. I don't know where I hit him, but hit him I did,
and he raced off toward the open sea.

When we reached shore, we found huts wrecked and the
natives in a panic. They told our boys that this had been
one of the worst earthquakes in their memory. They might
get the notion that we were the cause of it, so we continued
on our way as soon as the excitement was over and the sea
normal again.

We were rounding the southern end of Malekula in Father
Prin's boat, skirting the shore and stopping at villages which
the boys thought safe to visit. Martin was convinced that
here we should find what we were after and, if we kept our
wits about us, we could avoid trouble.

'Animals and primitive people are alike in one thing,' he
said. 'They know when you are friendly, they can sense it,
and we are going to prove it as well as get some fine pictures.
They can even smell fear. You just keep smiling at them and
I'll do the rest.'

We landed to get fresh water one morning, and followed
a small stream back a short distance into the bush to the
spring which fed it. Near the spring were several women and
children, gathering firewood. The women were so dirty I
knew they never bathed.

One of the women held a newborn baby. It smiled at me,
like a little black cherub, and I began making bird sounds
and talking to it. Then I held out my arms and, to my surprise, the mother handed me the child. I sat down and held
it very tenderly, as though it were my own, while Martin
looked on with some concern. Suddenly the woman bolted
into the jungle, followed by the others.

'That's a sweet kettle of fish,' said Martin. 'Either you've
adopted a cannibal baby or else something is going to happen.'

After a long wait, we started for the beach, carrying the
child. In this awkward situation we had better be near our

whaleboat. There was not a sound as we made our way through the bush. We reached the beach and Martin called the boys to stand by and keep the boat ready.

Time went on and the mother did not return. The baby began to fret. I bounced it and cooed to it, and kept one eye on the jungle. I wondered what on earth I should do with it. If I started away with it there would be an uproar, but I couldn't leave it on the sand.

Three young boys walked out of the bush. They looked as though they wanted to run away, but I motioned to them. They cautiously came near us and stood and gaped. Surely they must know who the mother was. I stepped toward them and held out the baby. They turned almost white with fright and ran away as fast as they could.

Just then the mother darted out of the bush, where I suppose she had been hiding all the time, and shyly came up and took her child. She grunted several words and gave me a haughty look and walked proudly away.

Martin chuckled and hurried me into the whaleboat. 'That proves what I was telling you,' he said. 'They know when you are friendly. She was flattered that you liked her baby and had no fear of you. She probably pities you for not having a child of your own and is just showing you her superiority.'

It was to be my experience among wild people, in years to come, that savages often doubted I was a woman because I had no baby in arms. That is their normal state.

The mountains of Malekula towered above us always as we sailed along the shore, often rising sheer from the sea and again retreating from broad beaches and foothills. They were heavily wooded and from the hillsides there rose numberless smoke columns from near and remote villages. But we saw few natives.

'I thought there were forty thousand people on Malekula,' I said. 'We haven't seen a hundred.'

'But they see you,' Martin replied. 'They build their huts

back there among the trees and the hills, so they are con-
cealed from us.   But they can watch the sea and every move
we make.   That gives them the jump on their attackers, in
time of war.'

I remembered what Markham had told us about the British
punitive expeditions.   Even they hadn't taken a chance on
landing.   They had sailed offshore and lobbed shells at the
smoke fires up there on the mountains.   That must have
frightened the natives almost as much as an earthquake.

Moored in a bay to rest one morning, and debating with
our boys whether to go ashore and investigate a village near-by
which its fires revealed, we heard the deep boom of boo-boos.
The sound continued and grew, and echoed from the hills out
across the water.   Martin asked the boys what they thought
was going on.

'It's either a show of some kind or they have spotted us,' he
concluded.   'I have a hunch it's all right.   Shall we have a
look?'

I could see that he had already made up his mind, so I
agreed and we paddled toward the beach.   Natives began
coming down to look us over and they seemed to be unarmed.
We watched them through the glasses for a time and decided
that they looked receptive, so we waded ashore.

The men were very black and bushy-haired and as unwashed as usual.   Some of them had lime in their hair which
had bleached white, giving them a kind of helmeted appearance.   Their noses were flat.   Their lips were thick and heavy
and slobbery.   Their eyes very shifty, either through fright
or mischief.   But they seemed more curious than malicious
and were soon asking us for 'tobac,' which we gladly gave
them, two sticks to each.   They at once began chewing on it
and went on jabbering to our boys, who seemed to understand
little more than we did.   In *bêche-de-mer*, our head boy told us
that the natives invited us to a feast.   The village was only a
few hundred yards into the bush, so we gathered our rifles and
cameras and accepted the invitation.

In the village the dance was already in motion. The place was a conglomeration of very shabby huts. Boo-boos stood around an open space and on them husky natives were beating out the South Sea rumba. In the center of a large ring of spectators, all men, a score or more of the dancers carrying war clubs were doing a lively movement. As they went on, they did individual acrobatic stunts which were a show-off of virtuoso steps they invented, but all were part of the principal dance.

Martin quickly set up his cameras, but, except for some of those nearest us, the natives paid little attention to him. Those who looked at him turned away with no show of interest. I knew they were not indifferent and were probably very concerned about what we had in the black box.

Other men, apparently from villages back in the bush, were coming in and joining the throng. Small groups were collecting about the edges of the settlement. After watching the dance for fully an hour, with the movement going on in the same monotonous routine, we began to move around the edges of the crowd. Here and there we now saw women, which was a reassuring sign, for their absence might have meant that trouble was brewing.

One group of men and little girls attracted our notice. We walked up to them. The men acted as though they were bargaining with each other. One of them was showing off a little girl to another, who finally gave him two boar's tusks, took the little girl and walked away with her.

'Martin, is he buying her for a wife?' I whispered, aghast. I had never been this close to such a transaction.

Martin and our head boy were talking in low tones.

'It's worse than that,' said Martin. 'Atree says she is for "kai-kai." Imagine fattening up a little girl like a pig and selling her to be eaten. It doesn't seem possible.'

But the others were continuing to bargain, and they were certainly trading those little girls.

As we walked down the trail to our boat, my mind went

back to Malaita and the youngster we had bought to save her from becoming 'kai-kai.' This was no place to be born a girl.

Three enchanting little islands lay offshore. Atree said that we would find a missionary there, so we made for them to put up for the night.

A young woman in a white cotton dress ran down to the beach as we landed. She stared at us, almost speechless with surprise and pleasure. Her plump cheeks were the color of pink roses and her blond hair, gathered back into a bun at the back of her head, and her shy blue eyes, reminded me of the farm girls back in Kansas. She was almost a picture of Martin's sweet sister, Freda.

An Australian missionary, she had been here, alone with her husband, since their marriage two years before. She had not seen a white person for several months, she said. When I kissed her, she broke into tears, and hugged me as though I were a long-lost sister.

Her young husband, an energetic little man, proved to be a doctor who had come from the Australian highlands. His father had been a missionary, but this was his first assignment. Although he was quite reserved, he was alert and evidently very capable and he had our respect at once.

We walked to their little frame house in the bush and they were soon begging us to stay for a genuine visit. They were a warm-hearted and ardent pair, and I saw in them the hardy spirit that had settled our West. Their kind has accomplished all the great pioneering work of the human race.

Two little native girls came in to serve us tea. They were cute little pickaninnies with great black eyes and short curly locks, bare legs and feet, and pot bellies showing under their white mother hubbards. I put my arms around them and gave them a squeeze. They rolled their eyes and smiled bashfully and ran off giggling. I asked the wife where she had found that lively pair.

'They were being traded on the mainland one day about a

year ago,' she said. 'Some of the Malekulans actually fatten their girl children like pigs and sell them to other tribes for food. We rescued these two. My husband paid for them in trade stuff and we brought them home. Nobody has ever asked whether we ate them. Nobody seems to care. But they are almost like our own children and we love them and are going to see them educated.'

We asked them if they had made encouraging progress in their work. The wife looked at her husband and smiled a little wearily.

'A very little encourages us a great deal,' she said. 'We have made converts here and the natives seem to thrive under protection and attention. Of course, we haven't any assurance that they won't relapse into their old ways if we leave, or if there is some other good reason we cannot prevent. But we aren't going to leave. And if you come back in ten years, I think you will see a very great change.'

I was somehow very sure of that.

'There is certainly cannibalism over there,' she said, looking toward Malekula. 'But the natives aren't really and deeply bad nor incurable. They are just children, and just as irresponsible. Our job is to teach them friendship and kindness, by example, and to give them as much respect for sanitation and medicine and a better way of life as possible.'

I admired her faith.

'The world will be surprised some day to see how they respond to Christian treatment,' she said. 'We have a great deal to live down out here, for some of the whites, especially the recruiters, have been brutal and untrustworthy and shameful. The natives, of course, think you and all of us are just as bad as those other whites they have had to deal with.'

'They are certainly star members of humanity,' said Martin as we left for our boat in the morning. 'Risking their health and their lives every day; living right next door to the cannibals. They have the kind of courage and ideals that real Christians are supposed to have. And if anybody is able to destroy cannibalism, it will be people with sweetness and patience like theirs.'

Sailing in a fine breeze along the shore of Malekula that afternoon, we spied a large smoke fire on a plateau in the foothills. The fire was too large to be an ordinary cooking-fire and too small to be brush. Martin's curiosity was provoked and I saw 'that look' coming into his eye, so I made the excuse for him, and suggested that we go and investigate.

After a half-hour's climb we came to a kind of meadow, on the far side of which, against the forest, was a small group of huts. Around a smudge fire sat and stood a number of natives. Not wishing to alarm them by striking straight across in their direction, we skirted the wood and did not seem to attract their attention until we were almost upon them. They stood up as they saw us, with their hands on their war clubs. They seemed more fascinated than afraid. All stared at me.

Close to the fire two men went on with their work. On long hardwood sticks they held in the smoke two human heads. My eyes froze. The natural hair was still on the heads, but the faces were clay masks.

For a moment one of the men withdrew a head from the smoke to examine it. He went over its features with his finger, feeling for flaws like a sculptor. And the work had a certain artistic quality, caricature though it was.

'Atree says they take off all the flesh,' Martin said. 'Then they build up the face to what the original looked like. It's a permanent clay image.'

He was busily setting up his cameras while the group of men stood and looked on wonderingly. The men at the fire paid no attention. They seemed absorbed in their art.

The heads were turned over and over in the smoke, like a chicken over charcoal, so that they would be equally exposed on all sides. They took care not to singe the hair, and evidently there was no shrinking here, as in Central America.

'He says he's the best head-dryer in the South Seas,' said

Martin. Atree chatted with the men at the fire, and interpreted what they said in *bêche-de-mer*.

'What did they do with the bodies?' I asked Atree.

'Him good fellah kai-kai,' he replied.

'Do you mean they *ate* them?' I asked.

'Him fellah, him no good. All time make trouble. Good fellah kai-kai,' said Atree, with a sheepish grin.

'He means they took their enemies in a skirmish, and here they are,' Martin said. 'Too bad we didn't get here sooner. Might pay to look around.'

But look as we did, we could see no evidence whatever of a long-pig feast.

'Funny, isn't it?' said Martin as we walked down the trail toward the beach. 'Much as we abhor cannibalism, here we are disappointed that we didn't find those fellows eating other human beings. But that's what we're after.'

My husband snapped out the last words with that Viking determination of his. And I knew that he was saying to himself, 'But find them we will.' What he went after I knew he would always get.

On the day following, we took Atree's advice and headed for a village, where he said we should find something worth seeing.

'My word, him head long fellah too much, all same boat belong Master,' he said.

Unable to make out just what he was trying to tell us, but overcome with curiosity, we landed.

The first person to appear on the beach was a little curly-headed boy, about ten years old. His head was distorted into a queer oblong shape, almost like a potato, and his forehead receded in a streamline backward from the eyes. Otherwise he seemed entirely normal and smiled at us in a very unafraid and friendly way.

He came over and looked me up and down and then fixed his eyes on Martin's gun and cameras with the intense curiosity of any boy. Atree began jabbering to him, but he made no reply, and continued to stare at us and smile. I thought he showed a great deal of personality and felt sorry for him with that misshapen head.

Other natives came out of the forest and edged toward us shyly. I saw at once that they were all smiling in the same easygoing manner of Markham's Polynesians back at Ong Tong Java, and, though very listless, they evidently had the same nice dispositions. But everyone had that distorted head. I was fascinated. They looked like imbeciles, but acted like the best people we had seen in the South Seas.

Several mothers joined the growing cluster, each with a baby riding on her back or held astraddle her hip. Each child seemed to have a basket on its head, but when I went to look, I saw that the heads were bound tightly round and round, with jungle vine. The binding made the faces look overfat and drew back the eyes, giving them a squinting appearance. Here was the cause of the head distortion, a deliberate beauty treatment. Their legs seemed to be very bowed, probably from riding their mother's hips, where they clung expertly, digging their little heels into the mother's flesh.

I asked for one of the babies, and the mother gave it to me without a moment's hesitation. It seemed very clean and its cheeks and hands and feet were dimpled. It had fine features and big, clear, lustrous eyes. Its skin was like brown satin, and when I patted it, the mother looked very proud at this attention, and the entire crowd laughed. But I suppose they were laughing at me and my funny round head and my white skin, like an albino's.

The boo-boos were booming and a festival was beginning in the village, so we went to watch, curious to see how these people would behave.

Several of the men were already in dance regalia. Their headdresses were bandeaus of colorful cockatoo feathers, which stuck out in a wide crown and bobbed about as they began to dance. Each man carried a heavy hardwood club with a knob or blade at the end that made a solid weapon.

Soon a group of men came up from the headhouse, wearing big, round, heavy masks, fitted over their heads like divers' helmets and with peep-holes in front, so that they could see where they were going. The masks were enlarged fantastic faces, smirking and leering, like the masks worn by Chinese actors. They were modeled out of clay, and baked.

Behind these men came others wearing smaller masks and carrying, on long sticks, dried human heads!

More than a hundred men and women joined the dance, spinning round and round in perfect rhythm, stamping with their calloused feet until the earth seemed to shudder. They were not listless now, and were dancing like normal wild men.

Martin was busy photographing them. Seeing him there made me sure that what I saw was true. It was almost incredible that these friendly looking people were cannibals. I asked Atree.

'Him no eatum,' said the boy. But I saw that he turned away and did not look me in the eye.

The long-headed people were hospitable enough, but by late afternoon, Martin had made ample films and I had several dozen stills, so we left them at the height of their festivity, without remaining for the feast, which we feared might excite them out of their good temper.

From our boat we could hear their chants and their boo-boos out across the water, almost indistinguishable from those we had heard elsewhere and equally sinister.

Martin was hungry after his long day's walk. I made him a hurried lunch of bully-beef and crackers. But the sound of the boo-boos and the thought of those heads struck me in the stomach, and I had no appetite.

On the following day, we sailed for hours along what seemed to be uninhabited mountain slopes, lush and heavily forested. Then we saw again a mass of smoke fires. Through the binoculars the beach seemed to be alive with natives.

We turned inshore and watched as we drew nearer. They

were evidently having a fish-drive, and this we wanted to see, for the New Hebrides natives were said to be so expert with spear and net that they scorned fishing lines and tackle. We landed on the beach and thought they looked as rough as any people we had seen. They continued their drive and paid little attention to us.

While the men gathered in their haul, Martin busily recorded their fine spearing technique on film. They almost never missed bringing up a fish with each thrust. The youngsters helped their elders in spearing and they piled up the catch on the beach.

The men were coming in from their labor when there was a shudder of the earth. There was a moment's pause and it began again, now prolonged. The natives howled and all fell on their faces in the sand.

Martin was trying to manage his cameras to keep them from falling. We all sprawled on the beach.

The tremors came again and again for perhaps fifteen minutes. I felt a sickish sensation all over and was glad I had eaten no lunch. I wondered if the sea would send in a tidal wave, and kept an eye on the water, but except for a very heavy surf that beat against our boat and washed it several yards up the beach, nothing further happened.

When the disturbance abated, we talked briefly to the men, but only to show our good will. We got away in the boat as quickly as possible. We were sure that sooner or later they would blame the tremor on us, and from their mutterings, we gathered that they already had their suspicions. They would probably tell their children about the visit of the white devils; and that the earth shook every time they put their feet down.

A tiny island some distance offshore seemed to be a fine place to put up for the night, and we made for it. As we sailed around it to find a proper landing, we saw that the sea had become gray in color, and was very calm. Then we cut into what looked like a floating crust. It was pumice. We seemed to be floating on sand, and the boat slowed so that we all had to man the oars to make any headway. We finally ground into the beach, which was already encrusted with the gray deposit.

'There has been a volcanic eruption, sure enough,' said Martin.

'My word, him devil-devil sing out too much,' commented Atree. 'Him cross fellah too much.'

I began to wonder if Atree himself would not think we had 'bad blood.'

From all the excitement, the little uninhabited island was a pleasant escape and we spent the following day there. Martin worked on his cameras, while I cooked over a real fire and caught up with mending and other chores. Our films were running low, and we should need to get on to Vao lest Father Prin think we were lost. But Martin was still hopeful of finding 'the real thing' on this side of Malekula.

We sailed on up the Malekula shore, sighting occasional villages, but no exceptional activity. Beautiful as it was, I was growing tired of Malekula and the endless array of dirty natives. The prospect of seeing a cannibal feast was growing slimmer each day. I knew that we might be here for years without finding exactly what we had come for, and we already had an enormous bag of fine pictures and proof enough of what the natives were like.

I didn't want to admit to Martin how I felt, for he often said my encouragement kept him going. But I was growing miserably homesick. Two years away were beginning to make me long to see my mother and dad and grandmother. I was dreaming by the hour of girlhood friends at Chanute.

We came to a spot which seemed to Martin worth exploring. There were great fires in the hills and quite a show of life.

Atree thought the people were not too friendly. He seemed anything but eager to go ashore, but Martin was all the more curious for that reason.

'Let me look around while you wait here,' he proposed to me.

But I was going with him wherever he went.

The men who met us on the beach were a dour lot. Some twenty of them stood and stared at us. They were husky and heavy-faced, and everyone's hair was covered with white lime. Atree told them we should like to make presents to their chief.

After we gave tobacco to each of them, they thawed and led us silently along a wide trail to the village, on a plateau about five hundred feet above the sea. The village was a large one and the huts were sturdy and well kept. Evidently the tribe was prosperous.

The chief was a pompous fellow, with a great shock of bushy hair and beetle brows and deep-set eyes. He looked at us suspiciously and without a smile.

We both smiled agreeably and I offered him tobacco and a mirror and pipe, which he accepted without any apparent appreciation. He seemed to resent us.

Martin thought that perhaps we had not been generous enough, so he asked me to hand out more tobacco, which I did. The chief looked me over with a scowl that made me uneasy, but I smiled as best I could.

I hoped Martin would get away from this place.

The chief and Atree made out a desultory conversation in *bêche-de-mer*, but we were all so uncomfortable that we decided to leave without our usual picture-taking. The old chief must have thought us recruiters and he had probably had his fill of them and of blackbirding experiences.

We said good-bye and shook hands, which seemed to mystify him further, and started back down the trail, without our guides.

We were soon off on a trail other than the one we had taken on our climb. Although we were descending, we came to several strange huts and there were no landmarks that we recognized.

As we struck through the bush, we heard the low sound of

boo-boos and stopped to listen. It was ahead of us on the trail. We crept along cautiously.

Through the foliage we could see a dozen or more natives about a fire, doing a lazy dance in a sort of hop-and-skip fashion. They were chanting something in time with the boo-boos.

Martin motioned and we stopped.

For some time he watched the proceeding with his binoculars from behind a tree.

He crept back to one of the boys and took a still camera and returned to the tree. I took my camera and tiptoed over to him to see what was so interesting.

'Osa, tell the boys to duck. I hope we aren't followed. I'm going closer. This looks like the real thing.'

We crouched in the bush and the boys hid off the trail. They all looked very scared.

Martin and I crawled through the bush and grass on hands and knees.

Although we tried to move quietly, we made some noise at every move, but it was not heard for the chanting.

I saw Martin feel for his revolver, to be sure.

He focused his camera more carefully than usual and made an exposure. Then he crawled forward a few more feet and I followed. He made another exposure and another.

We inched forward to the edge of the wood, so that only tall grass now separated us from the men at the fire. They were sitting down and some had begun to eat. Soon they were all greedily tearing at pieces of flesh snatched from the fire. They ate as though they had fasted for days.

We were now almost afraid to move, for the boo-boos had stopped, although there was considerable grunting from the men. My heart was thumping, and when Martin made another exposure the click of the camera seemed so loud I was sure it would attract the natives' attention.

I took the binoculars from Martin and turned them on the fire. Several large pieces of flesh lay there and the men were gnawing on others.

Then I saw, hanging from a spit, a human leg-bone and spleen. That is what Martin had seen, and, as always, he knew what he was doing.

'I want that,' he whispered. 'They have no guns. You cover me. I'm going after it.'

He took his revolver in his hand and, before I could restrain him, he was walking forward. I followed mechanically.

At sight of us the natives uttered a yell and bolted, stumbling over each other as they ran. Martin and I ran forward and in a moment he was taking close-ups of the remains of a feast of 'long-pig.'

We retreated to the cover we had come from. We had our boys ready with their guns and waited for something to happen. The forest was silent except for the flutter and calls of the cockatoos and pigeons.

Presently we struck off down the trail and made for the beach straight through the bush, fast. We ran to our boat and made the quickest of all our getaways.

From the hills rose a number of smoke fires, but there was no sound and no other sign of life.

The boys rowed us out to sea and the wind finally caught our little sail.

Martin and I sat quietly for a long time. He took my hand and held it so tight that it hurt, but I knew that he was too full of emotion to express what he felt in any other way.

After two years of persistence, we had got what we had come for and had actually seen a cannibal feast, with pictures of it to show the world.

Martin was looking back across the water at Malekula. I was enormously proud of him, of his courage and ambition, and sure I had married the most important man alive.

He put his arms around me and held me close.

'You've been a brick,' he said at last. 'If I could, I'd give you both those pearls you wanted at Penduffryn.'

My heart was not on pearls.

'Martin — I want to go home.'

One of the chief's wives, dressed as befits her position.   The grass covering is dyed purple and worn permanently.

Portrait of a Malekula native. Cockatoo feathers adorn his bushy curls.

Osa and Martin with Malekula natives.   Good feeling prevails despite the show of weapons.

In the market for a bride. A New Hebrides native with a hibiscus be-hind his ear and something on his mind.

Osa and the Big Numbers tribesmen. She makes a friendly beginning among the Malekula savages.

Something not to meet on a dark night. A cannibal brave — wild corn-flowers in his hair and a sliver of shinbone in his nose. The shark's teeth, dog's teeth and shells about his neck show that he is very wealthy.

New Hebrides cannibals cooking human flesh. Hanging from the spit are a human leg and spleen. Only tall grass separates the Johnsons from the men at the fire.

All that remains of a feast of long pig. *The natives and most of the victim have vanished.*

Glossary of
Bêche-de-Mer Words

Akkus: axe
Along fellah: with

Beacho: beach or shore
Belong: used as a possessive prefix, since there is no possessive pronoun. So:
> *Belong him:* his
> *Belong you:* yours
> *Belong me:* mine
Belly cry: hungry
Big fellah belong white mastah: Governor
Biggum: much
Billy can: teakettle
Bime-by: presently
Bokkus: box, camera
Bokkus belong bell: clothes box, with bell attached to cover as a 'burglar alarm'
Boxx: commissioner, Governor
Boy: servant
Bring him he come: to bring
Brokum bone along work: tired
Brother belong hammer: saw
Bullamacow: bully-beef

Cockoroco: chicken or fowl (derived from cock and rock; i.e., hen-laying rock)
Coppera: copra, dried coconut meats
Cow-oil: butter

Die finish: dead
Dinkum: the real truth, the 'lowdown,' and other colloquial uses

Eatum: to eat

Fellah: precedes every noun — 'one fellah' for singular and 'two fellah' for plural. Many natives count up to five or ten, after which description becomes vague and general — 'plenty fellah.' Others indicate numbers on fingers and toes. 'One fellah hand' is five; 'two fellah hand' is ten; 'two fellah hand, one fellah foot,' is fifteen.
Fennes: fence
Findum: to find
Finger belong foot: toe
Fokkus: flying fox or bat
Fright: fight

Gamman: lie
Good fellah: all right

Kai-kai: food
Ketchum: to get, to bring
Killum: to kill
Killum strong fellah too much: to receive a beating or spanking

Lickalick: a little bit
Long-pig: cooked human flesh
Lookum: to see

Mana: deity
Mary: woman
Matchisi: matches
Milliki: milk

245

Moon: month. So 'one fellah moon' means one month

Musket: gun

One fellah: see *Fellah.* A general singular prefix before a noun. Also used as singular pronoun, such as 'me fellah,' 'you fellah,' and 'he fellah,' to denote *he* or *she*

Pickaninny: child. Little girl is 'pickaninny Mary' and puppy bitch is 'pickaninny Mary belong dog.'

Plenty: many

Sailo: ship

Screw belong leg: knee

Shirty: shirt or jacket

Sing out: to pain or make noise

Shoot lamp: flashlight

Sokkus: sock

Speakum: to talk

Stop along ground: dead

Strong fellah: big, husky, strong

Sun he come up: sunrise

Sun he stand up: noon

Sun him go sleep: sunset

Taboo: forbidden, from the native word *tabu*

Take him he go: take

Talkum: speak

Time sun he come up: dawn

Tobak or *Tambak:* tobacco

Tush: starch

Two fellah: see *Fellah.* A general plural noun prefix and used with plural pronoun, 'we fellah,' 'you fellah,' and 'him fellah,' to denote *them*

Walkum: to go

Washee-washee: to paddle

What name: precedes almost any query, such as: 'What name belong you?' meaning, *Who are you?* Or, 'What name boy kai-kai he stop?' meaning, *Is dinner ready?* Used alone means *What?* Or, *What do you mean?*

Index

Index

Index